MAKING YOUR OWN

TOYS

PAMELA PEAKE

MAKING YOUR OWN

TOYS

PAMELA PEAKE

Rodale Press, Emmaus, Pennsylvania

Published in the United States by:
Rodale Press
33 East Minor Street
Emmaus, Pennsylvania 18049

ISBN 0-87857-623-1

2 4 6 8 10 9 7 5 3 1

Typeset by Wordsmiths, Street, Somerset
Origination by Adroit Photolitho, Birmingham
Printed and bound in Italy by New Interlitho, SpA, Milan

This book was designed and produced by The Paul Press
Ltd, 22 Bruton Street, London W1X 7DA

Contributors Pamela Peake (Consultant, Soft Toys), Paul
Collins (Wooden Toys), David and Frøydis Wellings
(Dollhouse), Ann Trudgill (Wooden Toys Paint Finishes), and
W.A. Hinckley (Paddle Steamer).

Art Editor Tony Paine
Project Editor Susanne Haines
Editorial Sally MacEachern
Emma Warlow, Elizabeth Longley, Barbara Horn
Designer David Ayres
Art Assistant Sarah McDonald
Illustrations Hayward and Martin Ltd
Photography Don Wood

Art Director Stephen McCurdy
Editorial Director Jeremy Harwood
Publishing Director Nigel Perryman

CONTENTS

FOREWORD

Toys are an essential part of growing up; from babyhood onwards, children need toys – not just as things to play with, but as tools to help them to learn more about the world and to aid in their physical and mental development. The next two pages tell you why play is such an important part of child development, so read these through before you start on the chapters devoted to practical toy-making, which form the core of this book.

Project by project, toy by toy, here you will find something to suit the needs of children of all ages. You will also find projects to match your growing toy-making skills. So that you can tackle each and every one of these with confidence in the end result, each of the main chapters – Making Soft Toys, Making Wooden Toys, Making Mixed Media Toys and Making Advanced Toys – starts with an introductory section, outlining the basic principles involved and telling you exactly what items of equipment you will need. When it comes to the toys themselves, you will find specific materials and equipment checklists, together with patterns and templates – all designed to make the task of toy-making really enjoyable.

For, above all, toy-making should be fun. Our hope is that you will find the projects as exciting and stimulating to make as they are to play with. You have a wide variety from which to choose – from cuddly elephants and kangaroos to rag dolls and jigsaws, from swings and a lunar space station to glove and string puppets and a home for a unqiue family of dolls – together with their furniture – whose design will fulfill every child's dreams. There is also a careful balance between indoor and outdoor toys.

Remember, though, that safety is of key importance. All the designs in this book have been devised with this in mind, so it is important that you are equally aware of potential danger, especially when it comes to the business of sewing on eyes, as in the case of some of the soft toys, or painting on decoration. If you are in any doubt at all about the suitability of a material you plan to use, check with your supplier before purchasing it.

INTRODUCTION

Play is a vital aspect of childhood, since it is through this that children learn about themselves and the world around them. It is an essential preparation for life, so you should appreciate its very real importance and provide your youngsters with every opportunity to express themselves in as many different ways as possible through it.

Children need to be able to play quietly as well as exuberantly; inside the home as well as outdoors; to combine freedom with organized games and other such activities; and to play with unstructured materials, such as paints, sand and water, as well as with manufactured toys. As a parent, you must recognize when it is time to join in, so helping your children to enjoy new experiences and activities to the full, and also when to stand back and simply keep a watchful eye on the proceedings.

Stages of play
Children pass through clearly recognizable stages of play; these stages are related to their physical and mental development. Specific toys are similarly appropriate to these various stages. But, though you will find that toy manufacturers often recommend certain toys as suitable for particular age groups, you should realize that not all children develop at the same rate. One child, for instance, may be in advance of his or her years; another may be mentally developed, but have poor physical coordination; and a few children may never be able to develop beyond a certain point at all.

A good toy is one that suits a particular child at a particular time. It should take into account the age, temperament and sex of the child, as well as the stage of mental and physical development. It should be stimulating and, above all, safe.

The tools of play
Toys are the tools of play. To a youngster, a toy may be something as ephemeral as a paper airplane, or an empty shoe box; it could be an improvised drum set, consisting of a pot and a wooden spoon; or it could be a craftsman-designed Noah's Ark or fully furnished dollhouse. Each of these will give a child pleasure in its own way, for it is a fact that children are seemingly unconcerned about whether their toys are the best that money can buy, or designed by experts and recommended by educationalists and psychologists! As far as children are concerned, toys work if they fulfill a purpose and are enjoyable. Consequently, such toys encourage children to learn about themselves and the world through play – undoubtedly, children learn best when learning is fun.

Your child's first toys
During the first months of life, all learning comes through stimulation of the senses – sight, hearing, touch, taste and smell. Babies need to be played with, cuddled and talked to; they are as yet too young for the majority of toys. As they grow older and become more aware of their surroundings, however, they should be given new experiences, which is where toys have a vital part to play.

Take something as simple as a mobile, for instance. Babies can derive hours of pleasure from simply looking at one of these as they lie on their backs in a crib. You can tie a string of toys across the crib as well, encouraging little fingers to reach out and touch. Then there are rattles to grasp and shake. This is the time to introduce your child to small clutch toys. Since these clutch toys have interesting surfaces and textures to explore, they will undoubtedly find their way to the mouth. Therefore, they must be washable and super-safe.

When movement begins
Once babies are sitting up and crawling around, they are ready for a whole new range of toys. Now, you can introduce them to lightweight balls, which help them to develop hand and eye coordination. Push-and-pull toys that move across the floor encourage a child to learn how to use its limbs, while a baby walker provides invaluable body support during these early walking days – that is, before it becomes a trolley, or pretend-wheelbarrow!

In broad terms, toys at this stage of life are generally designed to help your child control body movement and thus aid physical development. At the same time, stacking toys, building blocks, musical toys, and simple jigsaw puzzles will aid the development of intellectual skills by stimulating the brain and encouraging the child to experiment and think. Toys your child can play with in the bath will help to overcome any fear of water and promote a sense of security, so aiding the development of stable emotions. Likewise, encouraging a child to cuddle up with a soft toy at night is helpful if your child is afraid of the dark, or of being left alone. Soft toys are friends – in some cases, this means for life. After all, there are adults who still retain an attachment to their childhood teddy bear!

Group play
Once children are fully mobile, they will be in a position to play with others and starting to share their

experiences. This kind of play aids the development of social skills, which are so important when it comes to understanding and relating to others. However, having said this, in reality it is still not easy for two-year-olds to share either their parents or their toys. In both instances, they are fiercely possessive. They need to be really emotionally secure to understand that toys can be loaned, will be returned and that parents can talk to other children and be shared.

It is important to realize that physical, intellectual, emotional and social skills are all closely linked. They simply do not develop separately; and playing, almost by definition, involves more than one of them. Here, time is on your side. So-called 'difficult' children need more time to develop, so you should not be in a hurry to rush children ahead of their natural development rate.

Stretching the imagination
From about three years and onward children mix together more amicably and enjoy learning together. This is the great play period, when all the basic skills are being mastered and much exploration and experimentation is going on. Language and the ability to communicate are both improving quickly as well.

This is the time for make-believe, when children will spend endless hours imitating the activities that they see happening around them. It is a time of role-playing, when toys will be used to represent objects and situations in the adult world. Above all, it is a time for imagination – a cardboard box will become a boat, house, castle or a bed.

Playing with dolls and pretending to be mother is a typical make-believe game, while dressing a doll

provides a child with a less obvious way of practicing finger dexterity. Soon, children will want to dress up themselves and act out their chosen roles completely.

From home to school
At school, work and play gradually merge, until play becomes a recreational activity, something done in a child's spare time. Games become more important – they are generally structured with rules, as well as being competitive. Children are thus required to learn how to win and lose graciously.

Many of these games are centered around balls, thus bringing the story full circle. A ball, one of a baby's first toys, follows a child through life. Who knows, that child may become a baseball or tennis star!

Safety first!
Making sure that children are safe while they are playing should be of paramount importance to caring adults. Between them, toys and the play environment can present all manner of potential hazards. Consequently, all the obvious precautions and safeguards must be taken. Fortunately, outrightly dangerous toys are rare today, given the legal crackdown on toy safety.

Some hazards are obvious and therefore more easily overcome. Toys your child may chew or suck must not use any toxic elements in their manufacture. Paints must be lead-free. There should be no sharp edges or points on, or in, toys. Surfaces should be smooth and free from splinters, nail heads or screws standing proud.

Attachments such as eyes and noses on cuddly dolls and animals must be securely fixed, so that they cannot be pulled out in normal play conditions. Otherwise the danger is

that they could be swallowed, or, even worse, pushed up a nostril or into an ear.

Toys that can be sat upon must be stable, as well as strong enough to support a child's weight. Houses, tents and teepees should also stand securely; they must open from the inside as well as the outside and they must be ventilated.

Watch out for long strings that could become entangled around a youngster; equally, make sure that kites are flown well away from overhead wires.

Toy abuse
Despite all these safeguards, there are still accidents every year that involve toys. Some are caused by badly made toys and are the result of carelessness on the part of the maker. But, undoubtedly, most accidents are caused by toy misuse – that is, toys being played with by children for whom they were not intended, or being played with in the wrong way. Here, the responsibility lies with the person supervising the child.

The message is quite clear. It is essential for adults to choose toys carefully, making sure that they match the individual child's level of physical and mental development. This vigilance must be continuous, for toys must be maintained, kept clean and in a good state of repair. It also follows that toys must not fall into the wrong hands.

Children, toys and play are thus an inseparable mix. The early years of growing up are so important that we owe it to our children to enrich this period of their lives by providing them with a wide variety of carefully chosen toys with which they can play. The following sections of this book provide all the classics you will need to start you on your way.

MAKING
SOFT TOYS

No special skills are required to make soft toys – even knowledge of simple sewing procedures, though helpful, is unnecessary if you read the general instructions given here. Indeed you will discover that with little more than scissors, needle, thread and a handful of colorful fabrics you can make a simple, hand-sewn ball for a baby. The projects are graded: beginning with the simple clutch toys, they gradually increase in complexity, culminating in instructions to make a fully jointed teddy bear.

Tools and equipment

1. Scissors *A selection of sharp scissors is essential: dressmaking shears for cutting fabrics, embroidery scissors for working with threads and trimming fur, a pair for cutting paper and cardboard.* **2. Seam ripper** *Useful for removing wrongly positioned seams and embroidered facial features.* **3. Pins** *Avoid using pins whenever possible to lessen the danger of leaving any behind in a toy. Colored glass-headed pins are easier to see.* **Awl** *Used for making holes in fur fabrics for*

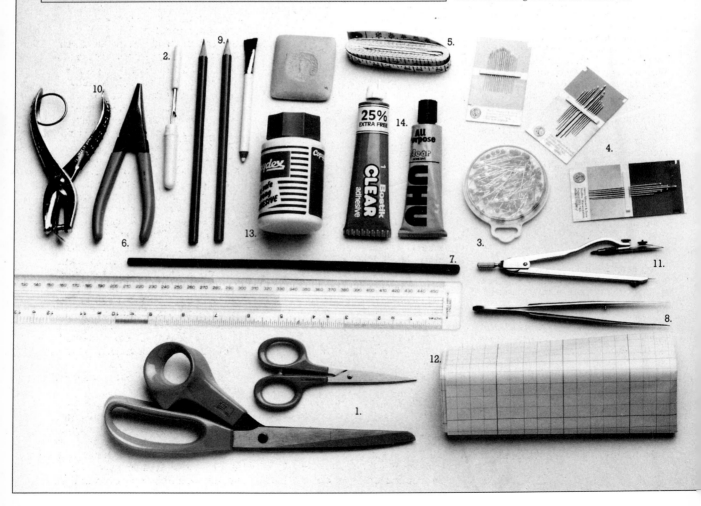

eye shanks and joints. *A knitting needle or the closed points of embroidery scissors can also be used.* **4. Needles** *A selection of hand sewing needles for seaming, embroidery and basting. Darning needles are used for needle sculpturing and for sewing on ears and tails with strong thread. Darning needles are also used when embroidering with tapestry thread or six-stranded embroidery cotton.* **Sewing machine** *Useful for speedy sewing but not essential. Use a strong needle when sewing thick fabrics.* **5. Measures** *Either tape measures or rulers can be used for measuring fabric. Use a ruler to copy patterns.* **6. Pliers** *Long-nosed electrician's pliers are used for bending cotter pins when making crown joints.* **Wire cutters** *Useful for cutting the metal washers when removing wrongly positioned safety eyes.* **7. Chopsticks** *Used for packing the stuffing into limbs. There are many alternatives, such as dowel rod, pencils, and rulers.* **8. Pincers** *Invaluable for inserting wisps of stuffing into extremities.* **9. Pencils** *Soft lead pencils are needed for preparing patterns and for transferring them to the wrong side of the fabric. Use yellow or white crayons or chalk on dark colored furs. Avoid using felt tip pens and ballpoint pens as these bleed into the fabric.* **10. Paper punch** *A single-hole paper punch can be used to punch holes for eye shanks in interfacing and felt.* **Cardboard** *Use thin cardboard to make full-size patterns, or templates. These can then be drawn around, so that pins do not have to be used with paper patterns.* **11. Compasses** *Essential for drawing circles accurately. There are many alternatives, such as egg cups and plates.* **12. Dressmaker's graph paper** *These ready-prepared grids are usually ruled with 2 in. (5 cm.) squares. To adapt one for use with the soft toy patterns you will have to rule in lines to make 1 in. (25 mm.) squares (see p.12).* **13. Rubber latex glue** *Used for sticking tracing paper onto cardboard when making the patterns and for gluing felt and wool to fabrics.* **14. Fabric glue** *Select a brand that bonds felt to fabric and dries clear.*

Threads

A variety of threads are needed for soft toymaking. Choose the correct quality and match the color carefully.
Sewing threads In general a natural cotton thread should be used with natural fabrics when sewing seams and a synthetic thread should be used with man-made fabrics. Basting can be done with a weaker thread, since it is usually temporary sewing. If an overcasting basting stitch is to be left in place in fur fabric toys, use the same thread as that used for sewing.
Strong thread Strong threads, such as carpet thread, button thread, upholstery thread or even crochet cotton must be used to attach the parts of the toy that are sewn onto the outside of the body, so that these parts can withstand the pulling and tugging that they will receive during play. General sewing thread is not strong enough. Strong thread should be used to close all stuffing openings with ladder stitch. Bracing stitches, such as those used for the elephant, *(see p.27)*, are worked with strong thread, as are the stitches used for knee hinges for the rag doll. Choose a natural colored thread.
Embroidery threads Six-stranded embroidery cottons are used to work facial features on the animals and the rag doll. Any number of threads can be used. For instance, a nose will require all six strands, an eye three strands. Interesting effects can be obtained by mixing strands of different shades, particularly effective for areas such as the iris of the eye.
Tapestry thread Dark brown and black tapestry thread can be used for working satin stitch noses on large bears. Persian yarn can be used as an alternative.
Invisible nylon thread This is ideal for working fine whiskers on animals.

Thicker whiskers can be worked using different grades of nylon fishing line.

Fabrics

All the animals have been made of fur fabrics, while the body of the rag doll is made from a firm woven calico. The clothes for the doll and the animals are all made from dress-weight cottons. Other fabrics are needed in smaller quantities.

Fur fabrics These man-made furs offer a wonderful choice of color, pattern and quality for the toymaker. They are usually made in widths of 54 in. (140 cm.) although shops will often precut the roll (or bolt) into smaller pieces that are easier to handle. The amount that you need to make each toy has been carefully calculated and is given in the list of materials. The most important measurement is the length, along which the pile of the fabric lies.
A good quality fur has a thick pile that covers the knitted backing. The backing should not be visible when the pile is flattened. A toy made from poor fabric will have bald seams, thus spoiling the appearance. Pile varies in length and in density. Thus a dense, short pile has the texture of a rich velvet, while a long, medium-dense pile makes wonderful fur for teddy bears. The fabric can be polished to give the fur a lovely sheen. Each toy has been designed with a specific fur in mind, consequently the finished appearance will not be the same if a different choice is made.
Interfacing This is a useful sewing aid for adding weight to lightweight fabrics, for strengthening weak felt and for protecting the edges of holes made for safety eyes and joints in fur fabrics. There are two basic interfacings: a sew-in variety and a

fusible, iron-on variety. Follow the manufacturer's instructions carefully. Always test iron-on interfacings on a scrap of fabric first, particularly if using fur fabric. Press lightly through a damp cloth rather than using a back and forth ironing action to avoid flattening the pile.

It is advisable to use interfacing to back pieces made of felt, such as paws and beaks. It helps to protect the felt from splitting when the toy is stuffed; it also bonds the felt and will protect it if the toy must be washed.

Calico This is a firm, woven cotton fabric that is ideally suited to making rag dolls. It is readily available in different qualities. Choose lighter weights for small dolls and firm weights for very large dolls. Alternative fabrics are any skin-colored firm woven cottons such as denim, poplin or a closed-weave muslin. Some curtain linings are also very useful for dollmaking.

Dress-weight cottons When making clothes for your toys, choose fabrics that drape well, are not too stiff and have attractive, small prints, such as fine cotton or poplin. The fabrics should be easy to wash and iron.

Velvet, velveteen and velour These shortpile fabrics are good alternatives to felt when making paws and feet. They have the advantage of not needing to be strengthened with interfacing, and they are easy to wash. Knitted velour is a stretch fabric, which makes it ideal for combining with fur fabrics in your toys.

Felt A very popular craft material much used by toymakers to make small animals. Its attractions are the great variety of color, ready availability all year round (velvet can be hard to find in the shops in the summer), and non-fraying edges. Felt is a non-woven fabric made from fibers either matted together by

MAKING A PATTERN

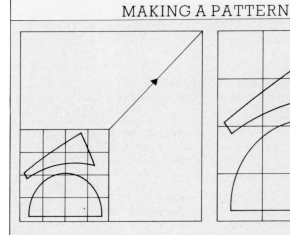
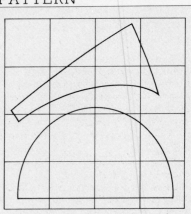

Pattern-making equipment
You will need: large sheet of paper (or dressmaker's graph paper), tracing paper, cardboard, glue, paper scissors, ruler and a pencil.
Enlarging a pattern grid
The patterns are given at half size, with each square of the grid representing a 1 in. (25 mm.) square at full size. The basic grid should be enlarged as a reusable master grid. To do this, rule a large sheet of paper accurately with ruler and set square into a grid of 1 in. (25 mm.) squares. Check that you have the correct number of squares. Dressmaker's graph paper (see p.11) will make the job easier.
Transferring the pattern *Lay a piece of tracing paper over the master grid, place* the book next to it and transfer the outline of the pattern, square by square. Care at this stage will pay off with pattern pieces that fit together comfortably. Cut out the pattern pieces and glue the tracing to the cardboard. When dry, cut out the cardboard. For some symmetrical pattern pieces only one half is shown. This is indicated by a note to 'place on fold'. To make a full-size template of this piece, simply transfer the enlarged pattern to a folded piece of paper, cut out, and you will have your full-size pattern piece.
Photocopying *If you have access to a photocopying machine that enlarges, then your work is over. Simply have the grid or pattern enlarged to twice its size.*

heat, moisture and pressure, or by artificial means such as an adhesive. There are different qualities; slipper felt is far too thick for general toymaking. Remember that felt can tear apart because it is not a woven fabric, and that washing can destroy the bonding of weaker felts.

Muslin An open weave muslin is used in toymaking to wrap noise units in so that they can be stitched to the inside skin of a toy.

Stuffing materials
Materials used for stuffing toys should be clean and hygenic, free from dirt and any foreign particles. There are several to choose from that meet these requirements, including polyester fiber, kapok,

acrylic fiber, foam chips and waste fabric.

Polyester fiber is the most popular of all present day stuffing materials and is used for all the toys in the book. It is readily available, lightweight and meets all the other requirements of a good stuffing material. It comes in various qualities, all of which are white, making it especially useful for fur animals and rag dolls made from pale fabrics.

Making pattern templates
No special skills are needed for making the patterns for these soft toys. However, it is important to measure and copy very accurately. While dressmakers use ready-

printed patterns on tissue paper, toymakers generally make a copy of a pattern on cardboard so that it can be used several times. In addition, a cardboard pattern can be used as a template, eliminating the need to use pins.

You will find pattern instructions given in two different ways:
1. Some very simple shapes, such as the petticoat for the rag doll, are given as measurements in the text. These should be ruled directly onto a piece of cardboard.
2. All of the patterns for the animals, the rag doll and for some of the clothes have been reduced to half size for reasons of space. You will have to enlarge them in order to make a toy that fits the measurements and materials given in the instructions. Note also that many of the pattern pieces overlap each other or are superimposed one on top of another on the grid. Make sure that you follow the correct outline for each piece when enlarging and transfer the matching set of markings for each.

Pattern layouts

The amount of fabric required is given in the list of materials for each toy. Always lay out the pieces first, finding the best arrangement before you mark the fabric and cut.

Layouts are done on the wrong side of the fabric and are determined by the nap of fur fabrics (the direction in which the fur lies) and the straight grain of cotton fabrics (parallel to the selvage), which is marked on the pattern with an arrow.

To determine the nap of fur fabric, stroke the fur and mark the direction in which it lies with an arrow on the wrong side of the fabric. Arrange the fur on the cutting surface so that the wrong side is uppermost and the nap

runs toward you from top to bottom. Arrange the pattern templates, matching the arrows with the direction of the nap.

Use the selvage as the guide for the direction of the arrows when cutting cotton fabrics. Felt does not have a grain, therefore pattern pieces are not marked with an arrow.

Lay out the longest pieces first, followed by the largest and lastly the smallest. Check that you allow for the correct total number of pattern pieces.

Take care to differentiate between cutting two and cutting a pair. Cut two means cut two exactly the same. Cut a pair means cut a right and a left sided piece. To cut a pair, draw around the pattern template, then turn it over and draw around it again for the second piece. You may wish to cut a separate template for every piece that you need to cut, which will help you to plan your cutting layout.

Cutting out

When you are satisfied with your layout you can mark around the edge of the template. Use a soft pencil held vertically and close in to the edge. Use a light colored crayon or chalk for dark fabrics, and do not use ballpoint or felt tip pens. Keep the pencil sharpened or it will affect the thickness of your line and thus the size of your pattern. It is more accurate to cut just inside the line. Correct any mistakes in a different colored pencil to show up the correct outline.

Use your sharp dressmaking shears for cutting out and always cut on a firm surface so that your scissors rest against the surface. Fur fabric needs care if you are not to destroy the pile. To avoid bare seams, slide the scissors between the pile and cut through the backing only.

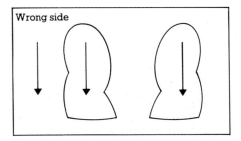

Pattern pieces arranged to cut a pair (ie a left and a right).

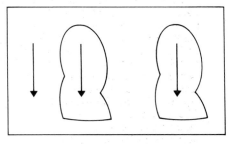

Pattern pieces arranged to cut two pieces the same.

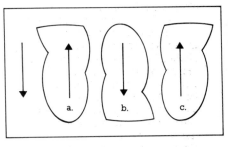

Example of an incorrect layout – a and c are a pair, but the nap lies in the wrong direction; b is placed correctly.

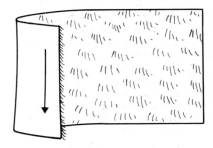

The arrow indicates the direction of the nap on fur fabric.

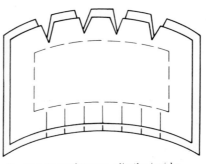

To ease curved seams, clip the inside curves and remove notches from the outside curves.

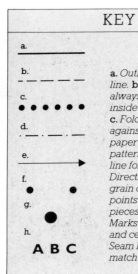

KEY

a.
b.
c. • • • • • •
d.
e.
f. •   •
g. •
h.
A B C

a. Outline or cutting line. **b.** Sewing line, always ¼ in. (6 mm.) inside the cutting line. **c.** Fold line. Place against folded edge of paper to make full-size pattern. **d.** Placement line for ears etc. **e.** Direction of nap or grain of fabric. **f.** Match points used in sewing pieces together. **g.** Marks position of eyes and centers of joints. **h.** Seam letters used to match pattern pieces.

the pattern template onto the fabric. There are several ways that this can be done:

1. Insert dressmaker's carbon paper between the template and the fabric, then trace over the placement lines with a tracing wheel and press firmly on the pattern with a pencil to mark the dots.

2. Make small holes in your pattern template and then use a pointed pencil to spot the marks onto the wrong side of the fabric. These same pencil marks can then be made more visible by sewing a tailor's tack on the spot, using colored thread.

It is not necessary to transfer the sewing line if you can sew accurately ¼ in. (6 mm.) in from the edge.

Sewing

The sequence of sewing a toy together is given in detail with each particular set of instructions, but it is important to know the basic methods of working that are common to all the toys.

In general, pieces are sewn on the wrong side, with the right sides together. Basting is used to hold fabric together temporarily, preparatory to sewing. When instructions tell you to baste, it will

usually mean overcast for a fur fabric and running stitch for non-pile fabrics. Sewing of seams may be by hand, using backstitch, or by machine, using straight stitch.

Darts are made first and then the parts of the body are assembled.

Openings for stuffing are left in inconspicuous seams wherever possible or in places that will be covered by another part of the body.

Before stuffing, the completed skin should be checked for seam strength and clipped at the corners and along the curves as shown.

Construction stitches

1. Running stitch The simplest of all the stitches. It is generally a small, regular stitch used for seams or joining edges when strength is not important. It is also used for gathering in fullness and in this instance is usually worked as two rows. A long running stitch is used for basting to hold edges together ready for sewing firmly by machine or hand, and it is always removed once the sewing is finished.

2. Overcasting This is a slanting stitch used by dressmakers when neatening the raw edges of darts and seams. Soft toymakers use overcasting for a different purpose and always work it from left to right. It is used as a basting stitch in place of running stitch when holding two or more fur fabric pieces together prior to seaming. The stitch enables the fur pile to be tucked in as the stitches are made. It can be left in place as it

is not in the way of the seam.

Take the needle over the edge of the fabric and insert beneath the edge, about ¼ in. (6 mm.) to the right. Pull through and repeat. Continue working along the edge in this way, tucking in the pile as you go.

3. Backstitch Used for sewing seams by hand, worked from right to left. Bring the needle up ⅛ in. (3 mm.) beyond the start of the seam. Take the needle and insert it at the start of the seam, then bring it up ⅛ in.(3 mm.) beyond the point at which it first emerged. Take the needle back to meet the first stitch and continue. Backstitches worked one on top of another are also used to secure a row of stitching.

4. Stab stitch Similar to running stitch in appearance, but worked in an up and down movement, one stitch at a time.

5. Hemming There are several stitches that can be used for hemming. The most useful is slipstitch. It is worked from right to left, taking a small stitch from the main part of the fabric and passing into the hem and along the fold for ¼ in. (6 mm.) before taking another small stitch.

6. Ladder stitch An ideal stitch for closing openings, attaching parts and bracing limbs because it is invisible. It is simply a running stitch worked on the surface. Always use strong thread. Secure the thread with backstitches in the seam allowance, then take the needle across the opening to the seam line on the other side; take a small running stitch, then pass it directly across the opening to the seam line on the opposite side, and repeat. Make several stitches and then pull up the thread, encouraging the raw edges of the opening to roll in, out of sight. For extra strength, work

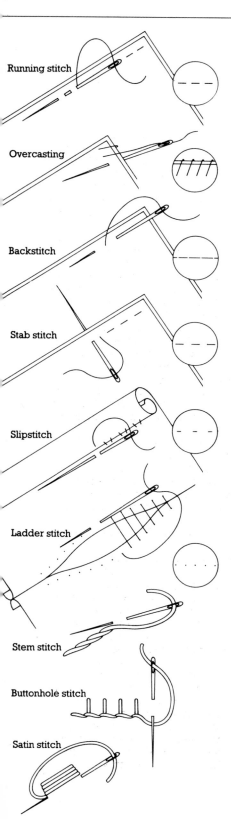

Running stitch

Overcasting

Backstitch

Stab stitch

Slipstitch

Ladder stitch

Stem stitch

Buttonhole stitch

Satin stitch

another row of ladder stitch along the seam line in between the existing stitches.

Decorative stitches

1. Stem stitch An outline stitch ideal for facial features. Bring the needle up at a starting point on the left side. Insert the needle a short distance ahead and emerge halfway between the two points. Continue in this way, always making stitches of the same length and keeping the thread either above or below the needle when working.

2. Satin stitch Straight stitches, worked closely side by side with no fabric visible between them.

3. Buttonhole stitch This stitch has the appearance of straight stitches with a rope edge connecting them all together. It is ideal for embroidering the irises of the rag doll, where it radiates from the center to form a circle. Bring the needle up on the outline of the eye, then insert it into the inside of circle and take a small straight stitch to emerge on the line again with the thread looped under the needle as in the diagram. Continue in this way until the circle is completely covered with buttonhole stitch.

Facial features

Treatment of the facial features will determine the character of the toy. Use the markings on the pattern as a guideline only. All the features can be embroidered.

Safety eyes These commercially made bright plastic eyes are designed so that children are not able to pull them out of the toy. They are attached before the toy is stuffed. Make a hole in the fur with an awl, then push the shank through from the right side to the inside of the toy. Now level the washer on the shank, making sure that the teeth on the

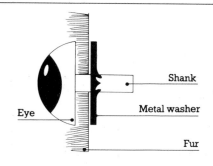

Eye · Shank · Metal washer · Fur

Safety eye in place. The shank is pushed through the fur fabric and held in place with a washer.

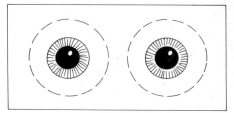

Eyes embroidered on interfacing. They are cut out along the dotted line. Gathering stitches are worked around the edge and pulled tight behind the eye.

washer are facing away from the back of the eye. Wrongly inserted washers can be removed only by cutting them away with wire cutters. Now, using finger pressure only, push the washer in place.

Embroidered eyes for animals
These eyes are perfect for toys for very young children where safety is of paramount importance. Draw circles of the required size onto a piece of firm interfacing. Embroider the irises first, then the pupils, with satin stitch. Lastly work a few stitches in white to represent the highlights. Now cut out the eyes from interfacing, leaving a border as shown. Gather around the edge of the interfacing and pull up a thread to draw the interfacing behind the

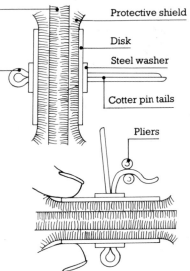

eye. Fasten off securely, then hem the eye in place on the toy. Check that the highlights are paired.

Embroidered noses and mouths

The noses and mouths of all the animals are embroidered. Noses are usually blocks of satin stitch while mouths are long straight stitches caught down in the center. The slightest change in position will alter the character of the toy.

Jointing

Joints allow parts of a body, like the head and limbs, to pivot around a central axis, and for selected positions to be held. They are quite unlike the stitched-hinge joints where limbs move only backward and forward and always return to a set position. To be successful, joints must be really tight – in fact so tight to begin with that they are difficult to move. The components for the joints are sold in sets. There are plastic safety joints available which are easy to assemble, but the size range is restricted. They are not of as good a quality as those made with hardboard or wooden disks, the type used for the jointed teddy bear described in this book.

Assembling a crown joint

Joints are available in several sizes, ranging from ½ in. (12 mm.) to 6 in. (15 cm.) in diameter. They are always referred to by standard measurements. They consist of two steel washers, two disks and a split cotter pin. The whole joint is locked in place by the cotter pin.

There is an art in making a firm joint, so it is worth practicing before working on the toy. You will need a 2in joint, an awl, long-nosed pliers and a piece of fur.

1. Cut the fur fabric into four pieces – two 6 in. (15 cm.) squares to represent the skin of the limb and the body wall) and two 3 in. (7.5

Use the pliers to bend the tail over so that it forms a loop and comes to rest on the disk.

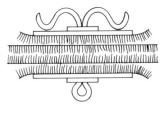

A finished crown joint.

cm.) diameter circles. The circles will act as shields to protect the skin from the abrasive action of the disks turning.

2. Use the awl to pierce a hole through the center of each square and circle. The hole should be just large enough to take the cotter pin. Protect or strengthen the hole with buttonhole stitch, a felt patch glued in place or a piece of iron-on interfacing.

3. Dismantle the joint into separate pieces and reassemble it with the fur fabric positioned between the disks. Do this by holding the eye of the cotter pin in your left hand and load on first a steel washer, then a disk with the smooth side upward, a protective shield and a fur square

with the pile facing upward, the second fur square and the second protective shield with the pile facing downward, the second disk with smooth side downward, and lastly a steel washer.

4. Press the disks together between the forefinger and thumb of the left hand. Spread the pins of the cotter apart, getting ready for the joining action.

5. With your right hand, slide the tips of the pliers down the longest tail of the pin until they rest ½ in. (12 mm.) above the disk and grip firmly. While maintaining the pressure of your left hand to hold all the parts together, use the pliers to bend the tail over so that it forms a loop and comes to rest on the disk.

6. Turn the sample around and form a loop in the same way with the second cotter tail. While bending the tails, you should be holding the joint firmly together as well as pulling up hard on the cotter tails.

7. Test the firmness of the joint by pulling on the fur squares. If the joint is not tight enough for your liking there are two things that you might try. Firstly, insert the pliers back in each loop, in turn, and twist down closer towards the disk. Secondly, pull each loop, in turn, out and away from its mate. If both these efforts fail, remove the cotter pin and start again. The cotter pin will have to be replaced when reusing the joint for a toy.

Squeaks and growls

Most of the devices used to produce sound effects are inserted into the body when the stuffing is nearly complete. They are held in place with a few stitches worked at the same time as you close the stuffing opening. In order to do this you must first wrap the chime or growler in muslin, or make a close-fitting muslin bag to fit over it. Push the unit into the body, with the unit positioned so that the holes of the cylinder or the hole for a winding key lies against the fur skin. Pack the stuffing closely around the unit, then close the opening, catching the muslin cover into the seam.

Most music boxes have a protruding shank into which a key fits. Remove the key, cover the box and push the shank through a hole in the muslin. The shank will protrude through the body as you close the opening. Screw on the winding key.

Bells can be tied on ribbons around the neck of a toy. However, if the toy is intended for a very young child it is much safer to insert the bell in an empty ear. In this way the bell can be heard without being muffled by the stuffing, yet the danger of it being swallowed is removed.

Finishing touches
Grooming Check over all the seam lines to see that no fur is trapped. Use a suede brush or a needle held horizontally in your fingers to tease out any trapped fur. Particular care is needed at the tip of ears and around curved seams. If longer pile furs have been used, you may want to trim fur away from the eyes. Trimming is best done with small embroidery scissors, snipping little bits at a time, cutting with the pile, rather than against it.
Bracing Occasionally limbs tend to splay out, and upset the balance of a toy. Push the offending limbs into the desired position and hold them there by working a row of ladder stitch between the limb and the body.
Tying a bow There is an art in tying an attractive bow and for this reason it is well worth practicing. Do a trial run by holding a bottle between your knees and pretending that it is a neck!

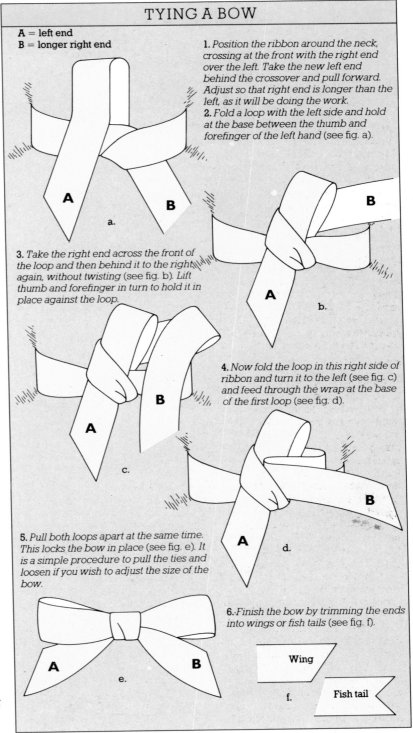

TYING A BOW

A = left end
B = longer right end

1. *Position the ribbon around the neck, crossing at the front with the right end over the left. Take the new left end behind the crossover and pull forward. Adjust so that right end is longer than the left, as it will be doing the work.*
2. *Fold a loop with the left side and hold at the base between the thumb and forefinger of the left hand (see fig. a).*

3. *Take the right end across the front of the loop and then behind it to the right again, without twisting (see fig. b). Lift thumb and forefinger in turn to hold it in place against the loop.*

4. *Now fold the loop in this right side of ribbon and turn it to the left (see fig. c) and feed through the wrap at the base of the first loop (see fig. d).*

5. *Pull both loops apart at the same time. This locks the bow in place (see fig. e). It is a simple procedure to pull the ties and loosen if you wish to adjust the size of the bow.*

6. *Finish the bow by trimming the ends into wings or fish tails (see fig. f).*

Wing

Fish tail

MAKING

SIMPLE CLUTCH TOYS

Feel and touch are among the first senses that very young children develop, so a set of clutch toys is an ideal introduction to the world of play. All such toys should have the following qualities in common; they should be small, lightweight, soft, easy to grasp, washable and safe. Whenever possible, they should also contain an element of surprise – a squeaker is hidden in the teddy bear's tummy, for instance.

Balls are always firm favorites, as they stimulate children in many different ways. Here, there are patterns for balls of different sizes, weights, textures and color – balls that your child can knock and roll to hear chimes, balls to reach out for in basic catch games, balls to kick and a puzzle ball for young fingers to explore. All the patterns are easy to follow and require a minimum of equipment and materials.

SOFT BALL
Preparing the pattern
This is a simple ball, consisting of just two segments. Its circumference is 12½ in. (32 cm.). Make a full-size pattern from the grid on a piece of cardboard and transfer the markings *(see p.12)*. Cut two pieces; one in each color.

Making the ball
1. Pin the segments together, matching the centers of the outside curves (A), of one segment to the centers of the inside curves (B), of the other segment *(see fig. a)*. Continue pinning between these centers.

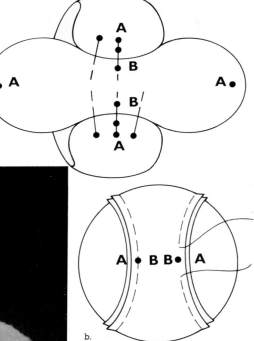

a.

b.

2. Stitch all around to make a continuous seam, leaving a small opening on one side *(see fig. b)*. Remove the pins.
3. Turn the ball right side out and stuff lightly, but using enough material to hold the shape. Close the opening with ladder stitch.

From left to right: the chime ball, soft ball, puzzle ball, nursery teddy bear and the patchwork ball.

PROJECT **2**

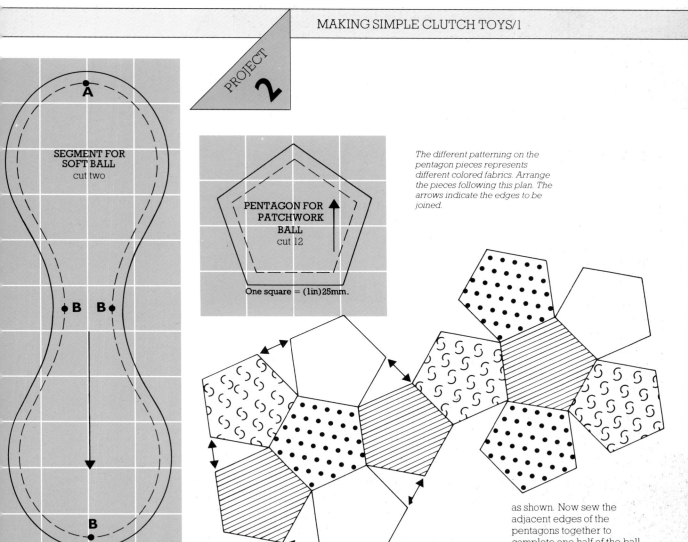

SEGMENT FOR
SOFT BALL
cut two

A

B B

B

One square = 1 in. (25 mm.)

PENTAGON FOR
PATCHWORK
BALL
cut 12

One square = (1in)25mm.

The different patterning on the pentagon pieces represents different colored fabrics. Arrange the pieces following this plan. The arrows indicate the edges to be joined.

MATERIALS

Soft ball
2   6 x 12 in. (15 x 30.5 cm.) pieces of short-pile fur
    fabric in different colors
    2 oz. (56 g.) stuffing

Patchwork ball
12 4 in. (10 cm.) square pieces of short-pile fur fabric in
    4 different colors
    3 oz. (84 g.) stuffing

EQUIPMENT

Dressmaking shears, pins, needles, thread, tape measure
or ruler, pencil, pattern-making equipment.

PATCHWORK BALL
Preparing the pattern
Make a full-size pattern of the pentagon shape on cardboard *(see p.12)*. Use the pattern to cut three pentagons in each color, making a total of 12 pieces. The finished ball measures 15 in. (38 cm.) in circumference.

Making the ball
Join all pieces with right sides together by hand sewing with a firm backstitch along the seam line.
1. Take one of the pieces and sew one edge of five other pieces to each of the five sides

as shown. Now sew the adjacent edges of the pentagons together to complete one half of the ball.
2. Repeat this process with the remaining six pentagons to make the other half of the ball. By following the diagram, which shows all the pentagons laid out flat, you will be able to arrange the different color patches so that they are evenly distributed over the ball.
3. Slip one half of the ball inside the other, with right sides together, making sure that they are correctly positioned. Sew together around the midline leaving two edges free. Turn right side out through this opening and stuff, taking care to form a firm, rounded shape. Close the opening with ladder stitch and remove any trapped fur from the seams.

PROJECT **3**

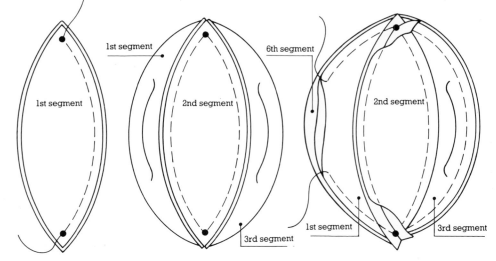

a. *Sew together two segments of different colors along one side between the dots.*

b. *Sew a third segment of a different color to the first two, making half the ball.*

c. *Place the two halves of the ball right sides together, and sew around the edge, leaving a small opening.*

CHIME BALL
Preparing the pattern
The ball consists of six segments and is 13½ in. (34 cm.) in circumference when completed. Make a full-size pattern *(see p.12)* of the segment shape on cardboard and use this as the cutting guide – you will need two segments in each color.

Making the ball
You can make this ball on a sewing machine – this is the quickest method – or by hand. When sewing the various segments together, make sure that the pile runs in the same direction, so that the textures match.
1. With right sides facing, sew two segments of different colors together between the dots *(see fig. a)*.
2. Sew a third different colored segment to the first two *(see fig. b)*. This completes one half of the ball.
3. Sew the remaining three segments together in the same way and following the same color sequence. This completes the other half of the ball.
4. Place the two halves together with dots matching top and bottom and sew around the edge, leaving an opening on one side *(see fig. c)*.
5. Turn the ball right side out and start to stuff it firmly. Insert the chime in the middle of the ball and pack the stuffing around it to hold it in place. Close the opening with ladder stitch.

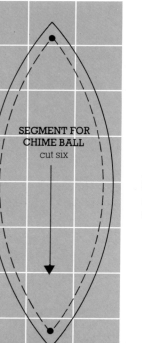

SEGMENT FOR CHIME BALL
cut six

One square = 1 in. (25 mm.)

PUZZLE BALL
Preparing the pattern
Make full-size patterns of the two shapes *(see p.12)* and use these to cut 12 of each from the fabrics. Mix the colors to make an attractive design. The red and blue ball illustrated here uses six different fabrics – each color having a dark and light patterned piece, as well as a plain, unpatterned one. The finished ball has a circumference of 19 in. (48 cm.).

Making the ball
The geometrical symmetry of this ball makes it appear something of a puzzle at first glance. However, it can be made quite easily, using a sewing machine.
1. Clip the seam allowance at B on a semicircular piece of fabric. Then take a gusset of a different color and lay it right sides together on the semicircle along a curved edge from A to B. Sew between the dots *(see fig. a)*. Leave the machine needle through the material at B.
2. Lift the machine foot and swing the fabrics around until

a. *Sew together a semicircle and a gusset of a different color, from A to B.*

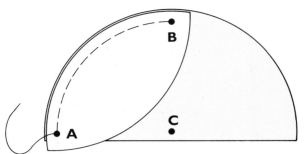

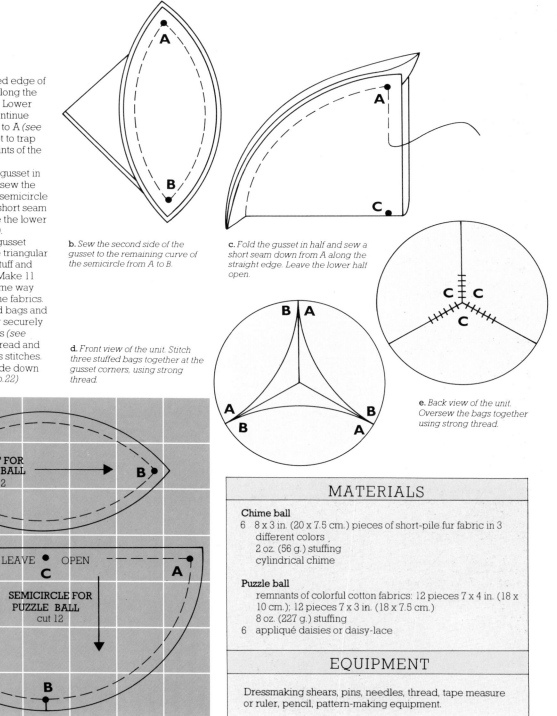

PROJECT 4

the unstitched curved edge of the semicircle lies along the other side of gusset. Lower machine foot and continue sewing from B back to A *(see fig. b)*. Take care not to trap any seams at the points of the gusset.

3. Carefully fold the gusset in half lengthwise and sew the straight sides of the semicircle together, making a short seam down from A. Leave the lower half open *(see fig. c)*.

4. Trim and cut the gusset seams, then turn the triangular bag right side out, stuff and close the opening. Make 11 more bags in the same way taking care to mix the fabrics.

5. Take three stuffed bags and stitch them together securely at the gusset corners *(see fig.d)*. Use strong thread and make inconspicuous stitches.

6. Turn the unit upside down and *(continued on p.22)*

b. Sew the second side of the gusset to the remaining curve of the semicircle from A to B.

c. Fold the gusset in half and sew a short seam down from A along the straight edge. Leave the lower half open.

d. Front view of the unit. Stitch three stuffed bags together at the gusset corners, using strong thread.

e. Back view of the unit. Oversew the bags together using strong thread.

GUSSET FOR PUZZLE BALL
cut 12

One square = 1 in. (25 mm).

LEAVE OPEN

SEMICIRCLE FOR PUZZLE BALL
cut 12

MATERIALS

Chime ball
6 8 x 3 in. (20 x 7.5 cm.) pieces of short-pile fur fabric in 3 different colors
2 oz. (56 g.) stuffing
cylindrical chime

Puzzle ball
remnants of colorful cotton fabrics: 12 pieces 7 x 4 in. (18 x 10 cm.); 12 pieces 7 x 3 in. (18 x 7.5 cm.)
8 oz. (227 g.) stuffing
6 appliqué daisies or daisy-lace

EQUIPMENT

Dressmaking shears, pins, needles, thread, tape measure or ruler, pencil, pattern-making equipment.

oversew the bags together at C *(see fig. e)*. Again use strong thread. This time, however, the stitches need not be concealed, as they will be hidden within the ball.

7. Make three more units in the same way, so that all 12 bags are stitched together into four units of three.

8. Now join two of these units together, stitching four gusset points together on the front and at C on the back. Join the remaining two units in the same way *(see fig. f)*. You now have the two halves of the ball.

9. Place the two halves together crosswise, so that all the Cs are in the center of the ball and all the gussets face outwards. Stitch the gusset points together at the Xs marked *(see fig. g)*. Cover the outside joining stitches with the daisies.

f. Join two units together, stitching four gusset points together on the front, and at C on the back. This makes up half of the ball.

g. Match all the Cs of both halves, so that all the gussets face outwards and stitch together at the Xs marked.

NURSERY TED
Preparing the pattern

Make a full-size pattern from the grid *(see p.12)*. Note that only half a back is drawn, so you will need to complete this. Transfer all the markings. Cut one each head back, head front, snout and body back. Cut two body fronts, reversing the pattern to get a left and right front. The finished bear is 8 in. (20 cm.) tall.

Making the bear

Because of its size, this toy is best made by hand sewing with a firm backstitch. The result is softer to cuddle than a machine-made bear would be.

1. Start by folding over the arm to sew the shoulder dart on the body front. Fold over the foot likewise to sew the ankle dart *(see fig. a)*. Make the darts on the other half of the front body. Trim the darts.

2. With right sides together sew both fronts down the center front seam.

3. Make the small seating darts on the body back and the two heel darts on each leg.

4. Place the body front and back together, right sides facing, and oversew around the edge, leaving the neck and the slit in the center back open. Take particular care to tuck in the fur when working along the underside of the arms and around the feet. You will also need to ease the fullness between the toes and the soles. Seam together.

5. Match A of the snout to A of the head with right sides together. Then, working each side in turn, ease the snout to fit the opening, pin and sew in place *(see fig. b)*. Complete the snout by sewing the two small darts.

6. Sew the dart on the head back then place the front and back heads together and sew all round the edge, leaving the neck open. Turn right side out and fix the safety eyes in place.

7. Carefully remove any trapped fur from the seams, especially around the ears. Stab stitch across base of each ear to seal off from stuffing.

8. Place the completed head inside neck of body with right

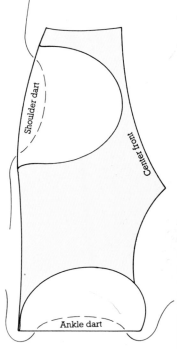

a. Sew the shoulder and ankle darts and clip the seams to release tension.

sides together and side seams matching. Sew in place. Some easing will be necessary to get a good fit. Turn the completed skin right side out through the back opening.

9. Stuff the head, arms, feet and legs in that order. Stuff the body cavity last, inserting the squeaker into the tummy area and making sure that it is surrounded by stuffing *(see p.16)*. Crease the top of the legs at body join, so that they flex. Sew up back opening.

10. Embroider a block of satin stitch for the nose and two straight stitches for the mouth *(see fig. c)*. Finally, tie a gaily colored bow around the neck.

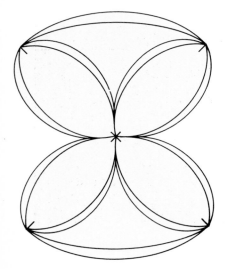

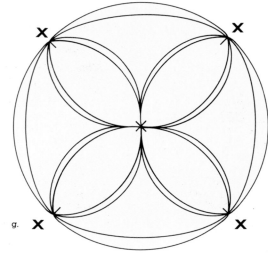

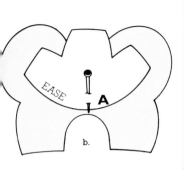

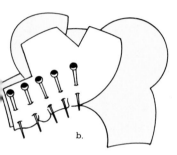

b. Pin the snout and head at A with right sides together. Ease the snout on one side to fit the curve opening and pin. Pin the other side before sewing.

c. The safety eyes are fixed in place before the head is attached to the body. The nose and mouth are embroidered when the teddy bear has been assembled.

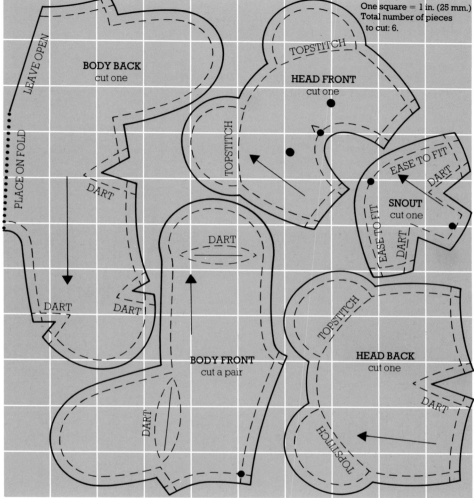

One square = 1 in. (25 mm.)
Total number of pieces to cut: 6.

BODY BACK
cut one

HEAD FRONT
cut one

TOPSTITCH

EASE TO FIT

SNOUT
cut one

LEAVE OPEN

PLACE ON FOLD

DART

BODY FRONT
cut a pair

HEAD BACK
cut one

TOPSTITCH

DART

MATERIALS

18 in. (45.5 cm.) square of short-pile fur
pair of ½ in. (12 mm.) amber safety eyes
3 oz. (84 g.) stuffing
brown embroidery thread for nose
squeaker
length of ribbon for bow

EQUIPMENT

Dressmaking shears, embroidery scissors, pins, needles, thread, tape measure or ruler, pencil, pattern-making equipment.

MAKING AN
ELEPHANT

The design of this elephant continues a tradition that started just over 100 years ago when Margarete Steiff made her first small gray felt elephant to sell in her shop in Giengen, West Germany. She gave one of these elephants to her young nephew Richard, who later joined his aunt in her toymaking business and designed the first European jointed teddy bear.

Preparing the pattern
Make a full-size pattern from the pattern grid and transfer all the markings onto your copy *(see p.12)*. Cut all the pieces from the main color, except for one pair of ears, which should be cut from the white fur to make the ear linings. The finished elephant stands 10 in. (25 cm.) tall.

Making the body
1. Start by placing an ear lining and an ear piece right sides together. Sew around the curved edge. Turn the ear right side out and carefully

24

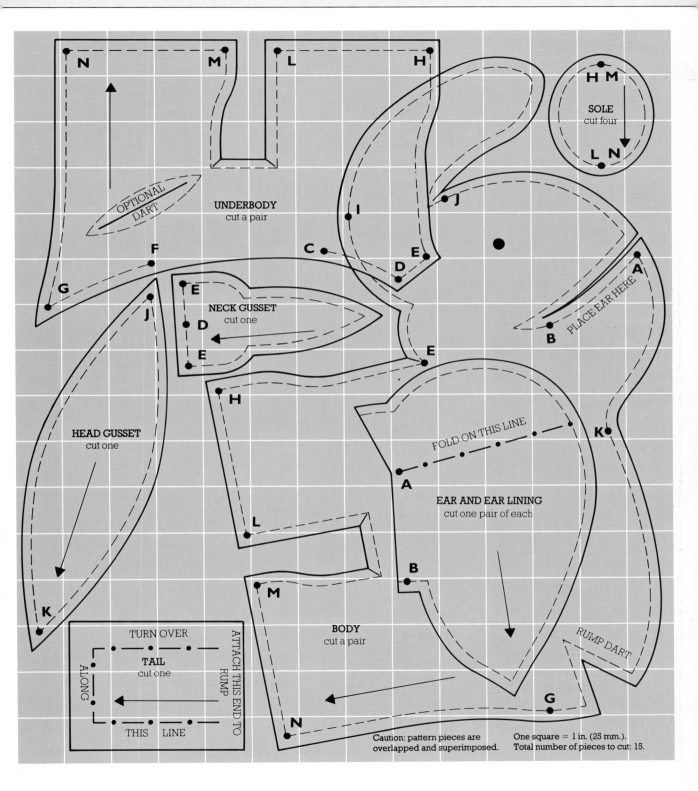

N M

L H

H M
SOLE
cut four
L N

I

J

C
E
D

A
PLACE EAR HERE
B

OPTIONAL DART

UNDERBODY
cut a pair

F

G

J

E
D
NECK GUSSET
cut one
E

E

H

HEAD GUSSET
cut one

FOLD ON THIS LINE

K

A

EAR AND EAR LINING
cut one pair of each

L

K

TURN OVER

TAIL
cut one

ALONG

ATTACH THIS END TO RUMP

THIS LINE

M

B

BODY
cut a pair

RUMP DART

N

G

Caution: pattern pieces are overlapped and superimposed.

One square = 1 in. (25 mm.).
Total number of pieces to cut: 15.

PROJECT **6**

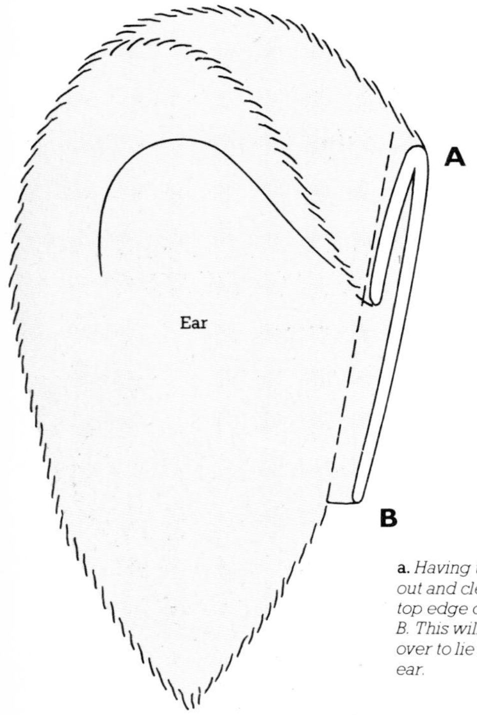

Ear

A

B

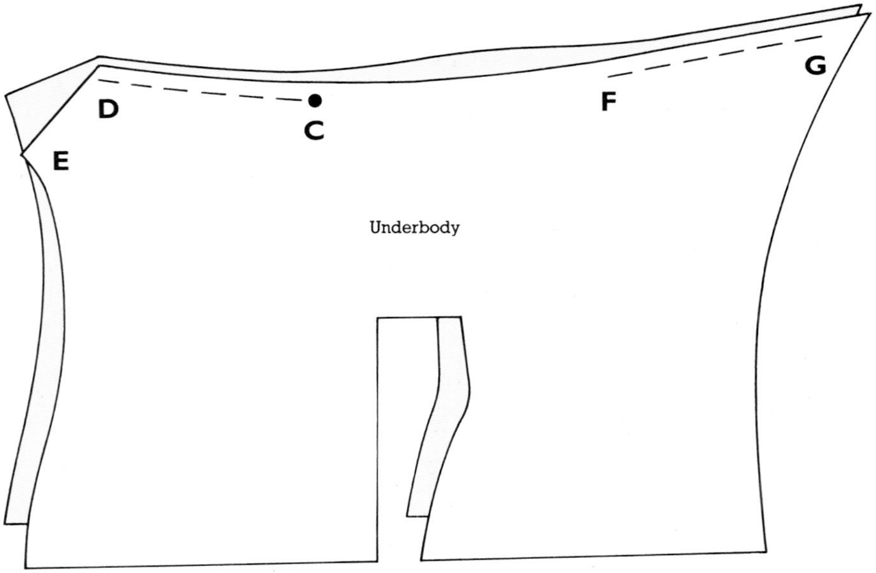

a. *Having turned the ear right side out and cleaned the seams, fold the top edge down and baste from A to B. This will bring the main color over to lie on the white front of the ear.*

D

C

E

F

G

Underbody

b. *Sew the underbody from C to D and sew in the neck gusset as shown in figure c. Then sew the seam from F to G.*

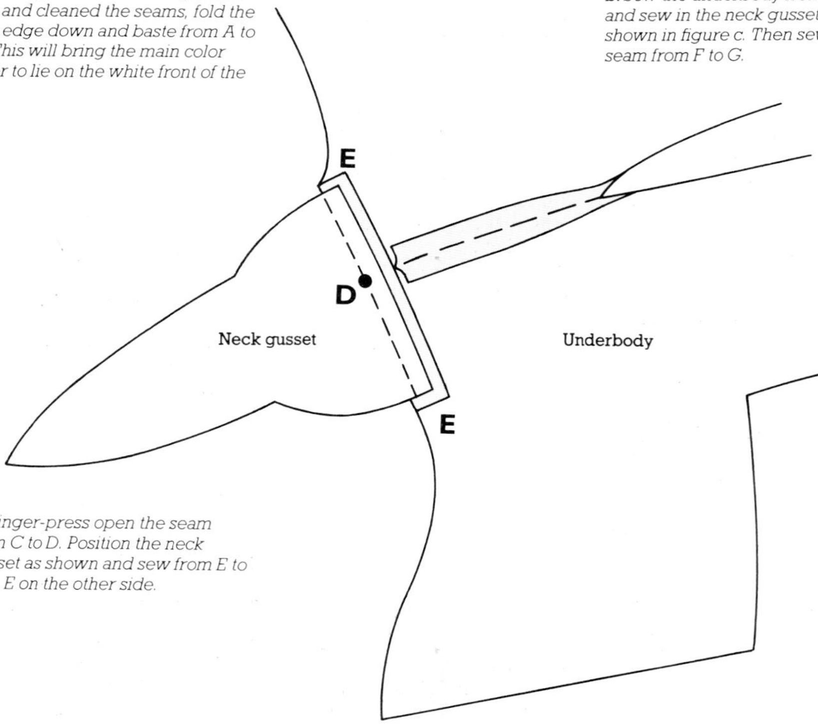

E

D

Neck gusset

Underbody

E

c. *Finger-press open the seam from C to D. Position the neck gusset as shown and sew from E to D to E on the other side.*

release any fur trapped in the seam. Fold the top edge of ear down along the fold line marked on the pattern and baste the open straight edges together from A to B *(see fig. a)*. The fold will bring the main color over to lie on the white front lining. Make a second ear in the same way, ensuring that you have a pair.

2. Place an ear against a body piece matching A to B and baste in place. Fold the body over to close the ear slot and sew the ear securely in the seam. Sew the remaining ear to the other side of the body in the same way.

3. Sew the underbody pieces, right sides together, from C to D *(see fig. b)*. Then finger-press the seam open and sew the neck gusset in place from E

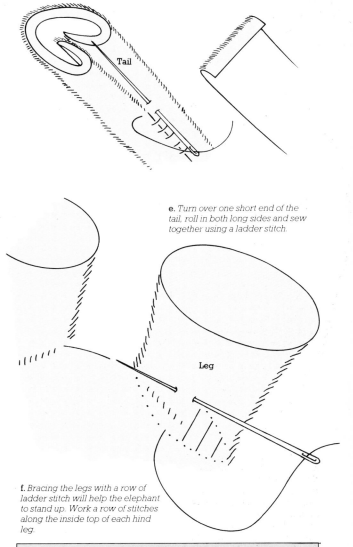

through D to E on the other side *(see fig. c)*. Continue sewing the underbody pieces together from F to G.

4. Now place the underbody against a body piece and with right sides together sew up the front leg from H, through E to the end of the neck gusset at I. Sew the remaining body to the other side of the underbody in the same way.

5. Sew the trunk pieces, right sides together, from I to J then insert the head gusset. After pinning and basting by overcasting, sew from J to K on each side in turn.

6. Make the darts on the rump of each body, then sew together from K back to G.

7. Finish joining the underbody by sewing from L to M on each side and then from N to G, again on each side in turn.

8. Insert the soles in turn, making sure that the fur lies in the same direction on each one. Pin, baste by overcasting, then sew, pressing open the leg seams as you work around the sole *(see fig. d)*.

9. Turn the completed skin right side out and fix the eyes in place.

10. Stuff the elephant, working on the legs first, followed by the trunk, head and body proper. Close the opening with ladder stitch.

Finishing touches

11. Catch the back of each ear to the head gusset seam with ladder stitch for about 1 in. (25 mm.)

12. Turn in one short edge of the tail piece. Then roll in both long sides and ladder stitch the folded edges together *(see fig. e)*. This makes a thin tail that is self-stuffed. Check that the pile runs down the tail before sewing it in place at G.

13. Finally, work a row of ladder stitch along the inside top of each hind leg *(see fig. f)*. This should pull the legs inwards on to the underbody, so bracing them to help the elephant stand securely. Without this bracing, the legs will tend to splay apart. Another way of achieving the same effect is to sew the optional dart marked on the underbody pattern piece, although this will mean predetermining the exact amount of bracing needed, which is not easy to judge.

14. Groom the elephant carefully, especially the soles, which are sure to have fur trapped in the seams.

e. Turn over one short end of the tail, roll in both long sides and sew together using a ladder stitch.

f. Bracing the legs with a row of ladder stitch will help the elephant to stand up. Work a row of stitches along the inside top of each hind leg.

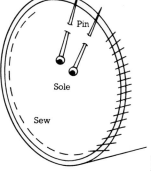

d. Pin a sole in position and baste by overcasting before sewing to the leg. Ensure that the fur lies in the same direction for all the feet.

MATERIALS

27 in. (69 cm.) wide by 24 in. (61 cm.) long piece of pink short-pile fur
10 in. (25 cm.) square of white, short-pile fur for ear linings
10 oz. (280 g.) stuffing
pair ⅝ in. (16 mm.) brown eyes

EQUIPMENT

Dressmaking shears, embroidery scissors, pins, needles, thread, tape measure or ruler, pencil, pattern-making equipment.

MAKING A
RABBIT

Rabbits, especially fluffy baby bunnies, are firm favorites in the nursery. Many of the best loved characters in nursery rhymes and stories are rabbits – the White Rabbit, Brer Rabbit, Little Gray Rabbit, Peter Rabbit, Flopsy, Mopsy and Cottontail are just a few of the most celebrated. As a result, rabbits are extremely popular soft toys. This pattern is for a simple sitting rabbit that can be dressed easily by young children.

Preparing the pattern

Make a full-size pattern and transfer all markings to the pattern *(see p.12)*. Cut out the body sides, base, ears, arms and feet from the short pile fur and the tail from the fluffier white fur. The finished rabbit will stand 11¾ in. (30 cm.) tall. The pattern for the dress is a rectangle with a neck ruffle. Simply cut the cotton into two strips, one measuring 7 x 24 in. (18 x 61 cm.) and the other 3 x 24 in. (7.5 x 61 cm.),

Making the body

It will be quicker to sew the body on the machine, but you must be careful not to trap fur in the center front seam that runs down the head and through the tummy.

1. Fold an arm in half and, with the right sides together, sew round the paw to the shoulder *(see fig. a)*. Turn the arm right side out and stuff it almost to the top. Keep the stuffing away from the opening with a pin. Make a second arm, using the same method.

2. Place one arm on a body side, matching A to A and B to B in the lower half of the dart and baste it in place *(see fig. b)*. Fold the body over to bring all the As together and then sew from C through A to B *(see fig. c)*. Check that the arm is securely attached. Sew the

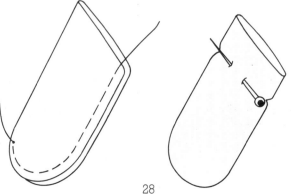

a. Fold each arm in half and sew around the paw to the shoulder, using backstitch. Turn the arms right side out and stuff them, keeping the stuffing in place with pins.

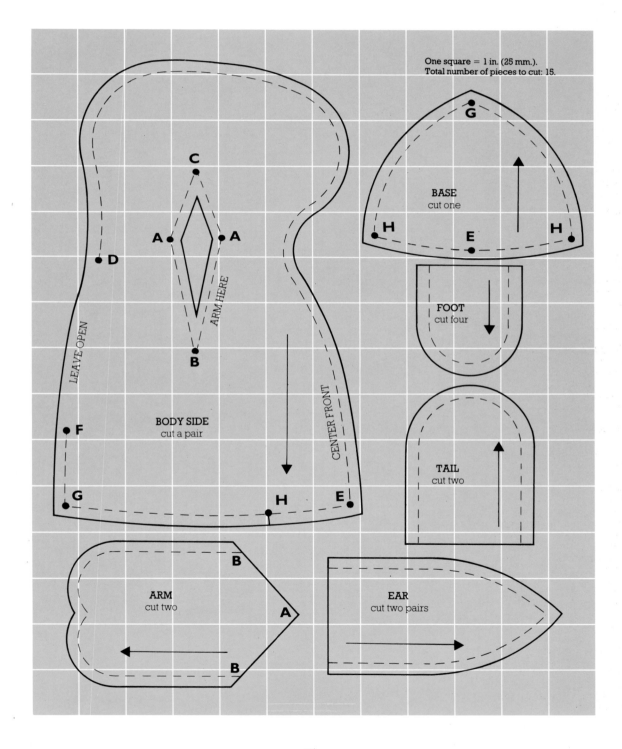

One square = 1 in. (25 mm.).
Total number of pieces to cut: 15.

G

BASE
cut one

H   **E**   **H**

C

A   **A**

D

ARM HERE

B

LEAVE OPEN

FOOT
cut four

BODY SIDE
cut a pair

CENTER FRONT

TAIL
cut two

F

G   **H**   **E**

B

ARM
cut two

A

B

EAR
cut two pairs

29

PROJECT 7

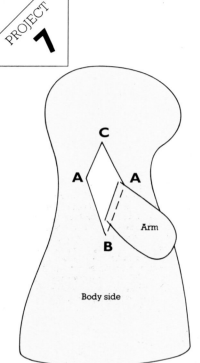

Arm

Body side

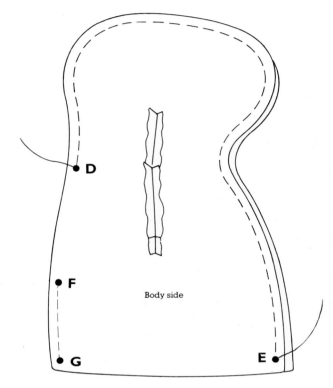

Body side

b. *Match As and Bs of one arm with one body side. Baste in place.*

c. *Fold the body over, match up all the As and sew from C through A to B. Repeat with the other arm and body side. Make sure that the arms are firmly sewn in to the seams and remember to remove the pins.*

d. *Sew the body sides together. First sew around the head from D, then continue down the center front seam to E. Sew from F to G and leave an opening in the back for stuffing.*

rabbit's second arm to the remaining body side in the same way. Then remove the pins from the arms.

3. Place both of the body sides so that their right sides are together, and sew from D around the head and down the center front to E. Leave an opening in the center back by sewing a short seam from F to G. Reinforce the stitching at the front of the neck by sewing a second row on top of the original seam line.

4. Place the feet pieces together in pairs, right sides facing, and sew around the curved edges. Turn them right side out and stuff lightly, so that they will flop forward when sewn in place. Position the feet on the right side of the base of the body, so that the straight edges of the feet align with the straight edge of the base. Sew the feet in place from H through E to H.

5. Position the base against the lower edge of the body and sew it in place from E to H to G on each side in turn. Do not forget to cut the seam allowance at H so that you can change direction without making puckers.

6. Turn the completed skin right side out and stuff, paying particular attention to shaping the cheeks and neck. The body must be firmly stuffed if the head is not to wobble. When you are satisfied with its appearance, close the opening with ladder stitch.

7. Sew the tail pieces together, right sides facing, around the curved edge then turn it right side out. Turn in the raw edges and insert a small amount of stuffing to give the tail some bulk. Ladder stitch it in place against the body.

Base

Foot

H   E   H

e. *Having stuffed the feet, position them on the base, aligning the straight edges, and sew from H through E to H.*

Tail

f. *Turn in the edges of the tail and attach it firmly to the body with ladder stitch.*

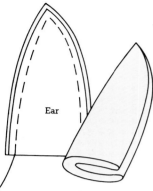

Ear

g. *Sew the curved edges of the ears together in pairs. Turn right side out, turn in the edges and shape the ears by folding in half and oversewing the lower edges together.*

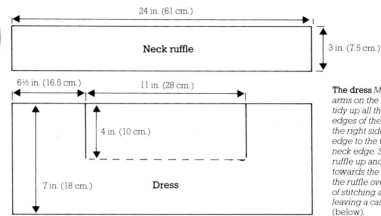

24 in. (61 cm.)

Neck ruffle

3 in. (7.5 cm.)

6½ in. (16.5 cm.)   11 in. (28 cm.)

4 in. (10 cm.)

7 in. (18 cm.)   Dress

The dress *Make two slits for the arms on the larger piece (left) and tidy up all the edges. Hem three edges of the neck ruffle and match the right side of the unhemmed edge to the wrong side of the dress neck edge. Sew together, turn the ruffle up and press the seam towards the ruffle (below left). Turn the ruffle over, press, sew two rows of stitching along the neckline leaving a casing between them (below).*

8. Sew the ears together in pairs, right sides facing, leaving the straight edges open. Turn right side out. Turn under the raw edges, then fold each ear in half and oversew the open base edges together.
9. Position the ear on the head and ladder stitch in place, with the fold next to center top seam. Use the same method to sew on the second ear.
10. Embroider a pair of brown eyes on interfacing with a diameter of ¾ in. (18 mm.). Sew them in place on the head.
11. Work a block of satin stitches for the nose and use straight stitches for the mouth.

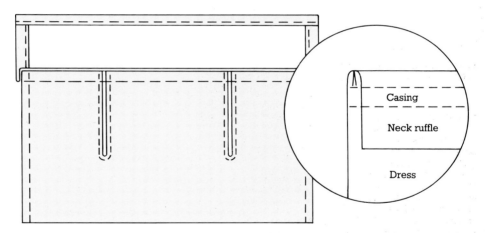

Casing

Neck ruffle

Dress

Making the dress
12. Cut two slits for the arms in the large rectangle of cotton print, as shown.
13. Make a narrow hem on both sides of the arm slits, as well as on both short sides of the dress. Trim the neck ruffle to the same measure as the neck of the dress, allowing for hems on both sides.
14. Now make a narrow hem along one edge and both short sides of the neck ruffle. Place the unhemmed edge of the neck ruffle right side to wrong side of the dress with neck edges matching. Sew along the

length of the neckline, then turn the ruffle up and press the seam towards the ruffle.
15. Turn the ruffle over and press. Sew two rows along the length of the neckline, making a casing for the ribbon as shown.
16. Thread the ribbon through the casing, pull it up and fit the dress on the rabbit. Finish by measuring the length required for the dress and hemming. Additional bows can be stitched to the front of the dress for decoration or, if you wish, tied around the ears.

MATERIALS

18 in. (45.5 cm.) square of short-pile fur
small piece of medium-pile white fur
4 oz. (112 g.) stuffing
pair embroidered eyes
embroidery thread for the nose
24 x 10 in. (61 x 25.5 cm.) piece of cotton print
24 in. (61 cm.) length of narrow ribbon

EQUIPMENT

Dressmaking shears, embroidery scissors, pins, needles, thread, tape measure or ruler, pencil, pattern-making equipment.

PROJECT **8**

MAKING A
DUCKLING

For a really cuddly duckling, choose a soft fur with medium-length pile to give the feel of real downy feathers. The thickness of the pile makes it necessary to baste by overcasting all the curved edges together before sewing, as otherwise they will slip and stretch. This method of working will give a professional finish to the toy and ensures that the duckling maintains its original shape.

Preparing the pattern
Make a full-size pattern and transfer all the markings on to your copy (see p.12). Remember to cut the slits for the wings and feet. Cut the beak and feet from velvet and all the other pieces from fur. The finished duckling will stand 12 in. (30.5 cm.) tall.

Making the body
1. With right sides together sew the feet, leaving an opening between A and B. Clip to the corners between the feet and turn right side out. Lightly stuff the toes of each foot. Baste the open edges onto the matching curve (A-B) of the right side of the body gusset, with the toes pointing toward the neck edge (see fig. a). Fold the gusset right sides together and bring all the raw edges together; sew from A to B to enclose the feet.
2. Place the wings right sides together in pairs and sew around the edges, leaving an opening between C and D. Take care to tuck in the fur on the tip of the wings, so that it is not trapped in the seams, as this would spoil the fluffy appearance. Turn the completed wings right side out and clean the seams.
3. Place a wing in position on the right side of a body side, matching points C and D (see fig. b). Fold over the top

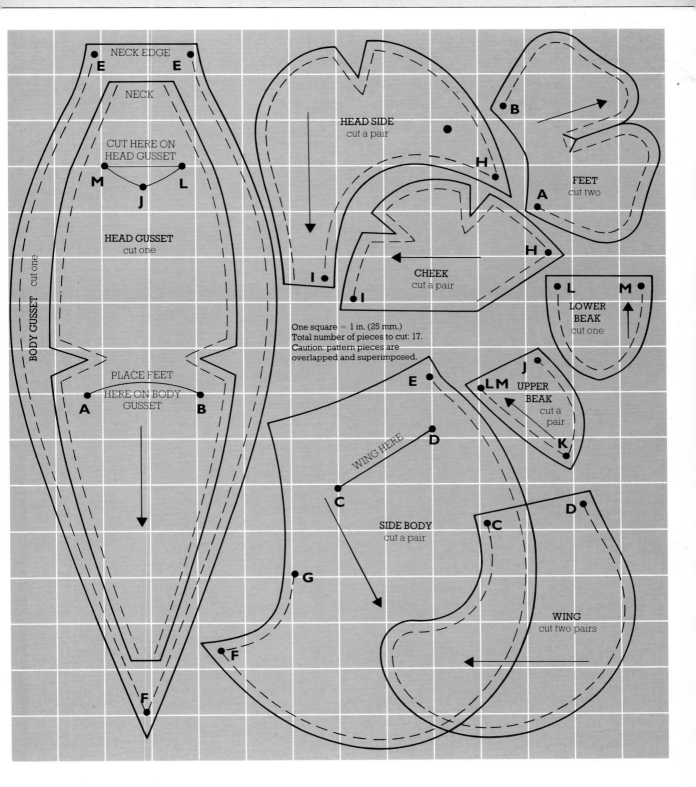

NECK EDGE

E   E

NECK

CUT HERE ON
HEAD GUSSET

M   L

J

HEAD GUSSET
cut one

BODY GUSSET   cut one

PLACE FEET
HERE ON BODY
GUSSET

A   B

F

HEAD SIDE
cut a pair

B

FEET
cut two

H

A

CHEEK
cut a pair

H

I

I

One square = 1 in. (25 mm.)
Total number of pieces to cut: 17.
Caution: pattern pieces are
overlapped and superimposed.

LOWER
BEAK
cut one

L   M

E

J

D

LM   UPPER
BEAK
cut a
pair

K

WING HERE

C

SIDE BODY
cut a pair

C

D

G

WING
cut two pairs

F

F

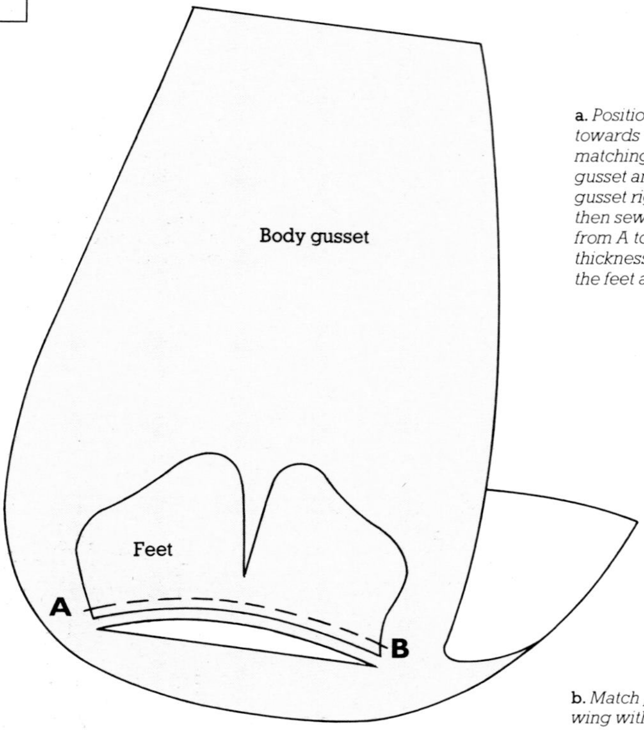

PROJECT **8**

Body gusset

Feet

A

B

a. *Position the feet, pointing towards the neck edge, against the matching curve (A-B) on the body gusset and baste in place. Fold the gusset right sides together and then sew the raw edges together from A to B through all four thicknesses of fabric. Ensure that the feet are securely attached.*

b. *Match points C and D of one wing with one body side. Fold over the body side and sew the wing securely in position.*

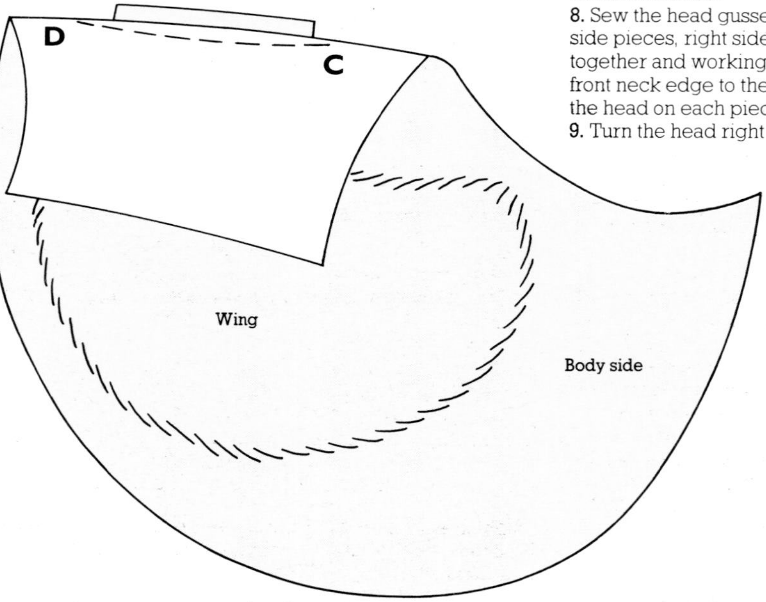

eight in all. With right sides together, pin one cheek to a head side at H and I and halfway between *(see fig. c)*. The pins must lie at right angles to the edges and the darts should be finger-pressed open to reduce bulk. Now pin again at intervals, gently easing in the fullness. Baste by overcasting and sew. Attach the second cheek to second head side and sew in the same way.

6. Sew the two upper beaks together, right sides facing, from J to K. Then sew them onto the lower beak from L through K to M *(see fig. d)*. Turn right side out and place in position in the head gusset. Baste in place before sewing. This is easier to do by hand with a small, firm backstitch.

7. Using all six strands of the black embroidery thread, work two straight stitches for nostrils on the upper beak. Fasten off the threads on the seam allowance.

8. Sew the head gusset to both side pieces, right sides together and working from the front neck edge to the back of the head on each piece.

9. Turn the head right side out.

portion of the body side (near E), bring all the edges together and then sew across. Tug the wing to make sure that it is firmly attached. Sew the second wing to the other body side in the same way.

4. Now attach the body gusset to the body sides. With right sides together, match point E of the right and left sides with E on the body gusset; with right sides together, baste by overcasting from E to F, working a little on each side in turn. Take care not to stretch the curved edges and so distort the shape. Sew the short center back seam from G to F. Turn the body skin right side out and check appearance. Put to one side.

Making the head
5. Start by sewing the darts on the head pieces. There are

D

C

Wing

Body side

34

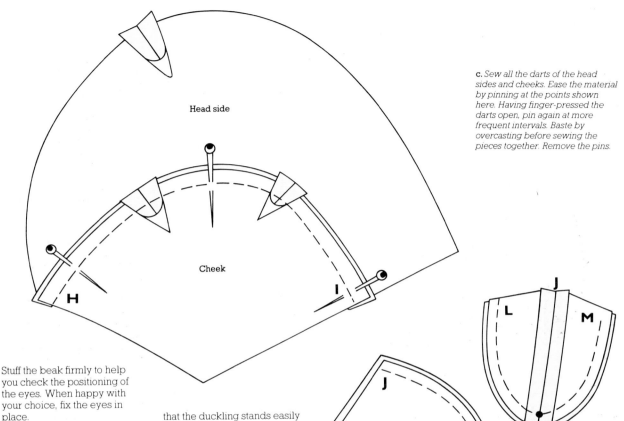

Head side

Cheek

H

I

J

L

M

J

K

K

c. *Sew all the darts of the head sides and cheeks. Ease the material by pinning at the points shown here. Having finger-pressed the darts open, pin again at more frequent intervals. Baste by overcasting before sewing the pieces together. Remove the pins.*

Stuff the beak firmly to help you check the positioning of the eyes. When happy with your choice, fix the eyes in place.

Fixing the head to the body
10. Now insert the head into the neck opening of body, so that neck edges are matching and the right sides are together. The head will be right side out, while the body will be inside out. There is a longer neck edge to the head, so ease in the fullness as you pin the edges together, checking that the center fronts and backs are matching. If you are not happy with pinning, run a strong gathering thread around the neck edge and gather until it fits the body neck edge. In both instances, baste before sewing either on machine or by hand-sewing a backstitch with doubled, strong thread.
11. Turn the completed skin right side out. Stuff the head first, then the body. Make sure

that the duckling stands easily and does not topple over. Close the opening with ladder stitch. As a finishing touch, tie a blue bow around the neck *(see p.17).*

MATERIALS

24 in. (61 cm.) long x 27 in. (69 cm.) wide length of white medium-pile fur
9 in. (23 cm.) square of old gold velvet or felt for beak and feet
8 oz. (240 g.) stuffing
1 yd. (1 m.) blue satin ribbon
pair ⅞ in. (22 mm.) blue eyes
black embroidery thread for nostrils

EQUIPMENT

Dressmaking shears, embroidery scissors, pins, needles, thread, tape measure or ruler, pencil, pattern-making equipment.

d. *Sew the two upper beak pieces together, first from J to K and then sew these two pieces to the lower beak (from K to M through J).*

PROJECT **9**

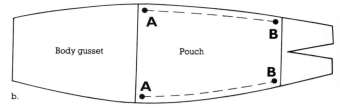

MAKING A
KANGAROO

Kangaroos make lovable and amusing toys – this one has the added attraction of a baby in its pouch. The mother kangaroo can be made by machine or by hand, but it is easier to sew the baby by hand, as he is so small. To complete the family, make a father kangaroo – without a pouch, of course!

Preparing the pattern
Make a full-size grid and mark out the pattern pieces on it *(see p.12)*. Cut out both kangaroos and keep the pieces separate. The mother kangaroo stands 15 in. (38 cm.) tall to the tip of her ears. The baby kangaroo is only 6 in. (15 cm.) tall.

Making the mother
1. Fold the pouch lengthwise to make a dart by bringing Ys together, right sides together. Sew from X to Y *(see fig. a)*. Sew the dart in the pouch lining in the same way. Press both darts open.
2. Place the pouch and the pouch lining right sides together, matching the top and bottom edges. Sew across the top from A to A and across the bottom from B to B. Then turn the faced pouch right side out.
3. Baste each open side of the pouch.
4. Make the center front dart in the body gusset by folding it lengthwise and bringing Ys together. Sew from X to Y. This leaves the lower part of the dart open so that the lower part

of the body can be stuffed later.
5. Position the pouch against the body gusset by matching As to As and Bs to Bs on each side, with the lining of the pocket against the right side of the body *(see fig. b)*. Baste in place down each side.
6. Position one inside leg to the

matching side of the body gusset and sew from C to D. Check this seam to see that the edge of the pouch has been caught in place securely. Sew the inside leg on the other side in the same way.
7. Place the gusset between the body sides and baste by overcasting on each side from

a. Sew a dart in the pouch flap from X to Y. Sew the lining in the same way. Press the darts open before sewing the pieces together.

b. With the pouch lining against the right side of the body gusset, match points A and B and baste down the sides of the pouch before attaching the inner leg pieces.

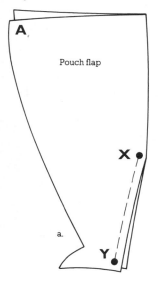

A

Pouch flap

X

a.

Y

b.

Body gusset

Pouch

A

B

A

B

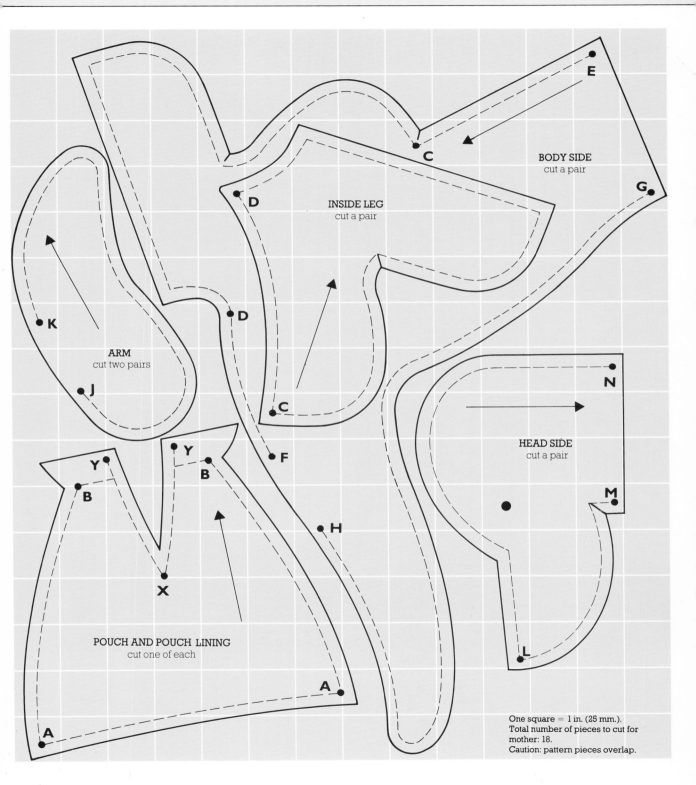

E

BODY SIDE
cut a pair

G

C

INSIDE LEG
cut a pair

D

D

C

ARM
cut two pairs

K

J

N

HEAD SIDE
cut a pair

M

Y

B

Y

B

F

H

L

X

POUCH AND POUCH LINING
cut one of each

A

A

One square = 1 in. (25 mm.).
Total number of pieces to cut for
mother: 18.
Caution: pattern pieces overlap.

PROJECT **9**

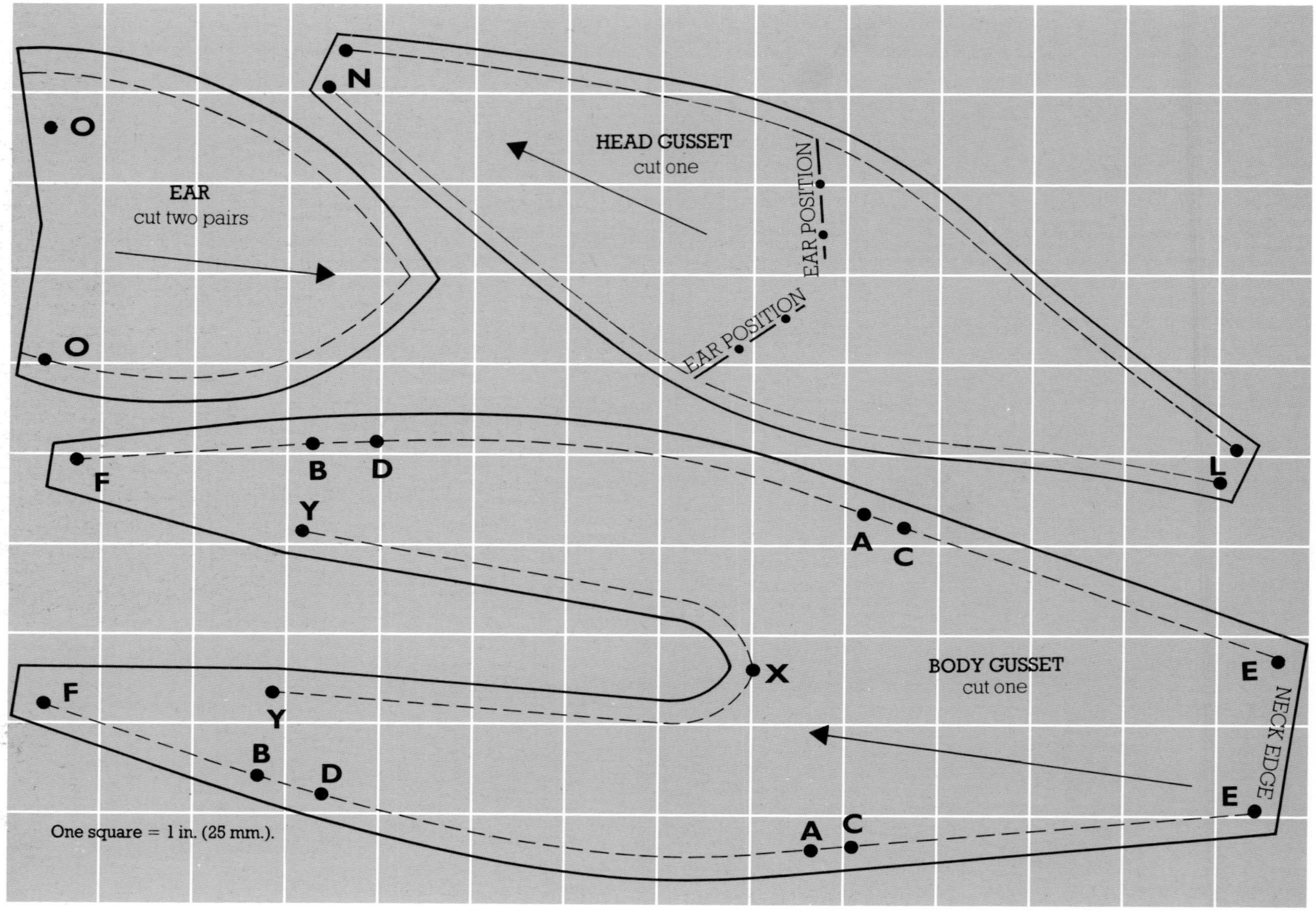

EAR
cut two pairs

• O
O

HEAD GUSSET
cut one

• N

EAR POSITION

EAR POSITION

L

F
B D
Y

A C

One square = 1 in. (25 mm).

F
Y
B D

X

BODY GUSSET
cut one

E

NECK EDGE

E

A C

E through C, around the leg and through D to F. Check on the right side for appearance, then sew in place.

8. Complete sewing the body sides together, right sides facing. Baste by overcasting and then sew from the neck edge at G, down the back and around the tail to H.

9. Turn the completed body skin right side out and begin stuffing. Push small pieces of stuffing into each leg and into the tip of the tail through the opening on the underside of the tail. Pack the stuffing in

really firmly, as these points provide the base on which the kangaroo stands. Stuff the haunches and then the rest of the body through the open neck.

10. Run a gathering thread around the neck edge and gather sufficiently to turn the raw edges inwards. Close the undertail opening and the lower edge of the pouch with ladder stitch.

11. Place the arm pieces together, right sides facing, in pairs and sew around the edges, leaving an opening

between J and K. Turn each completed arm right side out, stuff firmly then close the opening with ladder stitch.

12. Position the arms against the side of the body and ladder stitch to secure. Be careful not to have them outstretched, as otherwise they might get in the way of the baby while the imbalance could also throw the mother forward (see fig. c).

13. With right sides together, sew the under chin seam of the two head sides from L to M. Clip the corner.

14. Position the head gusset

between the head sides and baste by overcasting. Then sew in place from L to N on both sides.

15. Turn the head right side out and insert the safety eyes (see p.15). Now stuff the head, rounding it into a pleasing shape. Run a strong gathering thread around the neck edge, gather and fasten off. Place both neck edges together and ladder stitch the head to the body. Work around the neck several times to make sure that the head is securely attached.

16. Place the ears together in

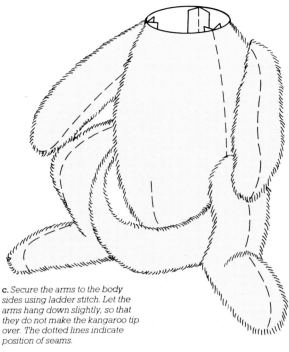

c. Secure the arms to the body sides using ladder stitch. Let the arms hang down slightly, so that they do not make the kangaroo tip over. The dotted lines indicate position of seams.

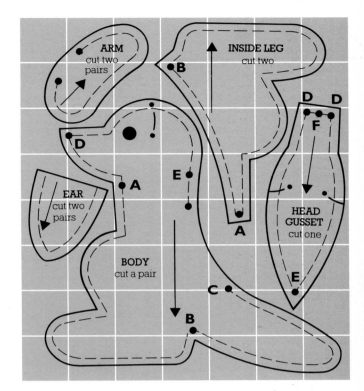

One square = 1 in. (25 mm.)
Total number of pieces to cut for baby : 13.

pairs, right sides facing, and sew the curved sides. Turn right side out and free any trapped fur from the seams, especially the tips. Fold one ear in half, so that the Os meet, and baste by overcasting the open edges together. Fold and sew the second ear in the same way.

17. Position the ears on the head gusset. Ladder stitch in place along the front sides first, then sew the back sides so that they are pulled back.

18. Embroider the nose by working a block of satin stitch (see p.15 and fig. d).

Making the baby
1. Sew the inside legs together from A to B.
2. Position the inside legs between the body sides and sew in place from A through B to C on each side in turn.
3. Match the head gusset at D on each side in turn and baste in place before sewing back to E and just beyond.

4. Fold the head gusset at F and sew under the nose from F through D to A.
5. Turn the completed skin right side out and insert the safety eyes.
6. Stuff the body through the opening on the back, then close it with ladder stitch, working back from C toward E. Pull slightly on the working thread to curl the tail upwards. Make the arms in the same way as for the mother.
7. Place the ear pieces together in pairs and baste by overcasting the curved edges together before sewing. Turn each completed ear right side out and baste the straight edges of each ear together. Ladder stitch in place the head gusset seam on each side.
8. Embroider the nose on the tip of the snout by working a small block of satin stitch.

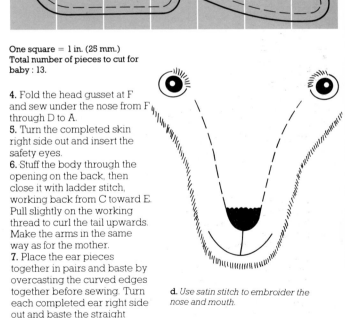

d. Use satin stitch to embroider the nose and mouth.

Finishing touches
Groom mother and baby carefully. Pinch the legs of baby together and sit him sideways in the pouch.

MATERIALS

24 in. (61 cm.) of 54 in. (136 cm.) wide gray or beige fur
10 oz. (230 g.) stuffing
pair ¾ in. (18 mm.) safety eyes for mother
pair ⁵⁄₁₆ in. (8 mm.) safety eyes for baby
six-stranded black embroidery thread

EQUIPMENT

Dressmaking shears, embroidery scissors, pins, needles, thread, tape measure or ruler, pencil, pattern-making equipment.

MAKING A
RAG DOLL

Children the world over have delighted in rag dolls of all shapes and sizes for thousands of years. This pattern is a popular twentieth century version worked with familiar everyday materials. The clothes can be changed, making the doll even more attractive as far as young children are concerned.

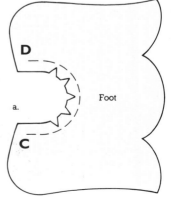

Preparing the pattern

Make a full-size pattern and transfer all the markings onto it *(see p.12)*. Notice that the pieces for the front and back of the body are very similar, so they are given together. The difference between them is that the front is shorter and lacks darts, while the back is longer with a pair of seating darts. Cut out all the pieces from calico, except for the face panel, which you should leave until the features have been embroidered. The finished doll stands 24 in. (61 cm.) tall.

Making the body

1. Fold the lower section of the back body so that the Ys on each side are together. Then sew each dart from X to Y and finger-press the seam open.
2. Sew the front and back bodies together from A on one side up to B at the top of the neck and down to A on the other side. Clip the neck curves and then turn the completed body right side out.
3. Sew a row of stay stitching around the ankle curve of each foot from C to D to strenghten the curve *(see fig. a)*. Now clip the inside curve so that you can stretch the foot piece to fit between C and D on the ankle edge of the leg. Sew together and repeat for the other foot.
4. Press open the ankle seam as much as possible. Fold the leg right sides together and sew the center back and under foot seam from E through C/D to F *(see fig. b)*.
5. Press open the edge of the

The pattern pieces for the front body and the back body are superimposed on the grid. These diagrams (left) show clearly the differences between the two pieces.

Back body

Front body

a. *A row of stay stitching will strengthen the ankle curve of the foot. Clip the inside curve so that it can be fitted onto the leg.*

D

C

Foot

a.

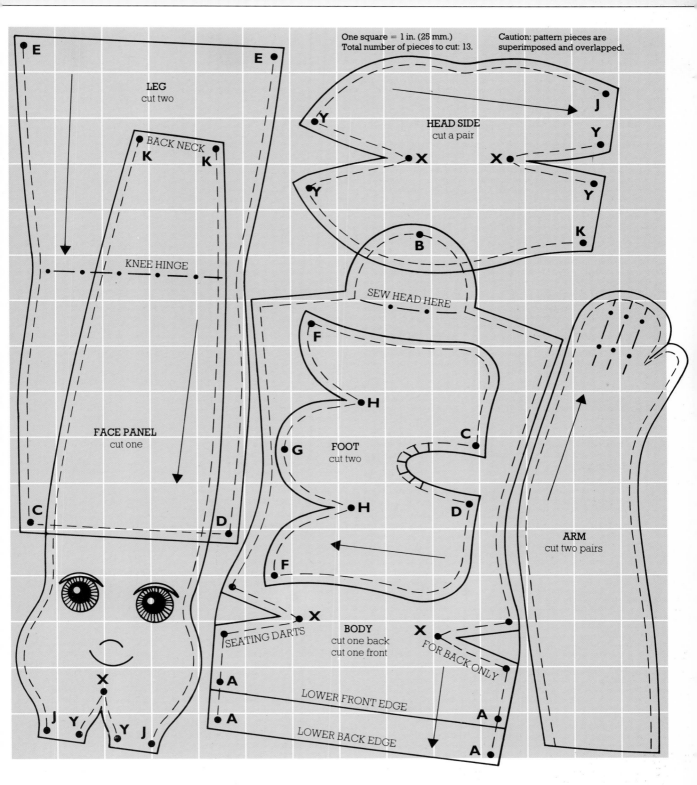

One square = 1 in. (25 mm.)
Total number of pieces to cut: 13.

Caution: pattern pieces are
superimposed and overlapped.

LEG
cut two

E

E

BACK NECK

K   K

KNEE HINGE

FACE PANEL
cut one

C

D

HEAD SIDE
cut a pair

J

Y

Y

X   X

Y

Y

K

B

SEW HEAD HERE

F

H

G   FOOT
cut two

H

F

C

D

SEATING DARTS

X

BODY
cut one back
cut one front

X

FOR BACK ONLY

A

A

LOWER FRONT EDGE

LOWER BACK EDGE

A

A

ARM
cut two pairs

X

Y   Y   J

J

b. *Press open the ankle seam and sew from E down the center back seam of the leg, under the foot to F.*

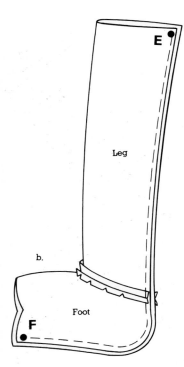

c. *Press open the edge of the foot flap to bring G and F together, then sew across from H to H, forming the toes.*

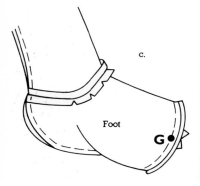

foot flap to bring G and F together *(see fig. c)*. Sew across from H to H, forming the toes. Complete the second leg in the same way.

6. Turn the completed leg right side out and stuff the foot firmly before stuffing the leg up to the knee line. Hold the stuffing in place with a pin *(see fig. d)* and then work across the knee line with stab stitches using strong thread. Pull up slightly on the thread before tying off. Continue stuffing the leg to the top, but not as firmly as the lower leg. Hold the stuffing away from the top of the leg with a pin. Complete the second leg to this stage.

7. With raw edges together, baste each leg in place against the lower edge of the front body. The legs should meet in the middle; toes should lie over the shoulders, so that when they drop down the toes point forwards. Sew across from one side to the other to attach the legs securely. Remove all the pins from the legs.

8. Stuff the body firmly, then turn under the lower back edge and ladder stitch the front to the back. Make a small pleat on each side at A to take in the fullness as you do this.

9. Sew the arm pieces together in pairs, right sides facing, leaving the top edges open. Clip between the thumb and forefinger, then turn right side out. To make the fingers, insert a small amount of stuffing into each hand and hold it in place with a pin as shown here.

10. Top stitch the finger divisions using strong thread. Work the fingers of both hands at the same time, so that you consciously make a pair. Remove the pins and stuff each arm firmly up to the top. Hold the stuffing in place with a pin while you turn under the raw edges of the opening, pleat

each side *(see fig. e)*, then overcast the edges together.

11. Lay the top of the arms over the shoulders, checking that the thumbs face forwards before sewing in place. Remove the holding pins. If the arms do not hang down beside the body, you will have to take them off and remove a little stuffing from the top before reattaching them.

Making the head

12. Before cutting out face panel, make a tracing of the facial features on tissue paper. Transfer your design to the face panel by tailor-tacking the outline through the paper onto the fabric. Pull the tissue paper away extremely gently.

13. Start by embroidering the

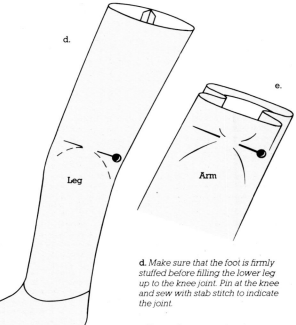

d. *Make sure that the foot is firmly stuffed before filling the lower leg up to the knee joint. Pin at the knee and sew with stab stitch to indicate the joint.*

e. *Form pleats on each side of the top of the arms to tuck in the excess fabric before oversewing the edges together.*

irises and then the pupils in buttonhole stitch, using three strands of embroidery thread *(see p.15)*. Use black for the pupils and green or blue for the irises. The highlights are made with a few white straight stitches worked as a small 'v' to cover the area marked out by the hands of a clock at 10 o'clock. The upper eyelids are worked in brown stem stitch; the mouth is worked with the same stitch but with a pink or rose colored thread. Now cut out the face panel.

14. Sew both darts on each head side piece and at the chin on the face panel by folding to bring Ys together then sewing from X to Y for each dart in turn.

15. Position the face panel

between the head sides, right sides together, and baste carefully before sewing from J at the front to K at the back neck edge on each side in turn. Turn the head right side out and check that the cheeks are level.

16. Turn under a narrow hem around the neck edge and baste in place. Now stuff the head firmly, carefully rounding out the fullness of the cheeks. Leave a hollow just large enough to fit the neck stalk on the body. Push the body and head together, screwing the neck stalk into position. Ladder stitch in place carefully, so that the head does not twist off-center. Remove the basting stitches from the neck edge.

17. Now make the hair. Cut approximately 80 strands of yarn, each 24 in. (61 cm.) long. Machine these lengths together through the middle, so that you make a wig about 6 in. (15 cm.) wide from front to back.

18. Cut an 8 in. (20 cm.) by 4 in. (10 cm.) piece of cardboard. Wind the yarn over this template, covering it evenly. Slip the loops off and without disturbing them stitch across three times (see fig. e). This part of the wig forms the hair at the front and back and is the first part to be positioned.

19. Lay the wool over the top of the head and backstitch in place at the front, then on the crown and finally at the back, making sure that it is pulled tight into place before sewing.

20. Now lay the long strands across the head so that they hang down the sides with the machine parting postioned centrally. Backstitch the central parting to the doll's head.

21. Catch the long hair down on each side of the head where the ears would be, and sew in place. Again pull the strands taut before stitching so that little fingers cannot pull the hair off. Cover the stitches with bows as a finishing touch.

22. The hair may be left in bunches or braided as you wish.

f. Wind wool around a piece of cardboard, then remove without disturbing the wool. Sew across by machine in the order given here.

g. Attach the hair first. Sew in position at the front, on the crown, and finally at the back.

MATERIALS

24 in. (61 cm.) of 36 in. (92 cm.) wide calico or doll skin fabric
12 oz. (340 g.) white stuffing selection of six-stranded embroidery threads in white, brown, black, blue, pink or rose for facial features
blusher for cheeks
approx 2 oz. (50 g.) brushed acrylic wool or mohair for hair

EQUIPMENT

Dressmaking shears, embroidery scissors, pins, needles, bodkin, thread, tape measure or ruler, pencil, tissue paper. pattern-making equipment.

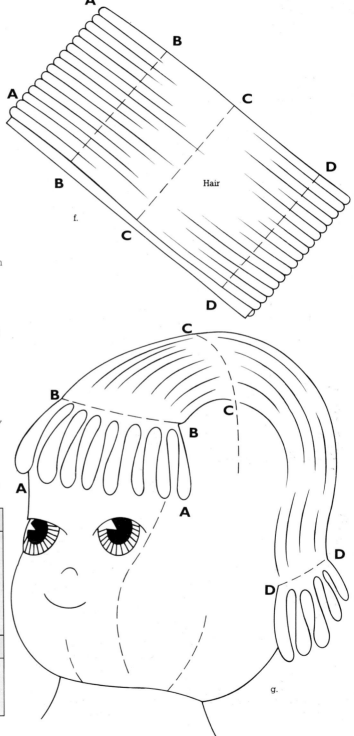

PROJECT

11

── DRESSING A ──
RAG DOLL

For many children, dolls are truly members of the family, taking their place as a make-believe sister, brother, baby or best friend. Half the fun comes from dressing such dolls and tending to all their needs. The removable clothes for this doll are all made from pure cotton, so that they may be easily laundered and maintained.

Preparing the patterns

Prepare a full-size pattern of the pantaloons *(see p.12)*, with a higher back waist edge and a lower front. The petticoat is a simple rectangle of cotton, 36 in. (92 cm.) wide and 11½ in. (29 cm.) deep, which can be cut without a pattern.

Prepare cardboard patterns for the back and front bodice and sleeves. The dress skirt is 36 in. (92 cm.) wide and 10 in. (25.5 cm.) long; the ruffle is made from two strips, each 5½ in. (14 cm.) by 36 in. (92 cm.). Cut a bias strip (a thin strip of material cut on the cross of the fabric) to neaten the neck edge.

The pinafore pattern can be made by cutting cardboard copies of the following sizes or by measuring directly onto the fabric. The skirt is 36 in. (92 cm.) wide and 9 in. (23 cm.) long, the waistband is 2½ in. (6.5 cm.) by 13 in. (33 cm.), while the two straps each measure 10 in. (25.5 cm.) by 1¾ in. (4.5 cm.). The two ruffles are each 18 in. (46 cm.) by 3 in. (7.6 cm.).

Prepare a cardboard pattern of the shoe pieces from the grid. Transfer all markings.

Making the underwear

1. Turn over a narrow hem to the right side at the lower end of each leg of the pantaloons, then cover the raw edges by sewing lace around the hem on the right side.

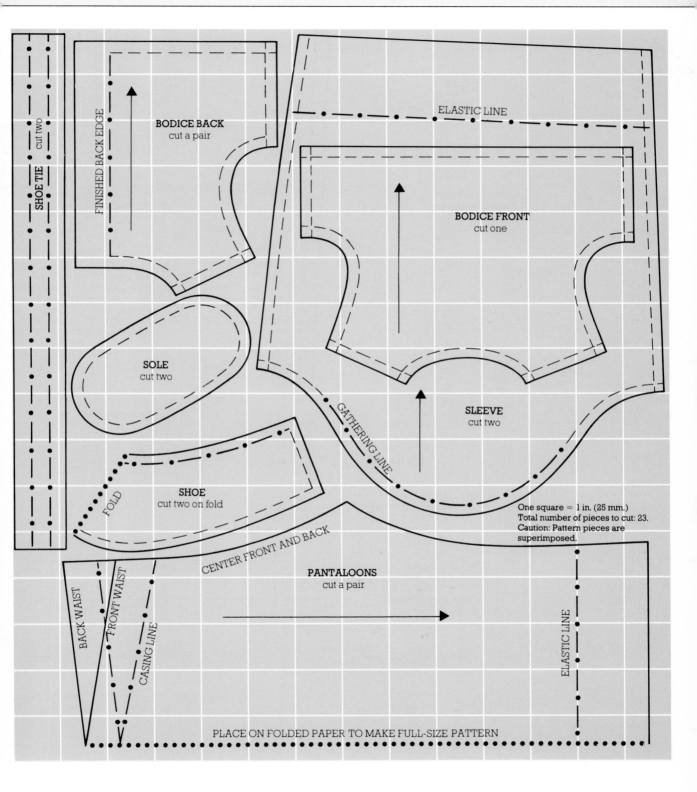

SHOE TIE
cut two

FINISHED BACK EDGE

BODICE BACK
cut a pair

ELASTIC LINE

BODICE FRONT
cut one

SOLE
cut two

SLEEVE
cut two

GATHERING LINE

FOLD

SHOE
cut two on fold

CENTER FRONT AND BACK

One square = 1 in. (25 mm.)
Total number of pieces to cut: 23.
Caution: Pattern pieces are
superimposed.

BACK WAIST

FRONT WAIST

CASING LINE

PANTALOONS
cut a pair

ELASTIC LINE

PLACE ON FOLDED PAPER TO MAKE FULL-SIZE PATTERN

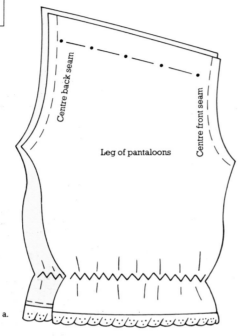

a.

a. Sew the lace and elastic on the pantaloons and then sew together along the center front and center back seams.

2. Stretch a piece of elastic across the line marked on each leg and sew in place either with zig-zag or straight stitching.
3. Join each half of the pantaloons together by placing right sides facing and sewing the center front and center back seams (see fig. a).
4. Fold the pantaloons right sides together and sew up one inside leg and down the other one.
5. Turn under a narrow single hem at the waist edge, then fold again to make a casing for the elastic. Sew, leaving a

b. Make a casing for the elastic in the waistband of the pantaloons. Leave a small opening at the center back.

c. Sew the bias strip to the right side of the neck edge, turn over to the wrong side of the bodice and hem in place.

small opening at the center back (see fig. b).
6. Cut a length of elastic to fit the waist, allowing for overlap. Thread through the casing, sew ends together and then close opening.
7. The petticoat is a simple half slip. Fold the cotton in half with wrong sides together and sew a narrow seam along the short end. Turn wrong side out and sew another narrow seam, enclosing the first seam. All the raw edges will now be enclosed in a French seam.
8. Make a narrow double hem along one long edge and

attach a row of lace to it on the right side.
9. Turn under a narrow fold to the wrong side along the waist edge and press. Now turn under again to make a casing for the elastic. This casing should be about ½ in. (12 mm.) deep. Sew around the edge of the casing, leaving a small opening.
10. Cut a length of elastic to fit the waist, again allowing for an overlap.
11 Thread the elastic through the waist casing and draw up to fit the doll. Overlap the ends and fasten off securely. Close the opening of the casing.

Making the dress

12. Sew the back bodice to the front bodice on both shoulder seams.
13. Run a row of gathering stitches along the top of each sleeve. Gather to fit the armhole opening and then sew in place.
14. Make a narrow double hem at the wrist edge of each sleeve.
15. Stretch a row of elastic across each sleeve, as marked on the pattern, and sew in place with zig-zag or straight stitching.
16. Fold front and back bodice, rights sides together, to bring the edges of the sleeves together. Sew each underarm and side bodice seam in turn.

17. Gather the waist edge of the skirt and draw it up until it fits the waist edge of the bodice. Distribute the gathers evenly, baste in place and then sew.
18. Make a narrow double hem down both edges of the dress from the neck to the lower edge. Turn a narrow, single hem to the front along the lower edge of the dress and sew to hold.
19. Prepare the dress ruffle by sewing the long strips together across one short end. Press the seam open. Fold the strip in half lengthways, right sides facing, and sew all along the long edge. Turn right side out and press. Turn in both short ends and ladder stitch or top stitch the edges together.
20. Run a double gathering thread along the folded edge of the ruffle – not the seaming edge. Gather to fit the lower edge of the skirt.
21 Position the ruffle along the lower edge of the dress and sew in place through the gathering stitches.
22. Cover the lines of sewing with a row of ric rac. Finish the wrist edges with a row of ric rac as well.
23. Fit the dress on the doll and check the fit. Make any necessary adjustments at the neck.
24. Finish the neck edge by attaching a bias strip (see fig. c).

b.

c.

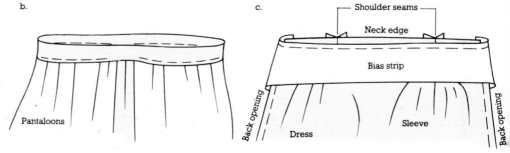

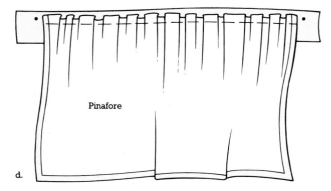

d.

d. Gather up the waist edge of the pinafore and pull up to fit the waistband between the dots. Sew in place.

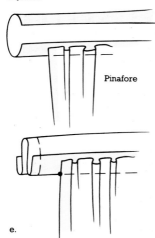

e.

e. Turn and press the top edge of the waistband, turning it to the wrong side. Fold in half and sew the ends together.

f. With right sides together sew the ruffle to the strap. Turn the strap over, fold the edge under and hem it to the back of the ruffle.

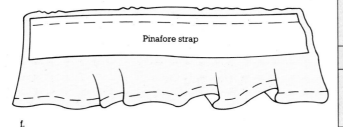

f.

25. Sew snaps in place on the back opening.

Making the pinafore
26. Make the skirt of the pinafore first by hemming both the short sides and the longer lower edge.
27. Run a gathering thread along the waist edge and gather to fit the waist band between the dots *(see fig. d).* With raw edges matching and right sides together, sew in place. Press seams.
28. Turn and press ¼ in. (6 mm.) of the long unstitched end of the waistband to the inside of the pinafore. Fold the waistband in half, right sides facing, and sew the ends together *(see fig. e)* with straight stitches.
29. Turn the waistband right side out and slip stitch the pressed edge in place.
30. Hem one long edge of each ruffle piece. Run a gathering thread along each unhemmed long edge and gather to fit the length of the strap.
31. Sew a ruffle to a strap with right sides together and raw edges level *(see fig. f).* Turn

the strap over, fold the edge under and hem it to the back of the ruffle. Attach the ruffle to the other strap in the same way.
32. Position both straps behind the front and back of the waist-band and sew in place.
33. Sew a hook and eye on the back waist opening.
34. Cut the daisies into separate units and arrange them over the apron, sewing in place, using straight stitches.

Making the shoes
35. Fold a narrow hem to the wrong side on the ankle edge of each shoe and sew in place in order to give the edge extra strength.
36. Sew a ⅛ in. (3 mm.) seam at the heel.
37. Baste and sew the shoe to the sole, easing in the fullness around the toes.
38. Fold the shoe tie in thirds lengthways and sew along its

length in the center to hold the fold in place.
39. Sew the tie to the back of the shoe on the heel seam.
40. Make a small pleat at the front of the shoe and cover with a bow or daisy.
41. Finish the second shoe in the same way.

Finishing touches
42. The clothes should all be pressed before dressing.
43. Put on the socks first, re-shaping the toes if they are too big.
44. Follow with the pantaloons and petticoat.
45. The dress goes on next (with a full back opening this should prove easy for any young child). The pinafore follows; lastly the shoes are tied in place.
46. Finally, brush the cheeks lightly with blusher to bring some warmth and color to the face of the doll.

MATERIALS

For the dress:
1 yd. (1m.) of 36 in. (92 cm.) wide cotton print
1½ yds. (1.5 m.) ric rac
4 snaps for back fastening
12 in. (30.5 cm.) of ⅛ in. (3 mm.) narrow elastic

For the pinafore:
18 in. (46 cm.) of 36 in. (92 cm.) wide dotted Swiss cotton
12 appliqué daisies or daisy-lace
1 hook and eye

For the underwear:
24 in. (61 cm.) of 36 in. (92 cm.) wide white lawn or cotton
2 yds. (2 m.) cotton lace
30 in. (76 cm.) narrow elastic

For the shoes and socks:
12 in. (30.5 cm.) square of felt
pair of first-size baby socks

EQUIPMENT

Dressmaking shears, embroidery scissors, pins, needles, thread, tape measure or ruler, pencil, tissue paper, pattern-making equipment.

— MAKING A —
TEDDY BEAR

Teddy bears have only been made since the beginning of the twentieth century, and yet in that time they have become firmly established as one of the world's classic toys. A fully jointed teddy bear is extra special, often becoming a lifelong companion and even a family heirloom.

Preparing the pattern
Make a full-size pattern and transfer all the markings onto it *(see p.12)*. Make sure nap is running down all sides, then cut the body pieces out of the fur and cut protective shields for the joints from the remnants. Dismantle the joint *(see p.16)*. The soles and paws are cut from velvet. Mark the joint positions with a soft pencil dot on the wrong side of the fur, then draw a cross through each dot, so that it can be easily located. The teddy bear stands 18in. (46 cm.) tall when finished.

Making the arms and legs
1. Sew the shoulder dart on an outside arm and finger-press open *(see fig. a)*. Repeat for the other arm.
2. Sew a velvet paw in place on an inside arm, matching As and Bs and finger-press the seam open *(see fig. b)*. Make a hole for the joint with an awl and then protect the edges of the hole. You can do this by working a row of buttonhole stitching around the edge, by pressing on an iron-on interfacing patch, or by gluing a felt disk over the area

a. *Sew the shoulder darts on the outside arms and finger-press them open.*

b. *Sew the paws to the inner arms. Match As and Bs, sew the seam and finger-press the seam open. Make holes for the joints and reinforce the openings.*

a.

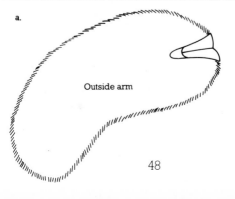

Outside arm

b.

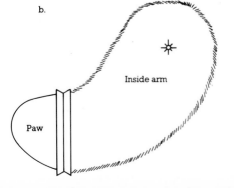

Inside arm

Paw

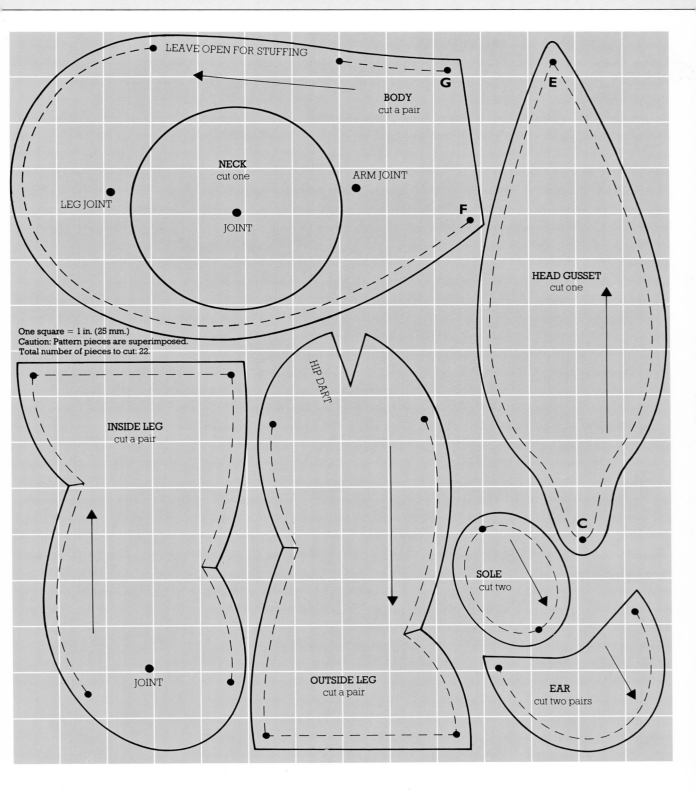

LEAVE OPEN FOR STUFFING

G

BODY
cut a pair

E

NECK
cut one

ARM JOINT

LEG JOINT

JOINT

F

HEAD GUSSET
cut one

One square = 1 in. (25 mm.)
Caution: Pattern pieces are superimposed.
Total number of pieces to cut: 22.

INSIDE LEG
cut a pair

HIP DART

C

SOLE
cut two

JOINT

OUTSIDE LEG
cut a pair

EAR
cut two pairs

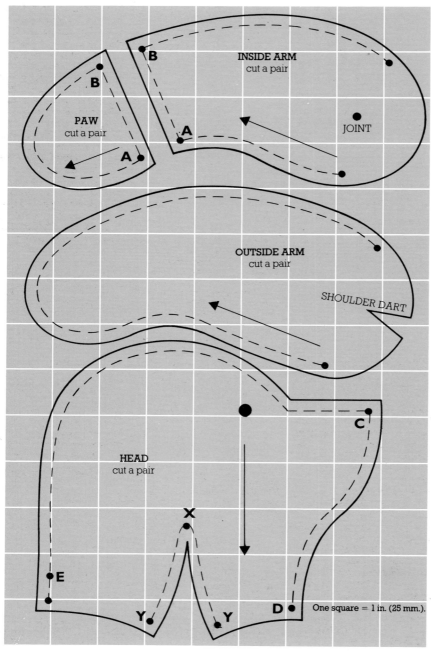

PAW
cut a pair

B

A

INSIDE ARM
cut a pair

B

A

JOINT

OUTSIDE ARM
cut a pair

SHOULDER DART

HEAD
cut a pair

X

E

Y   Y

C

D   One square = 1 in. (25 mm.).

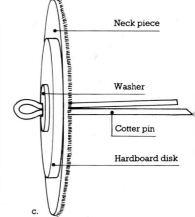

Neck piece

Washer

Cotter pin

Hardboard disk

c.

c. Assemble the neck joint. Hold the cotter pin in your left hand and thread a steel washer and a hardboard disk onto it. Push the pin through the neck piece from the wrong side. This piece will act as the protective shield for the joint.

(having first made a hole in the center of the felt). Repeat for the other arm.

3. Place one pair of outside and inside arm pieces right sides together and baste by overcasting the edges before sewing. Leave an opening at the shoulder. Repeat for the other arm.

4. Turn the arms right side out and stuff each firmly up to the joint mark. Load a cotter pin for each arm with a washer, hardboard disk and a protective shield *(see fig. b)*.

5. Insert a loaded cotter pin into each arm in turn and push it through the hole for the joint. Turn the protective shield over the disk edge and hold in place with stuffing as you finish stuffing the shoulder area.

6. Close the shoulders with ladder stitch and then remove any trapped fur from the seams. Put to one side while you work on the legs.

7. Make the hip darts on each outside leg piece and then

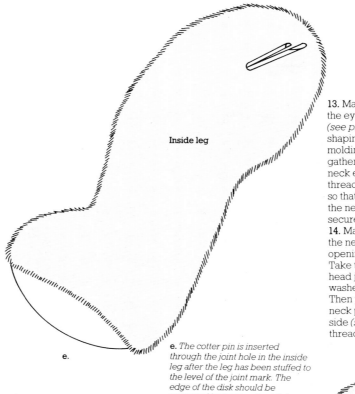

Inside leg

make a hole for the joint on the inside legs, protecting the openings in the same way as you did for the arms *(see step 2)*.

8. Match the pairs of inside and outside leg pieces (check that you have a left and a right one). Baste by overcasting the edges together for each leg, leaving the hip curve and the sole edge open. Sew together and clip the seam allowance at the corner at the top of the foot and behind the knees.

9. Pin each sole in place and baste by overcasting, opening out the back and front seam allowances of the legs, so that they lie flat *(see fig. d)*. Remove the pins. Sew the soles to the leg and turn right side out. Check that the two soles match in size and that the pile of the velvet lies in the same direction.

10. Stuff the legs firmly up to the jointing position. Insert loaded cotter pins into each

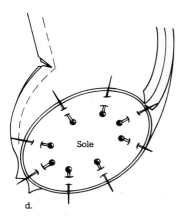

d. *Pin the sole in position on the leg and flatten out the seam allowances of the leg pieces before basting. Remove the pins and sew together with backstitch. Turn right side out.*

Sole

d.

e.

e. *The cotter pin is inserted through the joint hole in the inside leg after the leg has been stuffed to the level of the joint mark. The edge of the disk should be protected by turning the fabric shield over it before the hip area is stuffed. Close the limb with ladder stitch.*

leg, finish stuffing and close in the same way as described for the arms, steps 4-6. *(see fig. e.)*.

Making the head and body
11. Start by making the cheek darts in each head piece. Bring Y to Y and sew from X to Y. Sew left and right head pieces together, right sides facing, from C at the nose down to the neck edge at D.

12. Now insert the head gusset matching C to C and pinning back to E on one side first and then to E on the other side. Check that the gusset is even and straight and has not twisted the head. Baste by overcasting, remove the pins and sew in place. Close the remainder of the head seam from E down to the back neck edge. Turn the completed head right side out.

13. Make and protect holes for the eyes. Fix the eyes in place *(see p.15)*. Stuff the head firmly, shaping the cheeks and molding the head. Run a gathering stitch around the neck edge with strong double thread, gather up the opening, so that it is just big enough for the neck piece. Tie off securely.

14. Make a hole in the center of the neck piece. Strengthen the opening with buttonhole stitch. Take the cotter pin for the head joint and thread on a washer and a hardboard disk. Then push the pin through the neck piece from the wrong side *(see fig. c)*. Using strong thread, gather around the

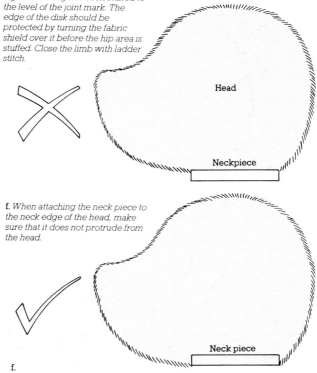

Head

Neckpiece

f. *When attaching the neck piece to the neck edge of the head, make sure that it does not protrude from the head.*

Neck piece

f.

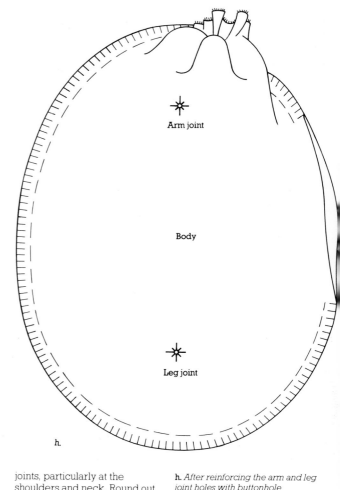

g. *Neck piece with cotter pin protruding, sewn in position on the neck edge of the head.*

edge of the neck piece and pull up gathers, so that the hardboard disk is enclosed. Tie off.

15. Place the prepared neck piece against the gathers of the head neck edge and ladder stitch it in place. Make sure that the neck disk nestles into the head; it must not be left protruding, as this would spoil the final appearance of the teddy bear *(see figs. f and g).*

16. Make and protect the holes for jointing the limbs on the two body pieces. Baste by overcasting and then sew the body, right sides together, from F down the tummy to G, leaving an opening on the back seam and at the neck edge for stuffing. Run a strong gathering thread around the neck edge, pull as tightly as possible and tie off *(see fig. h).* Turn the completed body skin right side out.

17. Carefully thread the cotter pin of the head through the neck edge of the body between the gathers. From inside the body, thread a protective shield onto the

cotter pin, followed by a hardboard disk and finally a washer. Spread the pins open and pull really tight with the pliers to make a crown joint *(see p.16).* This is the hardest joint you will have to work. There are two points to watch out for in particular: do not allow the neck disk to sink into the head and do not let the body neck gathers become too bulky, as this would force the head and body apart.

Attaching the arms and legs

18. All four limbs are attached in the same way, but it is easier to do the arms first, followed by the legs. Take up an arm and push the cotter pin through the body wall. Check that the paw faces forward and upward – in other words, the right arm is on the right side of the body and the left arm matches the left side of the body. Thread a protective shield onto the cotter pin, followed by the hardboard disk and washer. Bend the pins into a crown joint *(see p.16).* Attach the other arm and then the legs in the same way. Check that all the joints are secure before proceeding.

19. Stuff the body, taking care to pack the stuffing around the

joints, particularly at the shoulders and neck. Round out the tummy and the buttocks. Take time over the stuffing. It must be firm if all the joints are to work properly.

20. Close the opening with ladder stitch, using strong doubled thread. Clean the seam and tease out the pile.

21. Embroider claw marks on the paws and soles. Use all six strands of embroidery thread to work long straight stitches in each claw position.

h. *After reinforcing the arm and leg joint holes with buttonhole stitching, sew the two body pieces together. Baste by overcasting and then sew from F to G, leaving an opening at the back. Gather the neck edge, avoiding bulkiness at this point, so that the head can be attached closely and firmly.*

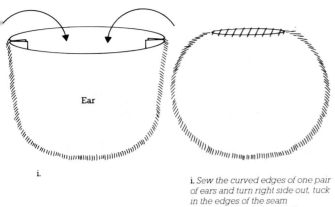

i.

i. *Sew the curved edges of one pair of ears and turn right side out, tuck in the edges of the seam allowances and overcast the opening.*

Finishing touches

22. Pin the ears together in pairs and baste by overcasting before sewing.
23. Turn the ears right side out and tease any pile away from the seams. Turn in the edges of the seam allowances on both sides of each ear and overcast the open edges together *(see fig. i.)*.
24. Position right ear on the head behind the right eye and just reaching up onto the head gusset seam. Ladder stitch in place on the front side first, taking care not to catch the fur on the back of the ear. Then ladder stitch along the back of the ear. By keeping the stitches ¼ in. (6 mm.) above the base you will spread the bottom of the ear, making a shorter ear that is really

securely attached. Sew the left ear in position in the same way.
25. Use all six strands of embroidery thread in a long darning needle to work a block of satin stitches for the nose.
26. The mouth is worked at the same time as the nose. Take a straight stitch down the center front from the nose for about ¾ in. (2 cm.), then pass the needle into the head and out on the lower left side to define one corner of the mouth. Thread the needle behind the base of the straight stitch and pass it back into the head on the lower right side, level with its emergence on the other side. This completes the mouth. If you are not satisfied with its appearance, simply unthread the needle, hook out the stitches and start again. Mouths are very expressive and will determine whether the bear is happy or sad, serious or mean.
27. As a final finishing touch, tie a lovely bow around your teddy bear's neck. If you like, you can follow the current fashion of tying a small bow around each ear for a girl bear.

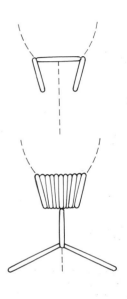

k.   Nose and mouth

k. *The nose is worked in satin stitch, using six-stranded embroidery thread. Define the outline and then fill it in. Continue to work on the mouth with the same thread.*

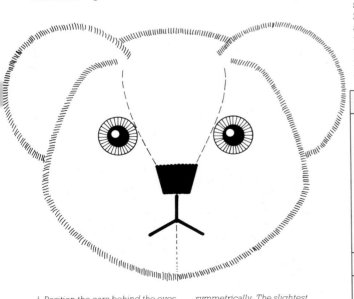

j. *Position the ears behind the eyes with the inside edges touching the gusset seam. Make sure that the features are arranged*

symmetrically. The slightest change in placement will alter the bear's character.

MATERIALS

18 in. (46 cm.) of 54 in. (137 cm.) wide medium-pile honey-colored fur
9 in. (23 cm.) square of velvet for paws and soles
pair ¾ in. (18 mm.) amber safety eyes
dark brown embroidery thread or tapestry wool for nose
2½ in. (6.3 cm.) joint for head
1¾ in. (4.4 cm.) joints for arms
2 in. (5 cm.) joints for legs
1 lb. 2 oz. (500 g.) stuffing
1 yd. (1 m.) of 1 in. (25 mm.) wide ribbon for bow

EQUIPMENT

Dressmaking shears, embroidery scissors, pins, needles, thread, tape measure or ruler, pencil, long-nosed pliers, awl, pattern-making equipment.

MAKING
WOODEN TOYS

To make the wooden toys in this section, you do not have to be an expert woodworker. The basic information in this introduction will prepare you with all the skills you need to follow the simple methods given for the projects.

The appeal of hand made wooden toys will always outlast that of their more modern metal and plastic counterparts. The natural beauty of the wood itself enhances the look of any toy and its durability makes shaping, construction and repair relatively easy.

Many people still enjoy using hand tools, and the illustration shows the ones you will need, as well as power tools, for those who prefer them.

Wood types
Wood falls into two categories: softwood and hardwood. There is also a wide range of manufactured wood materials available.

Softwood
Broadly, this is wood produced from evergreen, coniferous trees. It is easier to work, more readily available and generally cheaper than hardwood. The disadvantage of softwood is that it tends to deteriorate if exposed to the weather, unless it is well protected with paint or varnish. The exceptions are western red cedar and redwood, which weather very well.

Hardwood
Hardwood comes from deciduous trees, such as ash, beech, maple, oak and cherry. The most suitable for toymaking is beech. However, hardwood is expensive and also hard to work, so it is not recommended unless a particularly hard-wearing finish is required.

Choosing the wood
It is important to find a lumberyard

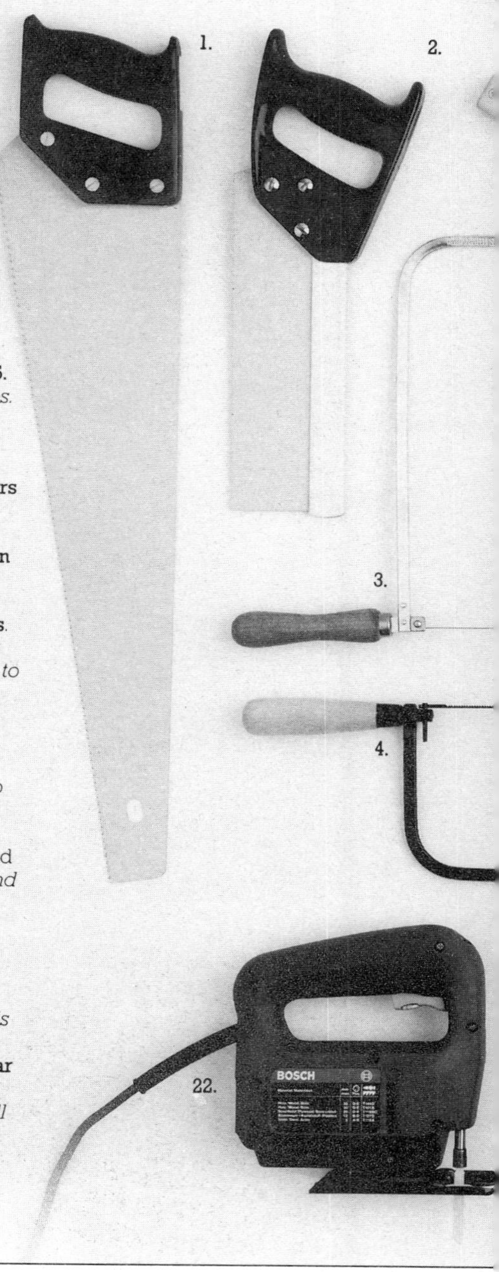

Hand tools and equipment
1. **Panel saw** *For making straight cuts along and across the grain.* 2. **Backsaw** *For cross cutting small sections and cutting joints.* 3. **Fretsaw** *For cutting curves.* 4. **Coping saw** *Similar to the fretsaw but with a more robust blade.* 5. **Keyhole saw** *For cutting internal shapes.* 6. **Smoothing plane.** 7. **Hand drill** *Drill which takes bits up to 1/4 in. (6 mm.) in diameter.* 8. **Brace and bit** *Drills larger holes than the hand drill.* 9. **Screwdrivers** *Flat-headed and cross head.* 10. **Claw hammer** *16 oz. (450 g.) For driving and withdrawing nails.* 11. **Cross peen** or **Pin hammer** *The tapered end is used for working in confined areas.* 12. **Chisels** *Available in a range of widths.* 13. **Pliers.** 14. **Mallet.** 15. **Awl** *Used to make starter holes before drilling.* 16. **G-clamp** *Used to hold two surfaces together.* **Bar or pipe clamp** *Used for clamping larger pieces.* 17. **Try square** *To measure right angles.* 18. **Tape measure** and **Metal ruler.** 19. **Modeling knife** 20. **Doweling jig** *Used to prepare holes for doweling joints.* **Sandpaper** *Three grades required. A cork sandpaper block is useful.* **Nails** and **Screws** *Brads, roundhead, oval head, and flathead wood screws are used.* **Workbench,** *preferably with a built-in vise.*

Power tools
21. **Power drill** *A general purpose two-speed drill with a 3/8 in. (10 mm.) chuck is quite adequate.* 22. **Saber saw** *Used to saw straight and curved cuts.* 23. **Circular saw** *For straight cuts across and along the grain.* 24. **Holesaw** *A specialized drill attachment for cutting circles.* **Router** *A high speed tool for cutting grooves and notches.* 25.**Countersink bit** *Fits a standard power or hand drill.*

1.

2.

3.

4.

22.

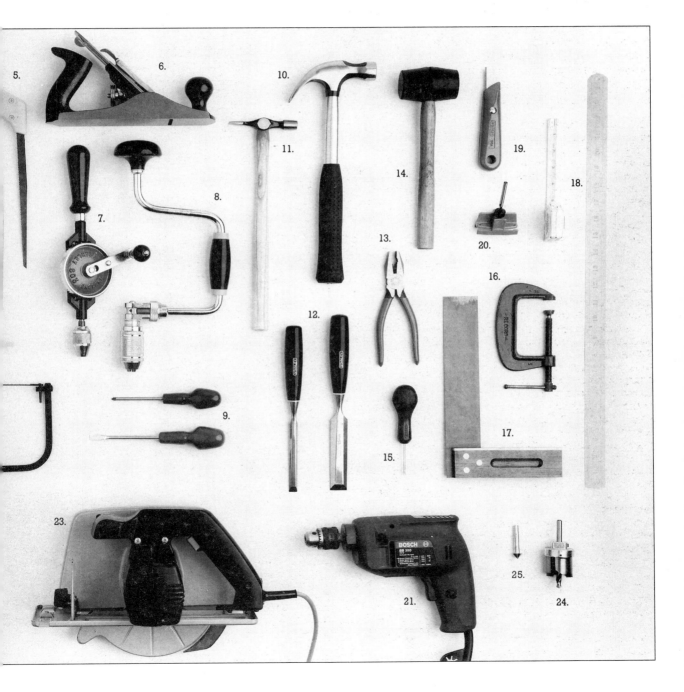

where you can rely on the quality of the wood. This depends chiefly on three factors: the way the wood has been dried, cut and stored. If wood has been well seasoned (either kiln-dried or air dried), its moisture content will have stabilized and been reduced. Check before buying that the wood is not warped and that there are no knots in it. Lumberyards classify softwood according to quality – Select or Common. For these projects you want Select B and Better or clear (B + BTR; clear).

Wood sizes

Softwood is stocked in a wide range of standard sizes. The standard thickness by width measurements refer to the nominal size of the 'rough sawn' wood, which is reduced with planing. For example, a 1 x 10 in. (25 x 250 mm.) piece actually measures ¾ x 9¼ in. (19 x 235 mm.). The measurements given for the projects are 'actual' rather than 'nominal'. You will need to plane down from a

The nominal size refers to the standard thickness by width measurements of the rough sawn wood. The lumberyard planes the rough sawn wood down to the actual size.

Nominal	Actual	Nominal	Actual
1 x 2	¾ x 1½ in.	25 x 50	19 x 38mm.
1 x 3	¾ x 2½	25 x 75	19 x 63
1 x 4	¾ x 3½	25 x 100	19 x 90
1 x 6	¾ x 5½	25 x 150	19 x 140
1 x 8	¾ x 7¼	25 x 200	19 x 184
1 x 10	¾ x 9¼	25 x 250	19 x 235
1 x 12	¾ x 11¼	25 x 300	19 x 286
2 x 2	1½ x 1½	50 x 50	38 x 38
2 x 3	1½ x 2½	50 x 75	38 x 63
2 x 4	1½ x 3½	50 x 100	38 x 90
2 x 6	1½ x 5½	50 x 150	38 x 140
2 x 8	1½ x 7¼	50 x 200	38 x 184
2 x 10	1½ x 9¼	50 x 250	38 x 235
2 x 12	1½ x 11¼	50 x 300	38 x 286
3 x 4	2½ x 3½	75 x 100	63 x 90
4 x 4	3½ x 3½	100 x 100	90 x 90

standard-sized piece or adapt the project to accommodate the standard sizes. Hardwood is available 'rough sawn' (timber sawn into planks) or 'dressed' (sawn and planed on all four sides to give a smooth finish, and ready for use). When ordering hardwood for the projects, ask for it 'cut and dressed to the finished size'. This means that it is sawn at the next size up and planed down to the desired dimension.

Manufactured materials

A variety of boards based on reconstituted materials are very useful to the toymaker. Their advantages over natural timber are that they are generally cheaper, more stable and less likely to warp. They are available in a range of thicknesses, and most of them are available with special finishes, suitable for indoor or outdoor use. They are essential for large panels.
Plywood This sheet material is made from thin layers, or veneers, of wood that have been glued together in such a way that the direction of the grain alternates in order to give the board strength and stability. Plywood meant for use indoors is called Interior, and is made with water-resistant (but not waterproof) glue. Plywood for use outdoors is called Exterior, and is made with fully waterproof glue.
Lumber-core plywood A sheet material made from rectangular strips of softwood glued together side by side and sandwiched between single or doubled veneers of wood.
Hardboard Made from softwood pulp that has been compressed under high pressure. Tempered hardboard is suitable for outdoor use as it has been impregnated with oil to make it relatively water resistant. Nonetheless, exposed surfaces

should be sealed.
Particle board Made from small wood chips that have been coated with glue and compressed into sheets.

Marking out wood from the template

The easier projects recommend that you have wood cut to size by your lumberyard. Templates are given as a guide to the pieces you will require, and you should use them as a pattern for the more complicated shapes. Where detail is required, as for the dog's head (see p.72), enlarge the pattern by squaring it up (see p.120) as a paper template and transfer it to the wood. Use a steel ruler and a try square to mark accurate 90° angles. If there are several similar pieces, identify each by labeling. Be sure to follow either the standard or the metric measurements, but do not mix them.

Cutting the wood

You can ask your lumberyard to cut the wood into manageable pieces, and tackle the rest yourself with a hand or power saw.
Straight saw cuts Cross-cutting (across the grain) and rip-sawing (along the grain) are done with a panel saw, a powered circular saw or a saber saw. To cut straight when using a panel saw, hold the wood steady and level and as you cut, look down, with one eye closed, at the top edge of the blade. If you can see either side of the blade, you are cutting at an angle and you will have to plane the wood square.

A backsaw is used for smaller straight cuts. To ensure a clean saw cut, first scribe the grain on the surface by marking it with a sharp modeling knife.
Curved cuts A fretsaw or saber saw will cut very tight curves and gives a fine, neat cut. A coping saw is useful

for cutting curves in thicker wood.
The blade can be set at any angle to
cut curves more easily. The wood
should be clamped to a workbench
or in a vise. The trick is to cut slowly,
constantly checking that a smooth
curve is being achieved.

Cutting internal shapes A keyhole
saw, fretsaw or coping saw can be
used. You must first drill a pilot hole
so that the blade can be inserted.
You must unscrew one end of the
blade of the fretsaw or coping saw,
push it through the hole and then
reconnect before you begin to saw.

Planing
Prepared wood should not require
further planing. However, if it does,
ensure that the blade of the plane is
set correctly and that it is very sharp.
Clamp the wood in a vise, protecting
the gripped surfaces with scraps of
wood. When you plane, it is essential
to keep the blade flat and to use a
smooth gliding action.

Drilling holes
A hand drill, a brace and bit, or a
two-speed power drill with a ⅜ in.
(10 mm.) chuck are all suitable for
toymaking.

Make a small starter hole with an
awl before drilling. If the drill binds,
ease it out of the hole to relieve the
pressure, remove the waste sawdust,
and try again.

If drilling to a specific depth, stick
a piece of masking tape around the
drill bit to mark the required depth.

Screwing
Steel wood screws should be
countersunk so that the top of the
screw is flush with the surface of the
wood. A countersink drill bit will
prepare a tapered opening for the
screw. If you do not have a
countersink bit, use a hand-held
countersink tool to make the tapered

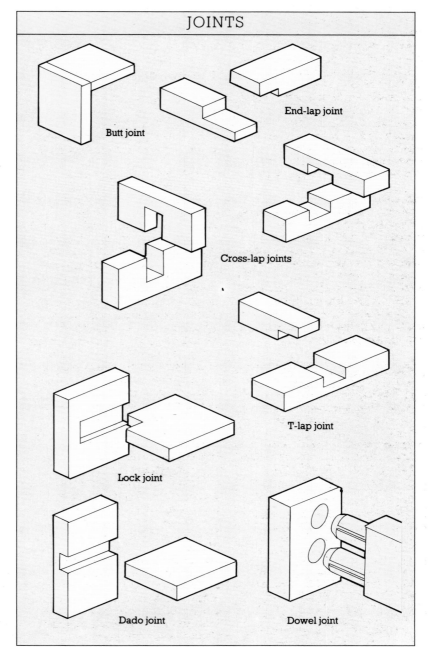

JOINTS

Butt joint

End-lap joint

Cross-lap joints

T-lap joint

Lock joint

Dado joint

Dowel joint

opening by twisting it around in the predrilled holes. Make sure that the holes you drill are small enough to allow the thread of the screw to bite firmly into the wood. Always screw into the cross grain, never into end grain as the thread has to cut into the grain, for a good fit. It will be easier to drive the screws into the wood if you first rub a little soap on the threads to lubricate them.

Nailing
Nails and brads should always be driven in at alternating angles, giving a much more secure joint than nailing at right angles. Never drive two or more nails along the same line of grain, as this may split the wood.

When using small nails or brads protect your fingers from injury by using a piece of thin cardboard to hold the nail in position while hammering. Use the tapered end of the cross peen hammer to start tapping in the nail and then drive it home with the large end.

Never nail directly into hardwood – always drill a pilot hole first.

Gluing
White or yellow glue is suitable for most applications. Ideally, resorcinol should be used for outdoor toys, as it is completely waterproof. Apply the glue to both surfaces, and if they are both wood surfaces, clamp them together under pressure. However, there is no need to clamp joints that have been glued together if they are also screwed or nailed.

Joints
All the joints used in the toys are easy to make. Accurate marking, scribing and sawing will ensure a good finish.
Butt joint The simplest joint used, it is made by nailing or screwing the end of one piece of wood to another. The

edges can also be glued for additional strength.
Lap joints The end-lap joint is useful for constructing frames. Mark and scribe the cutting lines and saw through half the depth of each corresponding piece of wood, both along and across the grain. Smooth the sawn edges with a chisel, glue the area and fix with wood screws. For cross-lap, and T-lap joints, saw across the grain and chisel out the wood from side to center.
Dado joint A strong joint where the end of a cross piece is recessed into the side of an upright. Mark and scribe the position of the channel, and saw across the width of the wood to a depth one-third of its thickness. Chisel out the wood, working from both edges. Glue the cross piece in position. Hammer nails in at an angle to hold the joint.
Dowel joint Accuracy in aligning the holes for the dowels, in drilling the holes vertically and to the exact diameter and half the length of the dowel is ensured by using a doweling jig. Shape the ends of the dowel, and saw a groove along its length to allow the excess glue to escape. Clamp it in position until set.

Fitting wheels
There are several types of wheels suitable for toymaking.
Proprietary wheel systems
Many cycle accessory shops stock wheel systems that come complete with axles, wheels and connecting bushes. All you need do is to specify the length of axle and size of wheel required, and simply buy them over the counter. In most cases they will come with fittings, including brackets and screws for attaching them to the toy.
Re-cycled wheels
Make use of existing wheels and convert them to a new use. Carriage

or stroller wheels, which come complete with axles, need only be removed from the unwanted stroller and refitted to the new vehicle, such as the go-cart *(see pp. 128-31)*.
Casters
Casters are made in a wide variety of shapes and sizes. The smaller sizes are suitable only for indoor use, but the larger casters, particularly those with rubber tires, can be used outdoors. Wheel sizes up to 8 in. (20 cm.) in diameter are available. Unlike the large universal casters, the smaller roller casters come in sets containing both right and left casters *(see pp. 72-5)*.
Wooden wheels
Wooden wheels for smaller toys such as the train and the truck *(see pp. 76-9 and 84-7)* can be purchased or cut from thick doweling, or from a section of handrail. However, you must be able to saw with sufficient accuracy to produce straight edges. Sandpaper all the surfaces. Mark the center of each wheel by drawing two bisecting lines across it, then drill the fitting hole – large enough to allow the wheel to rotate freely, but not so large that it wobbles. Attach the wheel with two washers and a roundhead screw.
Plywood wheels
You can draw circles on a piece of plywood with a compass and then cut them out with a fretsaw, coping saw or saber saw as for the hobby horse *(see pp. 80-1)*. The most accurate results, however, are obtained with a holesaw, attached to a power drill, preferably on a drill stand. The holesaw not only cuts perfect circles, but also drills a hole through the exact center of the wheel. It can be used for circles up to 3 in. (7.6 cm.) in diameter.

Wood finishes
Brightly painted toys appeal to

children, but a good finish is not purely decorative. Its practical function is to make the toy durable, and, when necessary, weatherproof. It is essential that you use only paints and varnishes that are non-toxic and meet the stringent regulations regarding the lead content of paint used for children's toys.

Preparing the wood
For both appearance and safety it is essential to give the toy a smooth finish. Sand all the surfaces, particularly edges that are cut across the grain, and fill countersunk holes with a commercially-made filler.

Gloss paint
First seal the wood with a primer (white latex paint is adequate). It will disguise any repairs that may have been done. Follow with an undercoat, and a final top coat of gloss. Gloss is too thick for fine detailed work but it covers large areas well and has a good depth of color.

Water-based acrylic paint
A wide range of ready-mixed, quick-drying colors available in small quantities make this a popular paint for toymakers. The paint covers well, and will also give a very delicate line when used with a fine sable brush.

First clean the surface of the wood with turpentine. Next, seal the surface of the wood with white latex, or to retain the grain of the wood, use a light varnish (made by diluting polyurethane varnish with an equal quantity of turpentine or other recommended dilutant). When dry, apply the acrylic paint. The paint will dry to a matt finish, so for a shiny protective coating, seal it with a full strength polyurethane varnish. This will darken the color slightly and give it a riche   uality.

Enamel paint
Enamel paint gives a hard-wearing, high gloss finish. It is available in

small quantities and in a good range of strong colors. However, it has a fairly long drying time. For finer, more detailed work, thin down the paint with enamel thinners.

Polyurethane varnish
This synthetic varnish can be used to give a clear gloss finish to toys painted with water-based paint, or used directly on unpainted wood to enhance and protect its natural features. When diluted it can be used as a primer before painting.

The varnish can be applied by brush or by spraying. When using a brush apply the first coat across the grain, allow it to dry overnight and sand with a fine grain sandpaper before applying the second coat, working along the direction of the grain. Clean brushes with turpentine. If you use a spray can, you will have to touch up areas with a fine brush, especially on the end grain.

Colored varnishes are available, that leave the grain visible, while still giving color to the toy.

Painting techniques
Attractive decorative effects can be achieved with a few simple techniques.

Masking
For a candy-stripe effect, stick strips of masking tape at regular intervals on a painted surface. Apply a coat of a second color and when dry, unpeel the tape to reveal perfect, crisp stripes of color.

Any shapes can be cut from adhesive film and treated in the same way.

Stenciling
Numbers, letters and decorative motifs can be stenciled onto toys. Cut your own stencil from special oil-coated stencil card, or buy one ready made. Use unthinned paint. Position the stencil carefully, and stipple the paint onto the design with

a short-bristled stencil brush. Work out the positions and spacing of your lettering before you begin stenciling.

Ruling fine lines
A ruling pen will produce fine lines for more detailed work. Mix paint until it is sufficiently fluid to flow from the pen and adjust the blades of the pen to give the required thickness of line. Practice before working on the finished toy – this technique requires confidence.

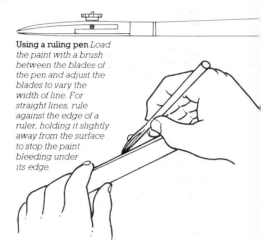

Using a ruling pen *Load the paint with a brush between the blades of the pen and adjust the blades to vary the width of line. For straight lines, rule against the edge of a ruler, holding it slightly away from the surface to stop the paint bleeding under its edge.*

Applied decoration
Instant transfer lettering and self-adhesive or gummed stickers can be used to add interest to toys. Give the toy a final top coat of varnish to seal the decoration.

Safety tips
Be aware of the hazards of working with wood – keep your workspace well organized and make sure that all wiring is safe. Keep saws, planes, chisels and drills sharp so that they do their job efficiently. Most importantly, keep all tools out of the reach of children, and remember that the finished toy must be safe for them to play with.

PROJECT 13

MAKING
BUILDING BLOCKS

The easiest of toys to make, these building blocks will give hours of pleasure to your young child, while at the same time teaching skills in hand and eye coordination. Play value and learning potential can also be increased by adding pictures, numbers or letters, by using dry transfers, or by gluing pictures on the six sides of the blocks. The more elaborate building blocks shaped as arches and columns require curved saw cuts, but they are also easy to make.

Making simple building blocks

1. That the blocks can be stacked is important, so use a try square and ruler to check that the sides are square and of equal size before cutting. You can ask your lumberyard to cut the cubes for you if you want to make the job easier.

2. Use a try square and a pencil to mark out the cubes at 2 in. (5 cm.) intervals, on all sides of the wood. Now go back over the lines on one side, line up the try square and scribe them with a modeling knife. This will sever the grain and ensure a clean cut.

3. The wood can be held steady by hand, but it is preferable to use a vise. Sandwich the wood between two pieces of scrap wood so that the jaw of the vise does not mark the surface of the wood. Use a backsaw to cut the cubes. Ensure that the cut is accurate by looking down at the blade from directly above. The sides of the blade should not be visible – if they are, it means that you are cutting at an angle.

4. When you have cut the 12 blocks, sand the sawn edges. Start with coarse sandpaper, then use a medium grade;

Add interest and educational value to the building blocks by choosing a theme for each cube. For instance, have a picture of an animal and the first letter of its name on one block, a number and the corresponding number of dots on another.

a. *Dry transfers give a professional finish. Align them accurately and rub down with a ballpoint pen.*

60

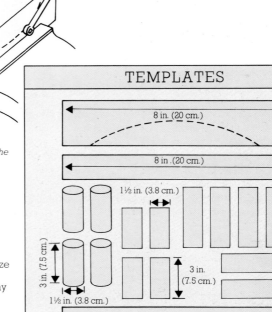

b. *Cut the curve carefully with a coping saw so that both parts of the wood can be used.*

TEMPLATES

8 in. (20 cm.)

8 in .(20 cm.)

1½ in. (3.8 cm.)

3 in. (7.5 cm.)

1½ in. (3.8 cm.)

3 in. (7.5 cm.)

5 in. (12.8 cm.)

1½ in. (3.8 cm.)

1½ in. (3.8 cm.)

1½ in. (3.8 cm.)

1½ in. (3.8 cm.)

3 in. (7.5 cm.)

finish with fine sandpaper. The best method for sanding is to lay the sandpaper on a smooth surface and to hold it steady while you rub the block of wood against it.

Decorating the blocks
5. Use a non-toxic varnish for a natural finish, or use brightly colored non-toxic paint *(see p.59).*
6. Cut out colorful pictures and glue them onto the cube; apply transfer lettering or numbers *(see fig. a)*; or stick on self-adhesive spots or shapes.
7. Give the blocks a final coat of varnish to seal the wood and decoration. If you have applied dry transfers, test first to see that the varnish does not make them blister.

Making columns and arches
1. Have the wood cut to the specified lengths by your lumberyard, or cut them to size yourself, using a backsaw.
2. Sand the sawn ends and any sharp edges.
3. Make a template for the curve of the arch on the two large pieces. The curve should begin at least 1¼ in. (3.2 cm.) from the end of the wood to allow the arch to be supported by the columns. Draw around a plate to get a smooth curve, or draw a section of a circle with compasses. Transfer the curve onto both sides of each piece of wood, making sure that they align.
4. Fix the wood in a vise and cut out the arch carefully, using a coping saw *(see fig. b)* or a saber saw.
5. Sand the curves smooth.

Painting and finishing
Use brightly colored non-toxic paint *(see p.59).*
6. Make sure that all the surfaces of the blocks are sanded smooth.
7. Apply one coat of water-based paint and allow to dry.
8. Sand the surface lightly, wipe away the dust and apply a second coat of paint.
9. For a glossy finish apply a coat of non-toxic varnish.

MATERIALS

For the cubes:
1 piece 2 x 2 x 24 in. (50 x 50 x 610 mm.) of knotfree softwood, or dressed hardwood (such as beech)

For the arches and columns:
Knotfree softwood or dressed hardwood:
2 pieces 1½ x 3½ x 8 in. (38 x 90 x 200 mm.)
2 pieces 1½ x 1½ x 8 in. (38 x 38 x 200 mm.)
6 pieces 1½ x 1½ x 5 in. (38 x 38 x 128 mm.)
4 pieces 1½ x 1½ x 3 in. (38 x 38 x 75 mm.)
Doweling:
4 pieces 1½ x 3 in. (38 x 75 mm.)

TOOLS

Ruler, sharp pencil, try square, backsaw, smoothing plane, various grades of sandpaper, coping or saber saw (for cutting arches), modeling knife.

PROJECT
14

MAKING A

JIGSAW PUZZLE

Jigsaw puzzles were invented in the middle of the 18th century, when they were illustrated with maps and used to teach geography. Today they are popular with adults and children alike. The puzzles that are most popular with very young children are those that incorporate a base, or tray, in their design. These can be simply made – use a favorite character as a basis for the painted design and cut around the contours to make large pieces that are easy to handle. A pattern is also given for traditional jigsaw shapes.

Making a tray jigsaw puzzle
1. Enlarge one of the designs given here by squaring up on a grid *(see p.120)* or by photocopy enlargement. Trace the outline onto a piece of birch plywood and mark where the cuts will be made with a heavier line. (If you choose a design that is more complex you will have to simplify it into large shapes.)
2. Trace the design onto one piece, leaving a border of at least ¾ in. (19 mm.).
3. Drill a small pilot hole at an intersection on the outline *(see fig. a)*. Unscrew the blade of a fretsaw, insert it through the hole and then reconnect it. Saw carefully around the outline *(see fig. b)* and then make all the other cuts.
4. Sand smooth all the edges of the puzzle pieces, the border and the piece of hardboard (which will form the base) with a fine-grade sandpaper.

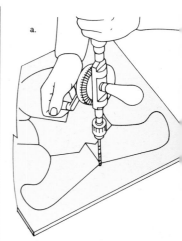

a.

a. *Use a hand drill to make a small pilot hole.* **b.** *Thread a fretsaw blade through the hole and cut out the shapes.*

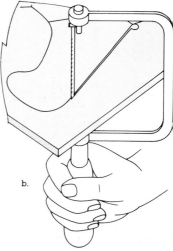

b.

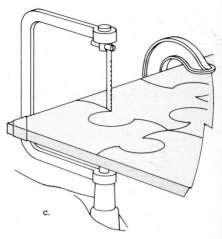

5. Apply a thin coat of glue to the underside of the border and place it in position on the base board. Weight it down and allow to dry.

6. Paint the base and the puzzle pieces and allow to dry. Use a non-toxic sealant if required.

Traditional puzzle shapes

Use the pattern for the interlocking pieces of a traditional jigsaw to make a simple six-piece puzzle for an older child.

1. Cut out a picture from a magazine.

2. Enlarge the puzzle pattern to the size you require and trace it onto a piece of plywood.

3. Cut out the pieces with a fretsaw *(see fig. c)*.

4. Assemble the pieces on a flat surface and glue the picture onto the wood, using white glue.

5. When dry, cut through the paper from the back, using a modeling knife.

c. *The tight curves of the traditional puzzle shapes can be cut with a fretsaw, or with a saber saw.*

c.

Left: *cutting patterns for the simple teddy bear and clown puzzles.* Above: *pattern for traditional puzzle shapes. Use these as templates and enlarge to the size you require (see p.120).*

MATERIALS

For the puzzle with a tray base:
1 piece ⅛ x 10 x 12 in. (3 x 255 x 305 mm.) hardboard
1 piece ¼ x 10 x 12 in (6 x 255 x 305 mm.) birch plywood
tracing paper
white glue
non-toxic paint
sealant

TOOLS

Fretsaw or saber saw, hand drill, modeling knife, ruler, soft pencil, paintbrush.

PROJECT **15**

MAKING A
DRUM, PIPE AND RATTLE

Making a drum, pipe and rattle for your children will help you to open up two related worlds for them – the worlds of sound and music. Here, you can utilize the lids of large cookie cans for the striking surface of the drum, while the rattle can be made from scraps of wood. When it comes to the traditional whistle, you can use bamboo cane, plastic or aluminum tube – the former is the more traditional material, but the other two are readily available. You will find the tube you require in most good hardware stores.

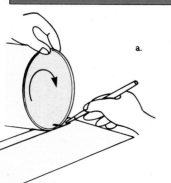
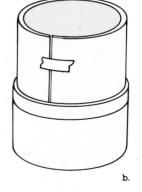
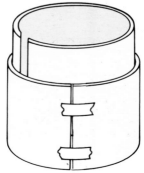

DRUM
Before you start, remember that the length of the cardboard is determined by the internal circumference of the lids you are using. You will need two of these; both must be of the same size. You will also need one of the cans, which will be used as a mold for the drum cylinder.

1. The easiest and most accurate way of measuring the required lengths of cardboard is to mark a point on the rim of the can and then roll it along the cardboard until you come to the marked spot again (see fig. a). This will give you the can's circumference; the cardboard should be cut about ⅛ in. (3 mm.) shorter so that it will fit inside the can. Each successive sheet should be slightly shorter than the previous sheet, so that it will fit inside.

2. To make the cylinder of the drum, curl the first sheet of cardboard into the can (see fig.

a. Use the can to measure the required lengths of cardboard.

b. Next, use the can as a mold to form the cylinder of the drum, making sure that the three joints are staggered.

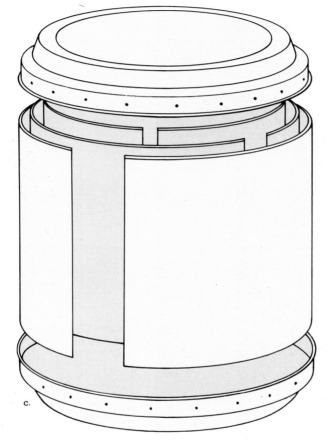

c.

the tape off and stick it around the circumference of each lid.

5. The size of the holes required will depend on the thickness of the cord you plan to use. The holes should be large enough to allow the cord to pass through easily. To prevent the drill from slipping, make starting indentations with an awl, center punch or a large nail *(see fig. d)*. The masking tape will also help to prevent the drill from slipping.

6. Glue the third sheet of cardboard in place and, when all the surfaces are completely dry, remove the cardboard cylinder from the can.

7. All three components of the drum should be painted before assembly, although the cylinder can be covered with a soft decorative vinyl, if preferred. Cut the vinyl to the correct length and glue it to the cardboard cylinder.

8. Lace the three components together with cord *(see fig. e)*. Finally, make a loop so that the drum can be carried.

9. Shape the ends of the doweling with a modeling knife and sandpaper to form drumsticks *(see fig. f)*.

e.

e. Lace the three components together with decorative cord.

f.

f. Using a modeling knife and sandpaper, shape the ends of the doweling to form drumsticks.

b). If necessary, carefully trim the edges until they meet exactly. Hold them together with a strip of masking tape.

3. Apply generous amounts of white glue to the inner surface of the cardboard sheet and insert the second cylinder of cardboard. Make sure that the joints are staggered for extra strength *(see fig. c)*. Press the two cylinders together and leave to dry.

4. It is important to mark the holes around the lids accurately before they are drilled. Apply two strips of masking tape to a suitable clean surface. Mark points for holes every 3 in. (7.5 cm.). Peel

d. *Make a pilot indentation for drilling the holes with a sharp point, such as a center punch, awl or nail.*

d.

MATERIALS

Drum

2	lids from metal cookie cans
3	pieces of flexible cardboard, approx. 10 x 29. (254 x 737 mm.)
1	piece soft vinyl, approx. 10 x 29 in. (254 x 737 mm.)
4	yards (4 m.) decorative cord
2	piece doweling ⅜ x 12 in. (10 x 305 mm.)
	white glue, non-toxic paint

TOOLS

Tape measure, pencil, modeling knife, awl, drill and bits, paintbrushes, masking tape.

PROJECT **16**

PROJECT **17**

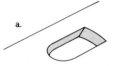

a.

a. First, cut or file the lower edge of the air hole until it is square, then file it to a 45° angle.

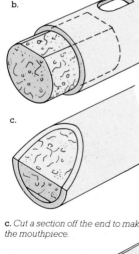

b. When the cork has been shaped to fit and the wind channel has been cut, insert the cork until the end aligns with the lower edge of the wind hole.

b.

c.

c. Cut a section off the end to make the mouthpiece.

PIPE

Whether you make a pipe from plastic, or from aluminum, you will use much the same methods of construction. The only real difference is in the internal diameter and, therefore, in the size of the cork needed.

1. Cut the plastic pipe to 11 in. (28 cm.) in length with a hacksaw.

2. Drill a hole ¼ in. (6 mm.) in diameter approximately 1⅜ in. (3.5 cm.) from one end of the tube. Square one side of the hole with a modeling knife and file the flat side to an angle of 45° *(see fig. a).* If you use a thin aluminum tube, then form a slight depression below the flat side of the hole, by tapping the tube gently with a ball peen hammer.

3. You can use a piece of wood, or a cork, to form a mouthpiece. Cork is preferable, as it is easy to shape with a modeling knife and can also be sandpapered. Pare the cork and sandpaper it smooth, until it fits snugly into the pipe without being compressed. Now cut a flat wind channel. Sand it smooth and insert it into the tube until the end of the cork is level with the top of the wind hole *(see fig. b).* If necessary, you can push the cork out of the pipe with a length of doweling.

4. Adjust the cork until you can blow a clear note. Cut off a slice at a sloping angle to form a comfortable mouthpiece *(see fig. c)* and sand until smooth.

5. Apply a length of masking tape along the top of the pipe. You can use it for marking the position of the holes. It will also help to prevent the drill from slipping *(see fig. d).* If you are using a metal tube, you should make pilot indentations with an awl or center punch before drilling the holes.

6. Drill the second hole 2⅜ in. (6 cm.) from the first and the remaining five holes at 1 in. (25 mm.) intervals. It is important to drill the holes in an absolutely straight line. Drill a thumb hole on the underside of the tube, 7 in. (18.5 cm.) from the open end of the tube.

7. Tune the pipe by carefully enlarging the finger holes one by one with fine sandpaper. The hole second from the open end should be the largest. If the pipe is out of tune, try adjusting the size of your air inlet. This may mean shaping another cork. Remember that you can flatten the pitch, but you cannot sharpen it. If the pipe is still out of tune, it is best to start again, since the materials do not cost much and the pipe is easy to make.

d.

d. Apply a strip of masking tape, mark off the holes, make pilot indentations with a sharp point and then drill the holes.

RATTLE

1. The rattle is an ideal project for using up any scraps of wood. Cut the wood and plywood to the measurements given on the templates. The grain of the wood should run with the length of the clicker. This will give it additional strength.

2. There are two ways of making the rattle wheel. The easiest is to cut a 1 in. (25 mm.) length off a piece of doweling with a diameter of approximately 2 in. (5 cm.). The second is to mark a circle onto each end of a block of hardwood, such as beech, and then round it off with chisels and sandpaper.

3. In either case, the next step is to divide the circle into six segments. Use a protractor to mark off angles of 60°. Draw lines from one point to the next until you have formed a star shape *(see fig. b).*

4. Use a backsaw to cut notches around the perimeter at the points marked, then carve out the ratchets with a sharp chisel. Sandpaper them until smooth.

5. Round off the bottom and top strips with a coping saw, or a fretsaw, and sandpaper the edges smooth.

6. Drill a ⅛ in. (3 mm.) hole in the top strip, a ⅜ in. (10 mm.) hole in the bottom strip, and four screw holes in the positions shown at the end of each strip *(see fig. a).*

7. Now drill a ⅜ in. (10 mm.) hole right through the center of the rattle wheel and a second ⅜ in. (10 mm.) hole, approximately ¾ in. (19 mm.) deep, into the top of the doweling handle.

8. Drill a hole in one clicker block *(see fig. a).*

9. Sandpaper all the edges and surfaces until smooth. Now paint all the components,

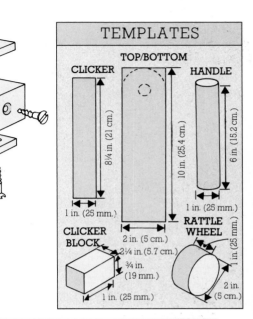

except the handle which should be varnished.

10. You can now assemble the rattle. First, glue the ⅜ in. (10 mm.) doweling into the handle, so that approximately 2¼ in. (5.6 cm.) projects.

11. When the glue has set, insert the doweling through the hole in the bottom strip of plywood and into the rattle wheel. Fix the wheel firmly in place with glue and a brad.

12. Screw the two clicker blocks in position, leaving sufficient space for the clicker strip. Screw the top strip in place. Use a cup washer with the screw that fastens the strip to the rattle wheel *(see fig. a)*. Adjust the position of the clicker strip so that the wheel ratchets hit the end. Fix it in place with a screw *(see fig. a)*. Any surplus length should be trimmed and the edge sanded smooth and re-painted.

TEMPLATES

TOP/BOTTOM

CLICKER 8¼ in. (21 cm.) — 1 in. (25 mm.)

10 in. (25.4 cm.) — 2 in. (5 cm.)

HANDLE 6 in. (15.2 cm.) — 1 in. (25 mm.)

CLICKER BLOCK 2¼ in. (5.7 cm.) — ¾ in. (19 mm.) — 1 in. (25 mm.)

RATTLE WHEEL 1 in. (25 mm.) — 2 in. (5 cm.)

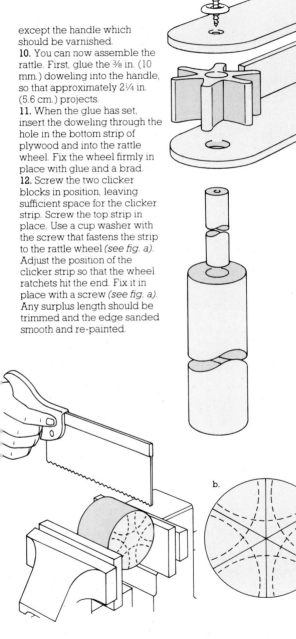

a.

b.

b. *Use a protractor to mark off six 60° angles. Draw lines from one point to the next until you have formed a star. Cut notches around the circumference and carve out the ratchets with a chisel.*

MATERIALS

Pipe
1 12 in. (30.5 cm.) length plastic pipe, with internal diameter of ¾ in. (19 mm.), or aluminum pipe, with internal diameter of ½ in. (12 mm.)
1 cork

Rattle
Softwood:
2 pieces ¾ x 1 x 2¼ in. (19 x 25 x 57 mm.)
Plywood:
2 pieces ¼ x 2 x 10 in. (6 x 50 x 254 mm.)
1 piece ⅛ x 1 x 8¼ in. (3 x 25 x 210 mm.)
Doweling:
1 piece 1 x 2 in. (25 x 50 mm.)
1 piece ⅜ x 3 in. (10 x 75 mm.)
1 piece 1 x 6 in. (25 x 152 mm.)
Hardware:
wood screws, brad, cup washer, non-toxic paint, white glue.

TOOLS

Pipe
Hacksaw, drill and bits, modeling knife, awl or center punch, masking tape, fine sandpaper, sandpaper, file.

Rattle
Backsaw, coping saw, chisels, mallet, drill and bits, screwdriver, paintbrushes, sandpaper, protractor.

MAKING A
BABY WALKER

This is basically a sturdily constructed box on wheels with a raised handle at one end. It is a simple toy, which is often a great favorite with toddlers who enjoy using it to ferry their other toys from place to place. It is a toy that also plays a large part in encouraging toddlers to walk. When the handle is grasped for support, the baby walker will start to move forward, inviting the toddler to walk in order to maintain a balance.

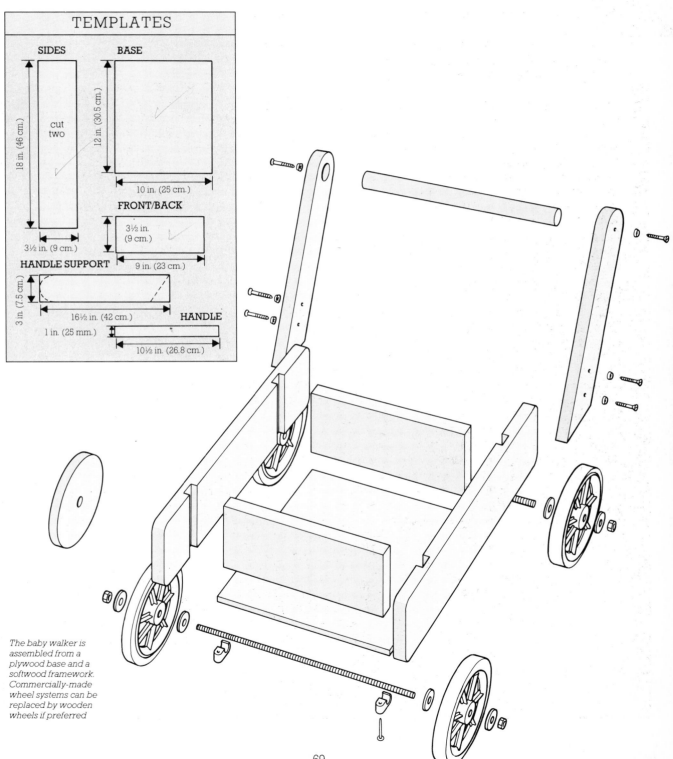

TEMPLATES

SIDES

18 in. (46 cm.)

cut two

3½ in. (9 cm.)

BASE

12 in. (30.5 cm.)

10 in. (25 cm.)

FRONT/BACK

3½ in. (9 cm.)

9 in. (23 cm.)

HANDLE SUPPORT

3 in. (7.5 cm.)

16½ in. (42 cm.)

HANDLE

1 in. (25 mm.)

10½ in. (26.8 cm.)

The baby walker is assembled from a plywood base and a softwood framework. Commercially-made wheel systems can be replaced by wooden wheels if preferred

Buying the wood

Have the wood cut to size when you buy it. Plywood is used for the base, and good quality knotfree softwood for the framework. If, in place of softwood, you use a hardwood, such as beech, you can allow for a reduction in the thickness used (about 20%) because of its strength. The commercially-made wheels can be replaced by wooden wheels if you prefer (see p.58).

Making the walker

1. If the wood has not been cut to size, saw it to the dimensions given, using a backsaw or a circular saw. Softwood may be further smoothed with a plane if necessary.

2. Draw around the base of a small jar or glass to mark the curves on the handle ends (see fig. a). Use a larger round object to mark the curves on the end of the side pieces. Cut the curves with a coping saw or an electric saber saw and sand smooth.

3. Center the side pieces with the base and mark the position for the four dado joints (see p.57). Use a try square and a modeling knife to score the edges of the ¾ in. (19 mm.) channels and cut with a backsaw to a depth of two-thirds of the width of the wood (see fig. b). Make a central cut and chisel out the wood,

c. Bar or pipe clamps can be used to hold the joints in position while the glue dries. However, joining the pieces with wood screws is just as effective.

working from both sides.

4. Now assemble the sides. Glue the grooves and slot the front and back pieces in. Drive two wood screws into each joint. If you choose not to use screws in the joints, use bar or pipe clamps to hold the joints fast until the glue has dried (see fig. c).

5. The base can now be fitted. Sand the edges of the plywood smooth. Glue the edges of the

d. Attach the base with nails driven at alternating angles.

base and place it in position. Nail the base to the frame, driving the nails at alternating angles to give additional strength (see fig. d).

6. The handle can now be assembled. Make pilot holes

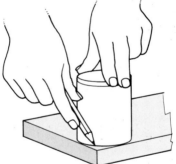

a. Draw around the base of a circular object for the curved ends of the sides and handle.

b. Cut the channels for the dado joints with a backsaw. Chisel out the wood from both sides.

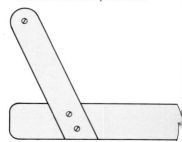

e. The handle sides are set at an angle. Make sure that you leave enough room for the wheels.

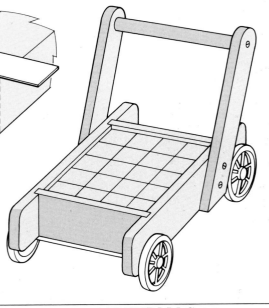

for the four screws at the base of the handle sides. Use a spade bit to drill a hole 1 in. (25 mm.) in diameter through half the depth of the handle sides at the curved end. Assemble the three handle pieces and check for length. Sand the ends of the doweling handle, glue and slot it into the holes. Countersink a screw into both sides to hold the handle firmly in place.

7. The position of the handle will depend on the size of your wheels. Allow a gap of at least

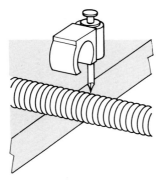

f. Use brackets to attach the axles to the base of the side pieces.

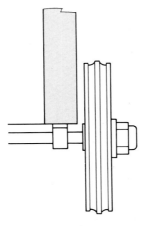

g. Fit the wheels with washers in position and secure them with commercial pushfit caps.

Make a set of blocks for your baby walker. Measure out blocks to fit neatly inside the box and decorate them with pictures, numbers or letters.

1 in. (25 mm.) between the wheel and the handle. Attach the base of the handle to the box with two flathead screws on each side *(see fig. e)*.

8. Before the wheels are fitted · the walker should be painted or varnished *(see p.59)*. Young children enjoy vivid colors so choose a bright color scheme, but remember that it is essential to use non-toxic paints.

9. Place the axles in position just beyond the edge of the base and make pilot holes for the brackets. Place the axles in position and screw down the brackets *(see fig. f)*. Fit the wheels, with a washer on either side, and secure with washer cap nuts. *(See fig. g.)*

Making a set of blocks for the baby walker

Make a special set of blocks for your toddler to carry around in the baby walker. From the measurements given, the box will carry 20 blocks, made from 2 x 2 in. (50 x 50 mm.) softwood. A simple method for making these building blocks is given on pp.60-1. Decorate the blocks by cutting out pictures and gluing them to the blocks. Give the blocks a coat of varnish to seal the wood and decoration.

MATERIALS

	Softwood:
2	pieces ¾ x 3½ x 18 in. (19 x 90 x 460 mm.)
2	pieces ¾ x 3½ x 9 in. (19 x 90 x 230 mm.)
2	pieces ¾ x 3 x 16½ in. (19 x 75 x 420 mm.)
	Doweling:
1	piece 1 x 10½ in. (25 x 268 mm.)
	Plywood:
1	piece ¼ x 10 x 12 in. (6 x 255 x 305 mm.)
	Hardware:
	white glue
2	wood screws 1½ in. (3.8 cm.)
4	wood screws 1 in. (25 mm.)
	cup washers
	nails
4	wheels at least 4 in. (10 cm.) in diameter
2	axles approx. 11½ in. (29 cm.) in length
4	brackets
	screws
	washers
	washer cap nuts
	non-toxic paint
	white glue

TOOLS

Ruler, pencil, try square and modeling knife, backsaw, set of chisels, smoothing plane, screwdriver, drill and drill bits, hammer, fretsaw or coping saw or saber saw.

MAKING A
PULL-ALONG DOG

This toy is most suited to very young children up to the age of three. It is big enough to allow two small children to ride on it while an adult, or an older brother or sister, pulls it along. Children older than three will be able to propel the dog along the floor or the ground with their feet, just as they would a scooter. The toy is easy to make, while its sturdy nature makes it suitable for both indoor and outdoor play.

Making a pull-along dog
1. Saw the wood to the dimensions given on the templates.
2. To draw the dog's head, enlarge the shape by squaring it up *(see p.122)* on paper to make the necessary pattern. Transfer the pattern to the wood. To cut out the head, saw in from the edge with a fretsaw or a saber saw *(see fig. b).* Sand the edges until they are completely smooth.

a. *The pull-along dog is simple to make and assemble. The casters must be good quality and, if the dog is to be played with outside, they should be fairly large.*

a.

PROJECT **19**

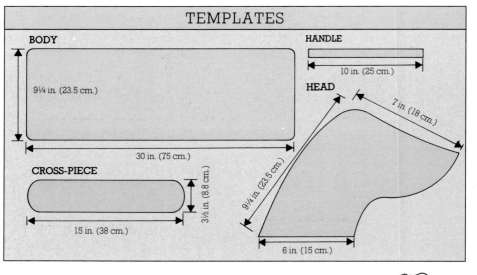

TEMPLATES

BODY

9¼ in. (23.5 cm.)

30 in. (75 cm.)

CROSS-PIECE

15 in. (38 cm.)

3½ in. (8.8 cm.)

HANDLE

10 in. (25 cm.)

HEAD

7 in. (18 cm.)

9¼ in. (23.5 cm.)

6 in. (15 cm.)

3. Drill a 1¼ in. (3.2 cm.) hole for the doweling that serves as a handle *(see fig. c)*.

4. There are two ways of attaching the head to the body. You can drill deeply countersunk holes underneath the body, glue the head in place and secure with screws. You can also cut the ⅜ in. (10 mm.) dowel into six lengths. Measure and mark the center points of the dowel holes in the head. Drill holes to half the depth of the dowel. The holes must be absolutely vertical. Insert dowels, place in position and mark the corresponding dowel points on the body. Remove dowels and drill another set of holes. Cut a groove along the length of each dowel to allow the glue to escape. Apply glue, insert dowels *(see pp. 57-8)* and clamp the pieces together until completely dry.

5. Glue the doweling handle in position.

6. Round the edges of the cross-pieces with a fretsaw and sand them smooth.

7. Drill holes in the cross-pieces, position them across the body, ensuring that they are square, as it is important for the casters to be straight. Fasten in position with glue and screws *(see fig. g)*.

8. Sand smooth all sharp or rough edges that might cause injury.

9. Paint and varnish. It is worth giving the dog several coats of varnish for a more durable finish.

10. When the paint has dried, you can attach the casters. If you buy a prepacked set of four casters, check to see that they are marked "l" and "r". You must use a left and a right caster on each cross-piece, or the casters will not operate properly. Screw them to the ends of the cross-pieces as shown *(see fig. h)*.

11. Cut out the fabric ears *(see fig. e)* and tail. Use tacks to attach the ears to the head and the tail to the back of the body. A staple gun is a useful alternative method of attaching the material.

12. Attach a screw eye to the front of the body and then tie a piece of rope or cord to it, if desired.

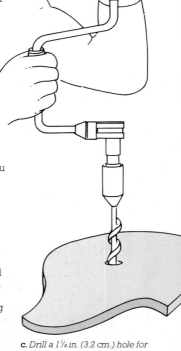

b. *Cut out the head by sawing in from the edge with a fretsaw.*

c. *Drill a 1¼ in. (3.2 cm.) hole for the doweling handle with a brace and bit.*

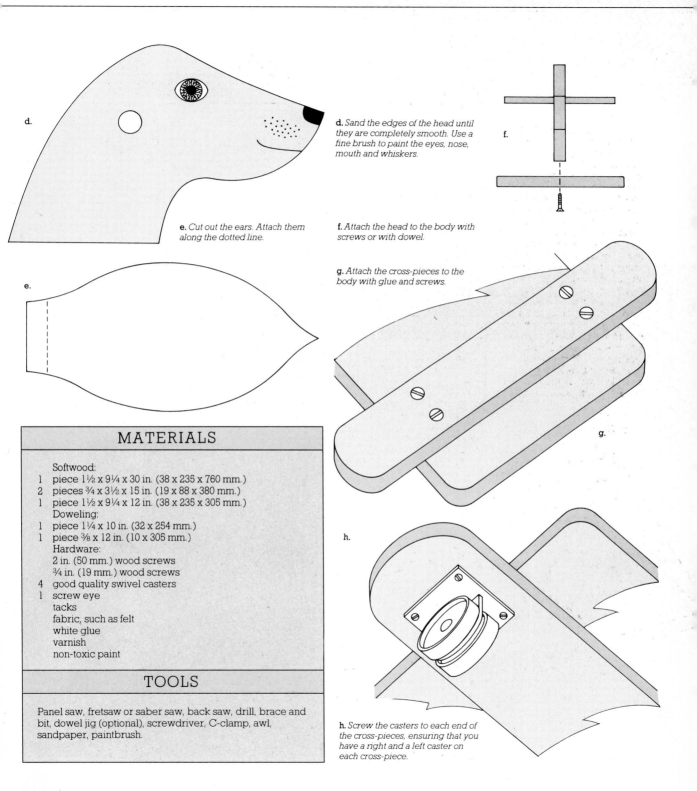

d.

d. *Sand the edges of the head until they are completely smooth. Use a fine brush to paint the eyes, nose, mouth and whiskers.*

f.

e. *Cut out the ears. Attach them along the dotted line.*

f. *Attach the head to the body with screws or with dowel.*

g. *Attach the cross-pieces to the body with glue and screws.*

e.

g.

h.

MATERIALS

Softwood:
1   piece 1½ x 9¼ x 30 in. (38 x 235 x 760 mm.)
2   pieces ¾ x 3½ x 15 in. (19 x 88 x 380 mm.)
1   piece 1½ x 9¼ x 12 in. (38 x 235 x 305 mm.)
Doweling:
1   piece 1¼ x 10 in. (32 x 254 mm.)
1   piece ⅜ x 12 in. (10 x 305 mm.)
Hardware:
2 in. (50 mm.) wood screws
¾ in. (19 mm.) wood screws
4   good quality swivel casters
1   screw eye
    tacks
    fabric, such as felt
    white glue
    varnish
    non-toxic paint

TOOLS

Panel saw, fretsaw or saber saw, back saw, drill, brace and bit, dowel jig (optional), screwdriver, C-clamp, awl, sandpaper, paintbrush.

h. *Screw the casters to each end of the cross-pieces, ensuring that you have a right and a left caster on each cross-piece.*

MAKING A
TRAIN

This pull-along engine and car are ideal as toddler toys. They have been designed with a low center of gravity, a wide track and large wheels, so that they will not overturn easily, even if traveling over carpets. Painting the train is fun and allows a great deal of scope for individual expression. You can, of course, add more cars, or you can adapt the basic car design to form a covered freight car, a flatcar or a passenger car, using scraps of wood from your workshop.

Making the engine
Saw the wood to the dimensions given on the templates. You can make the boiler from one piece of wood or from two pieces that you glue together.

Making the boiler
1. If you want a square boiler, all you do is sand the edges.

2. To make a round boiler, first draw diagonal lines across both ends of the piece of softwood. Place the compass point at the spot where the lines intersect and draw circles (see fig. b). Round off the corners with a rasp and sand with coarse sandpaper.
3. The boiler should have a flat base so that it will sit squarely

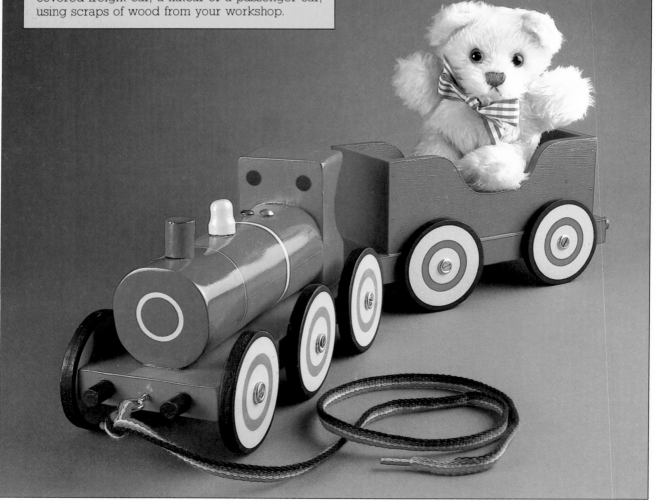

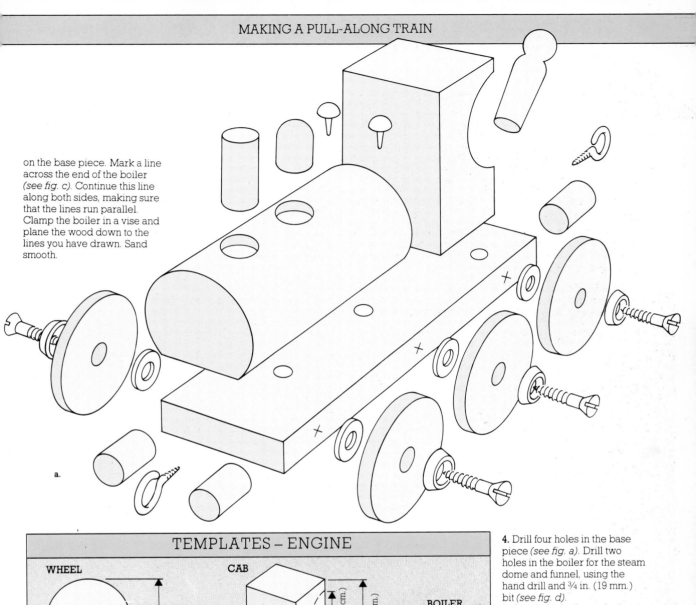

on the base piece. Mark a line across the end of the boiler *(see fig. c)*. Continue this line along both sides, making sure that the lines run parallel. Clamp the boiler in a vise and plane the wood down to the lines you have drawn. Sand smooth.

a.

TEMPLATES – ENGINE

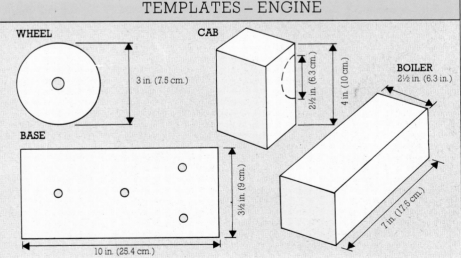

WHEEL

3 in. (7.5 cm.)

CAB

2½ in. (6.3 cm.)

4 in. (10 cm.)

BOILER
2½ in. (6.3 in.)

7 in. (17.5 cm.)

BASE

3½ in. (9 cm.)

10 in. (25.4 cm.)

4. Drill four holes in the base piece *(see fig. a)*. Drill two holes in the boiler for the steam dome and funnel, using the hand drill and ¾ in. (19 mm.) bit *(see fig. d)*.
5. Attach the boiler to the base with glue and screws *(see fig. a)*.

Making the cab

1. Draw a semicircle on each side of the piece of softwood.
2. Hold the piece steady in a vise and cut along the curve with a coping saw *(see fig e)*. Sand smooth.
3. You can insert the clothespin figures in one of two ways. If you want them to be removable, drill holes into the curve at an angle and insert the figures from the top.

PROJECT
20

Alternatively, you can drill holes through the bottom of the cab and insert the figures from underneath before attaching the cab. This will ensure that the figures stand upright in the cab, but it will not be possible to remove them.

4. Attach the cab to the base with glue and screws *(see fig. a)*.

Making the train crew
1. The best way make the train crew is to use old-fashioned wooden clothespins with a rounded top and split bottom *(see fig. f)*.

2. You can use felt-tipped pens or paint to draw on the features and clothes.

Making the wheels
1. It is important to make sure that the wheel edges are straight; if they are not, the appearance of the train will be

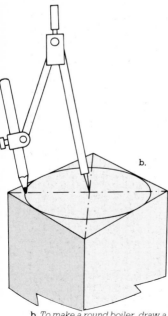

b. *To make a round boiler, draw a circle at each end of the block of wood with a compass.*

spoiled, and more important the wheels will not function properly. There are several methods of making the wheels.

2. You can make wheels up to 3 in. (7.5 cm.) in diameter with a hole saw attached to a power drill mounted in a drill stand. The hole saw automatically drills a hole in the precise center of the wheel.

3. If you can saw with sufficient accuracy, you can cut sections off a thick length of doweling with a back saw.

4. You can also draw circles on the sheet of plywood with a compass, and cut them out with a fretsaw or with a saber saw. Drill axle holes in each wheel, ensuring that they are exactly centered and straight. The hole should be large enough to allow the wheel to rotate, but not so large that the wheels wobble.

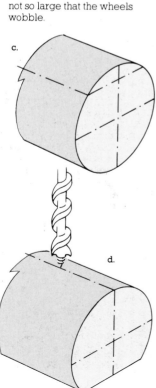

5. Paint both the wheels and the train before you attach the wheels to the base.

6. Using an awl, make starting holes for the wheel screws in the base. You will require a washer between each wheel and the base and a cup washer on the outside of the wheel *(see fig. g)*. Insert the screws. It is important to make sure that the screws are straight and that they are not turned in too tightly or the wheels will not rotate smoothly.

Finishing touches
1. Cut two lengths of doweling approximately 1 in. (25 mm.) long for the steam dome and the funnel. Shape the end of the steam dome with a modeling knife, sand and glue them in place.

2. Cut four lengths of doweling approximately ¾ in. (19 mm.)

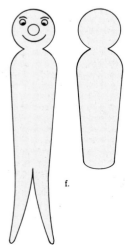

long for the buffers and stick them onto the base *(see fig. a)*.

3. Drive upholstery nails into the boiler top *(see fig. a)*.

4. Turn screw eyes into the front and back of the base. Tie a length of cord to the front eye.

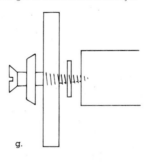

g.

Making the car
You make the car using the same basic methods as for the engine.

1. Saw the base and sides to the dimensions given.

2. Cut out the wheels, using the same methods as for the engine wheels.

3. Make a paper template for the curved sides of the car. Cut out with a coping saw. Sand the edges.

4. Attach sides to base with glue and brads *(see fig. i)*.

5. Glue the seats in position and secure with brads.

6. Attach the wheels, using the same method as for the engine.

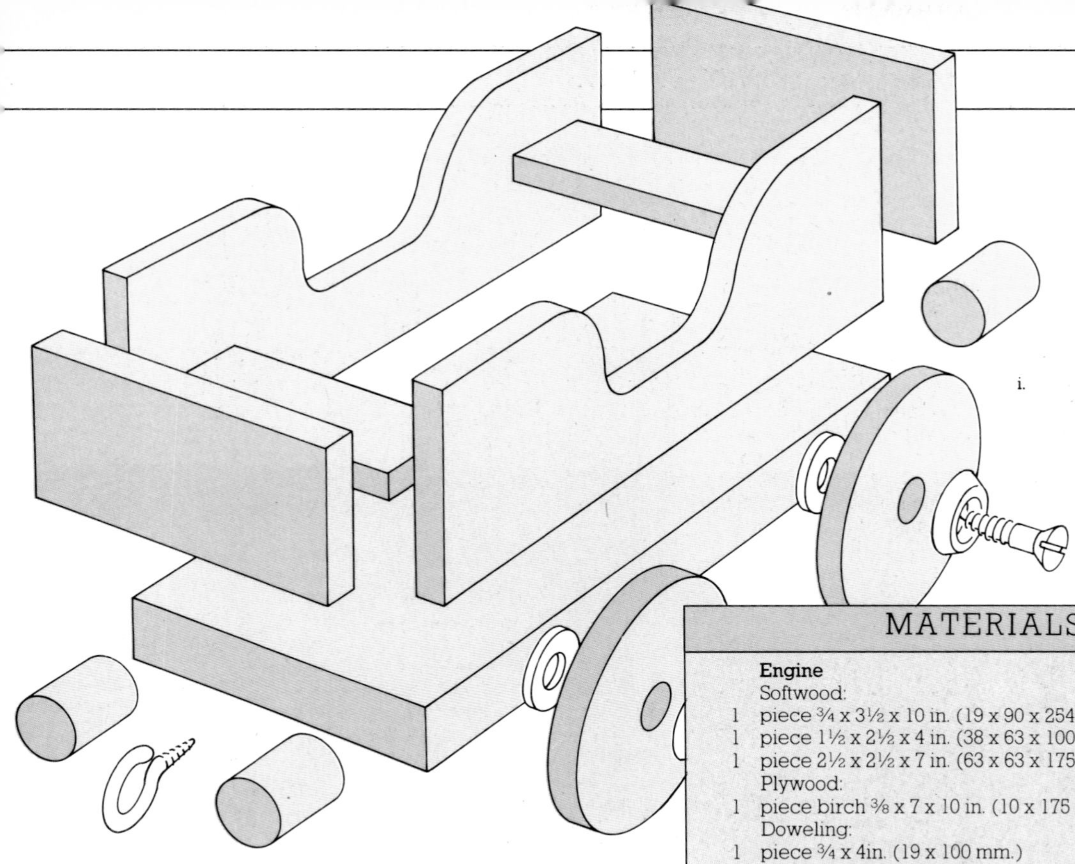

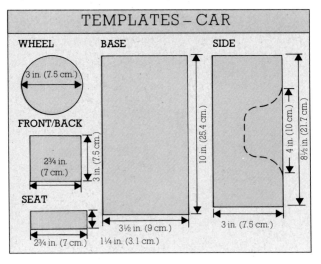

7. Cut four buffers from doweling and stick to the front and back of the base.

8. Make the coupling by screwing a hook into the front of the car base and linking it to the engine with the chain. The chain should be long enough to prevent the car from hitting the engine when turning a corner.

Painting

You can copy the color scheme shown in the picture or you can invent your own. Straight edges can be obtained by using masking tape and coachlines by using a ruling pen (see p.59).

MATERIALS

Engine
Softwood:
1   piece ¾ x 3½ x 10 in. (19 x 90 x 254 mm.)
1   piece 1½ x 2½ x 4 in. (38 x 63 x 100 mm.)
1   piece 2½ x 2½ x 7 in. (63 x 63 x 175 mm.)
Plywood:
1   piece birch ⅜ x 7 x 10 in. (10 x 175 x 254 mm.)
Doweling:
1   piece ¾ x 4 in. (19 x 100 mm.)
1   piece ⅜ x 4 in. (10 x 100 mm.)

Car:
Softwood:
1   piece ¾ x 3½ x 10 in. (19 x 90 x 254 mm.)
Plywood:
2   pieces ⅜ x 3 x 8½ in. (10 x 75 x 217 mm.)
2   pieces ⅜ x 3 x 2¾ in. (10 x 75 x 70 mm.)
2   pieces ⅜ x 1¼ x 2¾ in. (10 x 30 x 70 mm.)
1   piece ⅜ x 6 x 10 in. (10 x 150 x 254 mm.)
Doweling:
    piece ¾ x 4 in. (19 x 100 mm.)
    Hardware for engine and car:
    1½ in. (3.8 cm.) wood screws
    cup washers
    washers
    screw eyes
1   yd. (1 m.) cord, or shoelace
    screw hook
    chain
2   wood clothespins
    upholstery pins – brass finish
    white glue
    non-toxic paint

TOOLS

Fretsaw, backsaw, coping saw, hand drill, electric drill, try square, tape measure, plane, screwdriver, awl, compasses or hole saw, hammer, rasp, sandpaper, paint brushes, masking tape.

TEMPLATES – CAR

WHEEL
3 in. (7.5 cm.)

FRONT/BACK
2¾ in. (7 cm.)

SEAT
2¾ in. (7 cm.)

BASE
10 in. (25.4 cm.)
3 in. (7.5 cm.)
3½ in. (9 cm.)
1¼ in. (3.1 cm.)

SIDE
4 in. (10 cm.)
8½ in. (21.7 cm.)
3 in. (7.5 cm.)

PROJECT
21

MAKING A
HOBBYHORSE

The hobbyhorse is one of the most traditional of children's toys, its origins dating back over two thousand years. The basic concept of a stick horse has remained unchanged since those far-off times, although individual designs naturally vary considerably. This particular design is based on an 18th century hobbyhorse.

Buying the wood
Buy the best quality wood you can afford. Make sure that the softwood is knotfree.

Making the hobbyhorse
1. If necessary, cut the wood to size, using a backsaw or a circular saw. Plane the edges if they require it.
2. To make the horse's head you will need a piece of softwood trimmed to measure ¾ x 9¼ x 12 in. (19 x 235 x 305 mm.). Draw the outline of a horse's head *(see p. 120)* onto the wood and cut out with a fretsaw.
3. Using a drill and ¾ in. (19 mm.) bit, drill a hole in the horse's neck to take the handle.
4. Sand the head until it is completely smooth. It is worth spending time on the finish, as the head is the most prominent part of the hobbyhorse.
5. Use the ¾ x 2½ x 35 in. (19 x 63 x 890 mm.) piece of

a. *Draw diagonal lines across the plywood. Hammer a nail into the center and draw the circumference of the wheel using a pencil and a length of string.*

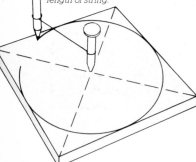

b. *Assemble the hobbyhorse, using white glue, screws, washers, a nut and roundheaded tacks as shown.*

c. *Details, such as the eyes, nostrils and mouth, should be carefully painted with a fine brush.*

e. *Knot short pieces of macramé rope around a length of ribbon. Fluff out with a comb.*

trimmed softwood to form the crossbar. To join the head to the crossbar, drill deeply countersunk holes underneath the crossbar, glue the head in place and secure with screws.
6. Use the ½ x 2½ x 9 in. (12 x 63 x 890 mm.) pieces for the wheel forks. Round off one end of each, using a fretsaw.
7. Make the wheel out of the square of plywood as shown *(see fig. a).* Cut out the wheel with a fretsaw. Drill a hole in the center.
8. Drill an axle hole in each of the wheel forks. Glue the

wheel forks to the crossbar, then drill four holes and insert the screws, countersinking them.
9. Insert the dowel handle and glue it in place with white glue.
10. Fill all screw holes with commercially-made filler. Paint and varnish the horse.
11. When the paint has dried, attach the wheel, using the 1¾ in. (4.4 cm.) carriage bolt, washers and nut.
12. To make the mane, tie a piece of ribbon between two chair backs. Knot lengths of macramé rope around the ribbon as shown *(see fig. e).* Attach the mane to the horse's head with roundheaded tacks.
13. Make a bridle *(see fig. d).*

d. *The bridle is made from macramé rope, or upholstery cord, and curtain rings. Attach with glue and roundheaded tacks.*

MATERIALS

Softwood:
1 piece ¾ x 2½ x 35 in. (19 x 63 x 890 mm.)
2 pieces ½ x 2½ x 9 in. (12 x 63 x 230 mm.)
1 piece ¾ x 9¼ x 12 in. (19 x 235 x 305 mm.)
Plywood:
1 piece ½ x 7½ x 7½ in. (12 x 190 x 190 mm.)
Doweling:
1 piece ¾ x 9 in. (19 x 230 mm.)
Hardware:
¾ in. (19 mm.) flathead screws
1 ⅜ in. (10 mm.) carriage bolt, 1¾ in. (4.4 cm.) long
washers
nut
roundheaded tacks
non-toxic paint
white glue
varnish
macramé rope, thick string, or chunky wool
ribbon
macramé rope, or upholstery cord
2 curtain rings

TOOLS

Ruler, sharp pencil, fretsaw, backsaw or circular saw, drill and drill bits, screwdriver, plane, sandpaper, paintbrush.

PROJECT **22**

MAKING A
SWING

Swings are easy to make and give enormous pleasure to children of all ages. If you are making a swing for a toddler it should have safety bars, but an older child will be quite safe on a traditional swing. You can suspend a swing from any tree with a sturdy branch or from a beam in your garage. It is important to test the strength of the branch or beam. The easiest method is to see whether it will bear the weight of an adult.

Positioning the swing
1. Before you buy your materials, you should first decide where the swing will hang, as this will determine the length of rope required.
2. Measure the precise distance between the support branch or beam and the swing seat. The swing should be approximately 22 in. (56 cm.) above ground level. Multiply by four, allowing a little extra for knots. This is the length of rope you will need to buy.

Making a swing
1. Swing hooks are specially made for the purpose, with a pronounced curlicue that prevents the swing from unhooking when in use. They also have a very coarse woodscrew thread, which enables them to be screwed securely into the underside of any suitable branch or beam.
2. Drill a generous pilot hole into the horizontal support. To ensure that the screws bite firmly into the wood, the hole should be the same size as the internal diameter of the thread. Screw the swing hooks into the wood.
3. Cut your length of rope in half. To prevent the rope ends from unraveling, play a lighted match or lighter over each end until the strands melt together.
4. Drill ⅜ in. (10 mm.) holes in

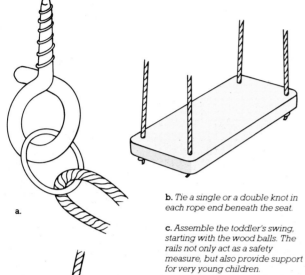

a.

b. *Tie a single or a double knot in each rope end beneath the seat.*

c. *Assemble the toddler's swing, starting with the wood balls. The rails not only act as a safety measure, but also provide support for very young children.*

c.

a. *Loop the rope through the steel rings.*

each corner of the piece of wood that will form the seat.
5. Round all corners and edges with coarse sandpaper. Sand all surfaces with medium and fine sandpaper and then varnish.
6. When the varnish is dry, loop each length of rope through a steel ring *(see fig. a)* and insert the loose ends through each pair of holes in the seat. Tie secure knots underneath *(see fig. b).*
7. Hook the two steel rings over the swing hooks.

Making a toddler's swing
This swing is made using the

same basic methods described above.
1. Round and sand the corners and edges of all the softwood and plywood.
2. Drill ⅜ in. (10 mm.) holes in each corner of the plywood and at each end of the eight safety bars. Varnish all the pieces.
3. Cut the plastic pipe into eight 3½ in. (9 cm.) lengths with a backsaw and sand the ends.
4. Varnish or paint the wood balls. These protect the toddler's hands from accidental rope burn.
5. Loop each length of rope through a steel ring and pass the ends of the rope through the wood balls, the plastic tube and the safety bars *(see fig. c).* Finally, insert the rope ends through the seat holes and knot as before.
Caution Remember to check the condition of the swing rope from time to time, as it may wear through.

MATERIALS

Swing
    Softwood:
1   piece 1½ x 9¼ x 18 in. (38 x 236 x 457 mm.)
    Hardware:
32   feet (10 m.) nylon rope, ⁵⁄₁₆ in. (8 mm.) in diameter
2   large swing hooks
2   large steel rings
    varnish

Toddler's swing
    Softwood:
8   pieces 1 x 2 x 14 in. (25 x 50 x 350 mm.)
    Plywood:
1   piece ¾ x 14 x 14 in. (19 x 355 x 355 mm.)
    Hardware:
32   feet (10 m.) nylon rope ⁵⁄₁₆ in. (8 mm.) in diameter
2   large swing hooks
2   large steel rings
1   14 in. (36 cm.) length of small bore plastic pipe
4   wood balls 2 in. (5 cm.) in diameter
    white glue

TOOLS

Backsaw, drill and ⅜ in. (10 mm.) bit, various grades of sandpaper.

MAKING A
TRUCK AND TRAILER

This toy is intended for very young children. It is robust and stable with large wheels so that it can be played with outdoors as well as inside the house. The construction of the truck and trailer is very similar to that of the pull-along train and car on pages 76-9. Decorating the truck and trailer allows great scope for individual design. Instant lettering and small colored sticky labels are useful for providing the finishing touches.

Making the trailer
1. It is important to use good quality knotfree softwood. Saw the softwood and plywood to the dimensions given on the templates. Sand all the edges.
2. Cut out the wheels, using one of the following methods. It is important to make sure that the wheel edges are straight, both for the sake of

appearance and to enable the wheels to function properly.
3. You can draw circles on the sheet of plywood with a compass and cut them out with a fretsaw or with a saber saw. Sand the edges smooth.
4. Drill axle holes through the center of each wheel. The holes should be large enough to allow the wheels to rotate,

but not so large that the wheels wobble. The holes should also be straight. It is advisable to paint the wheels and the trailer before you attach them together.

5. You can make wheels up to 3 in. (7.5 cm.) in diameter with a hole saw attached to a power drill mounted in a stand. The advantage of making wheels by this method is that the wheels are perfectly round and the axle hole is automatically drilled in the exact center. If neither method of making wheels seems suitable, you can buy commercially-made wooden wheels in different sizes from woodworking supply houses.

6. Attach the sides of the trailer firmly to the base with glue and brads *(see fig. b).*

7. Using an awl, make starting holes for the screws in the base. You will need a washer

between each wheel and the base and a cup washer on the outside of the wheel *(see fig. e).* Cup washers with a brass finish will give the wheels an additional sparkle. Insert the screws, ensuring that they go in straight and that you do not screw them in too tightly, otherwise the wheels will not turn smoothly.

8. Screw a hook into the front of the trailer base.

9. Paint with non-toxic paint. You will need a ruling pen *(see p. 59)* if you wish to draw coach lines. You can use instant lettering *(see fig. a)* to make up a logo for the sides of the truck.

a. *To apply instant lettering, first make a guiding line with masking tape, then line up the lettering and rub down with a ballpoint pen or a hard point.*

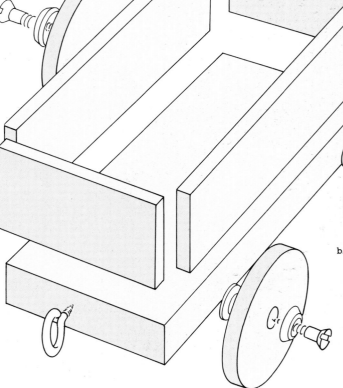

a.

b.

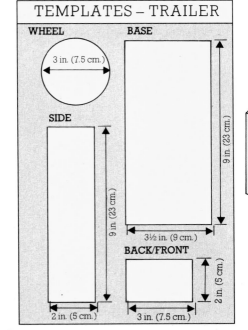

TEMPLATES – TRAILER

WHEEL

3 in. (7.5 cm.)

BASE

9 in. (23 cm.)

3½ in. (9 cm.)

SIDE

9 in. (23 cm.)

2 in. (5 cm.)

BACK/FRONT

2 in. (5 cm.)

3 in. (7.5 cm.)

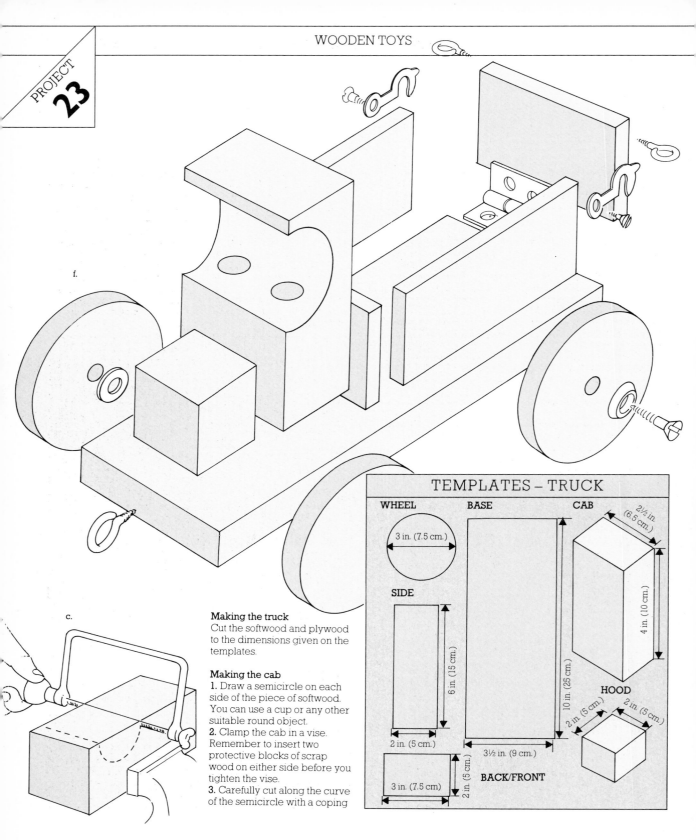

PROJECT **23**

f.

c.

Making the truck
Cut the softwood and plywood to the dimensions given on the templates.

Making the cab
1. Draw a semicircle on each side of the piece of softwood. You can use a cup or any other suitable round object.
2. Clamp the cab in a vise. Remember to insert two protective blocks of scrap wood on either side before you tighten the vise.
3. Carefully cut along the curve of the semicircle with a coping

TEMPLATES – TRUCK

WHEEL
3 in. (7.5 cm.)

BASE

CAB
2½ in. (6.5 cm.)
4 in. (10 cm.)

SIDE
6 in. (15 cm.)
2 in. (5 cm.)

10 in. (25 cm.)
3½ in. (9 cm.)

HOOD
2 in. (5 cm.)
2 in. (5 cm.)
2 in. (5 cm.)

3 in. (7.5 cm)
2 in. (5 cm.)
BACK/FRONT

saw. Sand the sawn curve smooth *(see fig. c)*.

4. You can insert the clothespin figures in two ways. If you want to make the train crew removable, drill holes into the curve at an angle and insert the figures from the top. Alternatively, you can drill holes through the cab from the bottom and insert the figures from underneath before you attach the cab to the base. This ensures that the figures stand upright, but you will not be able to remove them *(see fig. d)*.

5. Drill two holes in the base *(see fig. f)*. Attach the cab to the base with glue and screws.

Making the driver and mate

1. Old-fashioned clothespins with a rounded top and split bottom are ideal for making the figures. If you are inserting the figures from above, cut the clothespins to length so that they can be removed.

2. You can use felt-tipped pens to draw on the features and clothes. Alternatively, you can use paint.

3. Although the figures are too large for young children to swallow, you may prefer to glue them into the cab so that they cannot be chewed or lost.

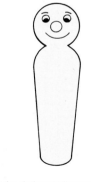

d. *Insert the clothespin figures through from the base of the cab. If you want to be able to remove the crew, cut off the base of the pins and insert them from above.*

Making the hood

Drill holes in the base and attach the hood block in position with glue and screws *(see fig. f)*

Making the open back

1. Attach the sides and back to the base with glue and brads *(see fig. f)*.

2. If you would like the back to open, each side should be ⅜ in. (10 mm.) shorter and the back piece ¾ in. (19 mm.) longer than the measurements given on the templates. Attach a hinge to the back and base with screws *(see fig. f)*. To

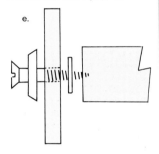

e. *Make sure that the wheels are screwed in straight. Have a washer between the wheel and the trailer and a cup washer on the outside.*

close the back flap you will need two small hooks and eyes. Screw them in position as shown.

Making the wheels

Make the wheels, using the same methods as for the trailer. Paint them and then attach them to the truck.

Finishing touches

1. Screw a hook into the back of the base for coupling the

trailer and a hook in the front so that the truck and trailer can be pulled along.

2. Paint and decorate. You can make headlights out of colored round, self-adhesive labels or brass-finish upholstery nails. For the radiator use smaller self-adhesive circles, for the radiator or punch holes in a small piece of colored paper and glue it onto the hood.

3. Knot a length of cord or a shoelace to the front eye.

MATERIALS

Trailer:
Softwood:
1 piece ¾ x 3½ x 9 in. (19 x 89 x 230 mm.)
Plywood:
2 pieces ⅜ x 2 x 9 in. (10 x 50 x 230 mm.)
2 pieces ⅜ x 2 x 3 in. (10 x 50 x 75 mm.)
1 piece ⅜ x 7 x 7 in. (10 x 175 x 175 mm.)

Truck:
Softwood:
1 piece ¾ x 3½ x 10 in. (19 x 89 x 254 mm.)
1 piece 1½ x 2½ x 4 in. (38 x 63 x 100 mm.)
1 piece 2 x 2 x 2 in. (50 x 50 x 50 mm.)
Plywood:
2 pieces ⅜ x 2 x 6 in. (10 x 50 x 150 mm.)
2 pieces ⅜ x 2 x 3 in. (10 x 50 x 75 mm.)
1 piece ⅜ x 7 x 7 in. (10 x 175 x 175 mm.)
Hardware for truck and trailer:
wood screws 1½ in. (3.2 cm.)
washers
cup washers
1½ in. (3.2 cm.) brads
2 wood clothespins
white glue
2 screw eyes
1 screw hook
1 hinge and screws (optional)
non-toxic paint
2 yards (2 m.) cord, or shoelace

TOOLS

Fretsaw or saber saw, backsaw, drill and bits, try square, tape measure, pin hammer, plane, screwdriver, awl, compass or hole saw, sandpaper, paintbrushes, masking tape.

──MAKING A──
PADDLE STEAMER

Bring the romance of Huckleberry Finn to life and make something special out of bath night with this miniature version of the traditional paddle steamers that still ply the Mississippi River today. The boat is sturdy and durable and will provide your children with hours of innocent fun.

The main requirement is for the boat to be completely waterproof. You can apply several coats of varnish or use waterproof non-toxic paints.

Making the hull
1. Cut the block of softwood to the dimensions given on the template and mark out the shape of the bow and the cut-out for the paddle on it. The classic riverboat has a round bow, though you can make it pointed or square, with a chamfered edge, if desired. A suitably-sized paint can will make an adequate template for the bow, though, for a really accurate curve, you should use the following method.

2. Mark a point which is half the width of the hull and an equal distance from the front and push in a thumbtack. Attach one end of a piece of string to the tack and a pencil to the other end. Keeping the string

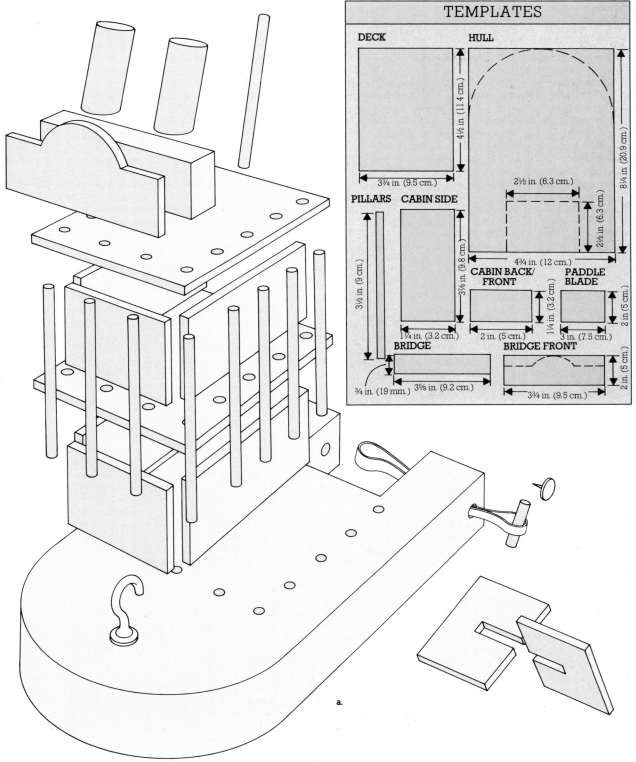

TEMPLATES

DECK

4½ in. (11.4 cm.)

3¾ in. (9.5 cm.)

HULL

2½ in. (6.3 cm.)

2½ in. (6.3 cm.)

4¾ in. (12 cm.)

8¼ in. (20.9 cm.)

PILLARS   CABIN SIDE

3½ in. (9 cm.)

3⅞ in. (9.8 cm.)

1¼ in. (3.2 cm.)

CABIN BACK/
FRONT

1¼ in. (3.2 cm.)

2 in. (5 cm.)

PADDLE
BLADE

2 in (5 cm.)

3 in. (7.5 cm.)

BRIDGE

¾ in. (19 mm.)   3⅝ in. (9.2 cm.)

BRIDGE FRONT

2 in. (5 cm.)

3¾ in. (9.5 cm.)

a.

taut, draw a semicircle *(see fig. b)*. Cut out the bow with a fretsaw or a saber saw and sandpaper the edge to produce a curve that merges smoothly with the sides of the hull.
3. Place the hull in a vise, remembering to protect the sides with pieces of scrap wood, and cut the two side slots for the paddle cut-out. In order to cut out the back of the cut-out, drill a hole on the inside of one of the slots *(see fig. c)*. Thread the fretsaw, or saber saw, blade through the hole and cut across the back of the paddle cut-out. Sand the three edges smooth.

Making the superstructure
1. Cut the decks from plywood to the dimensions given on the templates. On one piece, draw a line ¼ in. (6 mm.) in from the edges, around two sides and the front. Starting ¼ in. (6 mm.) in from the unmarked side, mark off 1 in. (25 mm.) spaces along the lines you have just drawn. These marks indicate the positions of the pillars.
2. To make sure that the holes you drill for the doweling pillars in the decks and the hull line up exactly, position the two decks carefully on the hull and hold them temporarily in place with a couple of brads. The back of the decks should align with the back of the paddle cut-out. Drill ¼ in. (6 mm.) holes through both decks and about ¼ in. (6 mm.) into the hull *(see fig. e)*. To make sure the holes in the deck are all the same depth, wrap a piece of tape around the drill bit to mark the position down to which you should drill. In setting the pillars in the hull make sure that the superstructure is firmly anchored.

b. Mark a point which is half the width of the base and equidistant from the front edge and draw a semicircle with a pencil attached to a thumb tack with string.

3. The cabins are simple plywood boxes. Cut the sides to the measurements given on the templates. Glue and nail them together, with the front and back pieces butting against the inside edge of the sides. Check for squareness with a try square.

Attaching the superstructure
1. Mark the position of the cabin on the hull, making sure that it aligns with the edges of the paddle cut-out, and glue it in place.
2. Glue the corner pillars into the holes drilled in the hull *(see fig. f)*. The pillars should be cut slightly long, so that when the top deck is in place, the ends of the pillars can be sanded down to fit flush.
3. Using the corner pillars as a guide, glue the lower deck on top of the cabin. Next, glue the upper cabin and the top deck in place, making sure that they

c. Cut out the side slots for the paddle cut-out and drill a hole for the fretsaw blade.

all line up and that the holes are directly above each other. You can now insert the remaining pillars through the decks and glue them into the hull.
4. Glue the bridge block in position at the front of the upper deck. Mark out the front of the bridge and name board *(see templates)* and cut out with a fretsaw. Sand the edges smooth and glue it to the softwood block.
5. To make the funnels, cut the ⅝ in. (16 mm.) doweling into 1½ in. (3.8 cm.) lengths. Cut one end of each funnel at a slanted angle, so that they rake back slightly when glued in place. Use a scrap of doweling for the flagpole, drill a hole in the deck and glue it in place.

The propulsion system
1. You will need two pieces of plywood for the paddle blades. Cut the pieces to the dimensions shown. Draw a line through the center of each blade and cut a slot, to the thickness of the plywood, half way across each one as shown *(see fig. a)*.
2. Apply glue to the blades and slide them into place, checking

90

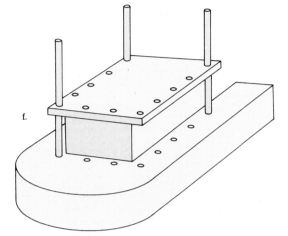

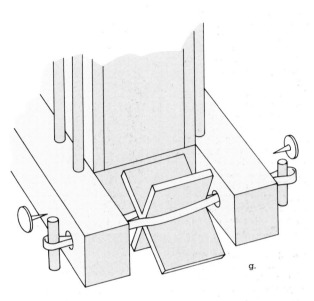

to see that they are at right angles to one another, as this ensures an even rotation. Drill a hole through the hull on each side of the paddle cut-out in the position shown *(see fig. g)*. This is important as the position of the rubber band holding the paddle-wheel governs the depth at which the blades bite into the water.

3. The paddle is powered by a rubber band. Use a fairly thick one that stretches across the width of the hull. It is held in place on either side by a piece of doweling *(see fig. g)* and is looped across the center of the blades, holding them in position. You may find it necessary to insert a nail next to each piece of doweling, to stop it spinning back as the rubber band is wound up.

Decoration

If you want to keep the natural wood finish, apply at least one coat of clear varnish – you may have to apply further coats on the end grain of the wood to ensure that the boat is completely waterproof. Before doing this you can easily decorate the boat with colored stickers if you like. Remember

these must be applied before you varnish the boat as they will soak off in water. Alternatively, you can devise whatever color scheme you like and paint it with waterproof non-toxic enamel paints.

A simpler version

If you feel that this paddle steamer design is too complex to build, or that it may not stand up to the rigors of a very young child's bath night, you can simplify the boat's superstructure by using softwood blocks for cabins. Make sure that the blocks are not too heavy or the boat may become unstable.

The maiden voyage

With your riverboat painted or varnished, sea trials can now take place. You may find that the boat needs trimming to make it sit squarely in the water. To deal with this problem, you can add weight to one side or the other. Another option is to drill out small pieces from the underside of the hull. You can also add a cup hook so that your child can tow the boat.

MATERIALS

Softwood:
1 piece 1¾ x 4¾ x 8¼ in. (44 x 120 x 209 mm.)
1 piece ¾ x ¾ x 3⅝ in. (19 x 19 x 92 mm.)
Plywood:
2 pieces ¼ x 3¾ x 4½ in. (6 x 95 x 114 mm.)
4 pieces ¼ x 1¼ x 3⅞ in. (6 x 32 x 98 mm.)
4 pieces ¼ x 1¼ x 2 in. (6 x 32 x 50 mm.)
2 pieces ¼ x 2 x 3 in. (6 x 50 x 75 mm.)
1 piece ¼ x 2 x 3¾ in. (6 x 50 x 95 mm.)
Doweling:
2 pieces ⅝ x 1½ in. (16 x 38 mm.)
12 pieces ¼ x 3½ in. (6 x 89 mm.)
Hardware:
1 rubber band
1 cup hook
   wood glue
   brads
   clear varnish, or waterproof non-toxic paint

TOOLS

Backsaw, coping saw, fretsaw or saber saw, drill and bits sandpaper, paintbrush, try square.

MAKING A
LUNAR SPACE STATION

Children can travel to the stars with this interstellar galactic space station and save Earth from alien invasion before bedtime. The space station is equipped with the latest triple cluster search and destroy missiles, capable of blasting the alien armada into the terrifying black hole under the coffee table.

Although this toy can be made exactly as shown, it can also be adapted to use up pieces of scrap wood in your workshop. If you have a very young child, you can easily disarm the launcher.

Making a space station
1. Make paper patterns of the various shapes, using the dimensions given on the templates and then trace them on the wood and plywood. Saw out the pieces. You can substitute scrap pieces left over from other toys for any of the pieces listed, or adapt the design to suit the pieces of scrap in your workshop. Sand the edges smooth.
2. Draw a line across the base, 23 in. (58 cm.) from one end. Mark the center point of the near edge and draw two lines from that point to the line you have just drawn (see templates). Saw along the lines

a.

to form a pointed rocket nose.
Sand the edges smooth.
3. Drill a hole through the base
for the missile launcher
mounting as shown *(see fig. a)*.
Note It is essential to paint all
the missile launcher pieces
before assembly.

Making the tail
1. The first step in assembling
the tail is to attach the
horizontal fin to the base with
glue and brads *(see fig. b)*. The
fins should project an equal
distance on each side of the
base.

2. Using a sharp modeling knife, scribe the edges of the cross lap joints on the vertical tail fins and the flying bridge. Cut along the waste edges of the scribed lines with a backsaw. Remove the unwanted wood with a chisel until the three pieces fit together neatly.
3. Now attach the vertical fins to the tail support with a butt joint, glued and screwed together *(see fig. c)*.
4. Glue and screw this assembly in position.
5. Slot the flying bridge into place and glue it *(see fig. d)*.

Making the missile launcher
1. Cut the plastic pipe into three equal lengths of 6 in. (15.2 cm.). The plastic is not difficult to cut, but you should use a fine-toothed saw. A hacksaw is ideal, but a backsaw can be substituted. Sand the edges with fine grades of sandpaper. Cut slots in one end of each section with a modeling knife *(see fig. a)*. Sand until smooth.
2. Mark the circumference of the circle on the square piece of plywood with a compass. If you do not have a compass,

you can draw diagonal lines from corner to corner and then hammer a nail into the center point. Attach a pencil to the nail with a piece of string and draw the circumference *(see pp. 80-1)*.
3. Drill holes in the barrel mounting large enough to take the plastic tubes.
4. Drill two screw holes above each barrel hole, plus one on each side of the block. Insert the plastic tube and screw in roundhead screws until the points just catch the tubing, but do not actually penetrate it. Screw a roundhead screw into each side of the barrel mounting, so that rubber bands can be looped around them *(see fig. f)*.
5. Drill a hole through the smallest block of softwood for the carriage bolt. Then glue the block to the center of the barrel mounting.
6. With a fretsaw, shape the

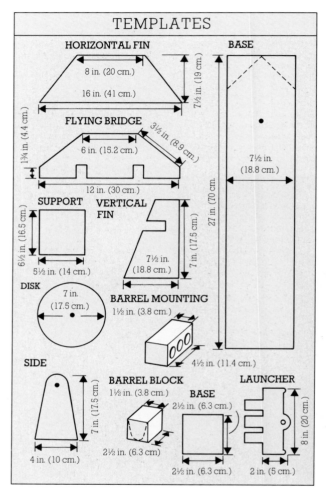

TEMPLATES

HORIZONTAL FIN — 8 in. (20 cm.) / 16 in. (41 cm.) / 7½ in. (19 cm.)

BASE — 7½ in. (18.8 cm.) / 27 in. (70 cm.)

FLYING BRIDGE — 1¾ in. (4.4 cm.) / 6 in. (15.2 cm.) / 3½ in. (8.9 cm.) / 12 in. (30 cm.)

SUPPORT — 6½ in. (16.5 cm.) / 5½ in. (14 cm.)

VERTICAL FIN — 7½ in. (18.8 cm.) / 7 in. (17.5 cm.)

DISK — 7 in. (17.5 cm.)

BARREL MOUNTING — 1½ in. (3.8 cm.) / 4½ in. (11.4 cm.)

SIDE — 7 in. (17.5 cm.) / 4 in. (10 cm.)

BARREL BLOCK — 1½ in. (3.8 cm.) / 2½ in. (6.3 cm.)

BASE — 2½ in. (6.3 cm.) / 2½ in. (6.3 cm.)

LAUNCHER — 8 in. (20 cm.) / 2 in. (5 cm.)

c.

b.

d.

To assemble the tail, first attach the horizontal fin to the base, then butt joint the vertical sides to the

support, screw in place and attach the flying bridge with a cross lap joint.

sides and then cut out the multiple launcher. Sand the edges smooth.
7. Drill holes in the sides and through the centers of the bottom softwood block and the plywood disk. Attach the sides to the bottom block, with glue and countersunk screws. Position this assembly on the plywood disk and attach to the base with a wood screw and cup washer. The screw should be loose enough to allow the

missile launcher to be swiveled to find its target. Now attach the barrel mounting between the side pieces with the carriage bolt, washer and wing nut as shown *(see fig. e)*.
8. Drill three holes in the multiple launcher – in the handle to give a better grip, and the other two to take the rubber bands, which propel the missiles. Attach the launcher to the mounting barrel with rubber bands *(see fig. f)*.
9. The range of the missile launcher can be altered by adjusting the length of the rubber bands. With safety considerations in mind, make sure that the range of the missiles does not exceed 1 yd. (1 m.), so experiment with different rubber bands until you have the right range. If you have very young children you may prefer to disarm the missile launcher by removing the bands.

Making the missiles (optional)
1. Cut the ⅝ in. (16 mm.) dowel into three lengths of approximately 3 in. (7.5 cm.).
2. Round off one end of each missile with coarse sandpaper *(see fig. g)*.

Decorating the space station
As mentioned earlier, all the missile launcher pieces should have been painted before assembly, but you can now give the space station its final coat of paint and add all the fine detail. Create your own spectacular galactic space station design with the help of self-adhesive paper, or self-adhesive plastic film in different colors, stick-on stars, and strips of thin, white, sticky tape.

e. Assemble the missile launcher, using a carriage bolt with washers and wing nut, countersunk screws and glue.

f. Attach the multiple launcher to the barrel mounting with rubber bands.

g. Round off the ends of the dowel missiles with coarse sandpaper.

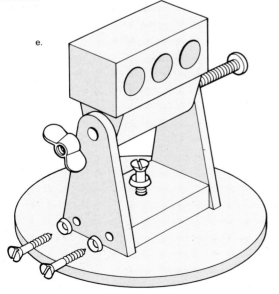
e.

MATERIALS

Softwood:
1   piece ¾ x 7½ x 27 in. (19 x 188 x 700 mm.)
2   pieces ¾ x 7½ x 7 in. (19 x 188 x 175 mm.)
1   piece ¾ x 5½ x 6½ in. (19 x 140 x 165 mm.)
1   piece ¾ x 3½ x 12 in. (19 x 89 x 305 mm.)
2   pieces ½ x 4 x 7 in. (12 x 100 x 175 mm.)
1   piece 1½ x 1½ x 4½ in. (38 x 38 x 114 mm.)
1   piece 1½ x 1½ x 2½ in. (38 x 38 x 63 mm.)
1   piece 1½ x 2½ x 2½ in. (38 x 63 x 63 mm.)
Plywood:
1   piece ⅜ x 7 x 16 in. (10 x 175 x 406 mm.)
1   piece ⅜ x 7 x 7 in. (10 x 175 x 175 mm.)
1   piece ¼ x 6 x 8 in. (6 x 150 x 200 mm.)
Doweling:
1   piece ⅝ x 9 in. (16 x 225 mm.)
Hardware:
1   18 in. (46 cm.) length plastic pipe with ¾ in. (19 mm.) inside diameter
    roundhead screws
    woodscrews
    carriage bolt, with washers and wing nut
1   cup washer
    brads
    rubber bands
    white glue
    non-toxic paint

TOOLS

Panel saw or electric circular saw, coping saw, fretsaw or saber saw, backsaw, drill with drill bits, screwdriver, try square, hammer, chisels, mallet, modeling knife, sandpaper, paintbrushes, compass.

— MAKING A —
SNAIL CLOCK

This bright, cheerful snail clock will make it fun for young children to learn to tell the time. You can stand it on the floor, or on any other suitable flat surface. You can hang it on a wall. It is extremely easy to make and can be adapted if you wish to use up odd scraps of plywood in your workshop. In addition, using the methods for drawing patterns described on p. 120, you can change the snail base to any design you prefer.

Making a snail clock
1. Draw the outlines of the clock pieces on the sheet of plywood. You can use the dimensions given, or alter them to suit the size of your plywood sheet.
2. Start by drawing the circular clock face, leaving enough space for the snail's body. Decide where the center of the circle will be and, if you do not have a compass, drive a nail in at that point. Attach a 6 in. (15 cm.) piece of string to a pencil and then to the nail. Draw a circle (see fig. a).
3. Draw the outlines of the

96

a. *If you do not have a compass, draw the clock face by attaching a length of string to a pencil and a central nail.*

a.

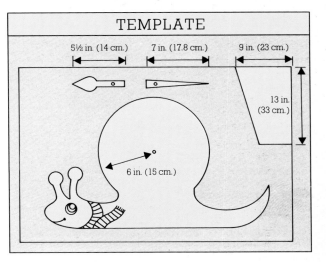

TEMPLATE

5½ in. (14 cm.) 7 in. (17.8 cm.) 9 in. (23 cm.)

13 in. (33 cm.)

6 in. (15 cm.)

snail, the clock hands and the support bracket by enlarging the shape on a paper pattern *(see p.120)* to the measurements given and transferring it to the sheet of plywood.

4. Cut out the shapes with a fretsaw, or a saber saw. Sand the edges until smooth.
5. Drill holes through the center of the clock face and in the clock hands.
6. Hinge the support bracket to the back of the clock *(see fig.*

b. & c. *Fasten the support bracket to the clock back with hinges and the hands to the clock face with a bolt, washers and wing nut.*

b.

c.

c). Use an awl to make starting holes for the hinge screws. If the ends of the screws project, file off the sharp points until the ends are flush with the plywood.
7. The clock is now ready for painting. You can use a stencil to paint on the numbers, or instant lettering. You can also mark the minutes on the clock, if desired.
8. When the paint is dry, attach the clock hands to the face, using the ¼ in. (6 mm.) bolt, two washers, and a wing nut *(see fig. c).*
9. If you wish to hang the clock on the wall, attach screw eyes or picture hooks to the back.

MATERIALS

Plywood:
1 piece approx. ¼-⅜ x 19 x 28 in. (6-10 x 480 x 710 mm.)
Hardware:
2 small brass hinges, with screws
2 small screw eyes, or picture hook
1 ¼ in. (6 mm.) bolt 1¼ in. (3.2 cm.) long
2 washers
1 wing nut
non-toxic paint

TOOLS

Pencil, tape measure, try square, fretsaw or saber saw, drill and drill bits, screwdriver, awl, compasses, sandpaper, paintbrush, hammer, file.

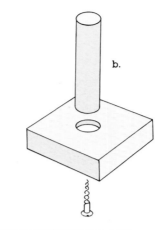

MAKING
MIXED MEDIA TOYS

Because so many different materials and skills are required to make the puppets in this section, they have been used to demonstrate the principles of mixed media toymaking. Once you have mastered the techniques involved, you can apply them to other toymaking areas.

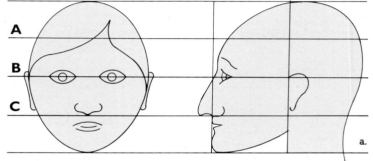

Using mixed media for making puppets

Start with some hand puppets, as these are less complicated to make than the other varieties. Children also find them relatively easy to operate, so even the simplest design can provide them with many hours of amusement and fun. String puppets or marionettes, on the other hand, are more sophisticated. Because of their size, their intricate articulation and their stringing, they are complex to make and correspondingly difficult to operate. They thus present a bigger challenge.

In both cases, however, the very wide range of modern materials that can be used makes the task less demanding. Though puppets are traditionally made of papier mâché, wood and cloth, for instance, why not use self-hardening clays, plastic foam and silicon tile-sealant as speedier alternatives; modern adhesives and paints also help to make life easier. Let your imagination run free as well – you can use all sorts of junk materials to create instant, low-cost characters that will appeal to children of every age group.

Making puppet heads

Traditionally, papier mâché is an excellent medium for making lightweight yet durable puppet heads. What you do is to model the basic shape you need in modeling clay or self-hardening clay and then

cover this with pieces of paper. When the paper dries, the resulting hard shell is cut in half, removed from the modeling clay and pasted together again. Allow sufficient time between the various stages for drying out.

You do not have to be an expert modeler to model the face – the important thing is to get the proportions of the various features more or less correct. Here, the following guidelines will help you. Remember that all puppets should have relatively large heads to make the face more visible to an audience. Consequently, the features should be bold and simple, so that they can convey the various kinds of emotion. Think of the head as an oval divided into four equal parts (see fig. a). The eyes lie halfway down the head and are separated by a distance equal to their width. Line A represents the hairline; the nose lies between B and C together with the ears, which can be seen in the side view. Thus the

bottom of the ears are level with the tip of the nose. The mouth lies in the lower quarter section of the head – model this partly open so the puppet looks as if it is speaking.

These guidelines apply to both hand and string puppets, but, when it comes to the neck, things are different. A hand puppet's neck should have a flange to help secure the puppet, while you should allow sufficient room to accommodate the fingers that will be manipulating it. The design of a string puppet's neck depends on the type of movement required and the media used to make the head.

Making the modeling stand

A modeling stand is an essential prerequisite before you get down to business. Such a stand makes the task easier, as it provides a steady base of exactly the right height on which to work. You will need a 1 in. (25 mm.) thick wooden block about 6 in. (15 cm.) square; a length of dowel

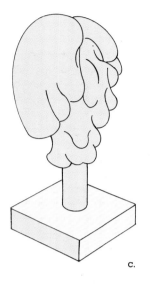

c.

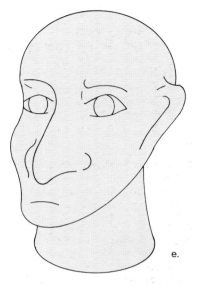

d.

e.

rod or broomstick approximately 8 in. (20 cm.) long and ¾ in. (19 mm.) in diameter; woodworking glue; a hand drill with ¾ in. (19 mm.) spade bit; a hammer or a screwdriver and 2 in. (5 cm.) screw.

1. Drill a hole through the middle of the block and smear a little glue inside the hole and around the rod's base *(see fig. b)*. Then hammer the rod home into the hole. Another approach would be to butt the rod to the center of the block, then drive a screw through the base into it. Countersink the screw, as otherwise the base will wobble.

Working with modeling clay

You will need a stand; newspaper, clear plastic kitchen wrap, about 1½ lbs. (681 g.) of modeling clay and a few modeling tools.

1. Scrunch up a few sheets of newspaper to make a ball about 4 in. (10 cm.) tall.
2. Cover the ball with a layer of plastic wrap and place it on top of the stand. Hold it in place by covering with more wrap, tightening

Modeling clay *The newspaper core is held in place on the stand with plastic wrap. Features are built up with sausages of clay and then modeled in an exaggerated style.*

the ends around the rod *(see fig. c)*.
3. Work the clay in your hands until it is warm and pliable. Roll out a strip just long enough to wrap around the rod. This is the neck.
4. Cover the paper core with clay, smoothing into the neck.
5. Add clay to the head piece by piece to build up the basic shape.
6. Press the eye sockets out with your thumbs. Then roll out two eyeballs and gently push them home.
7. Use clay sausages to build up the eyebrows, the lips and the ears *(see fig. d)*.
8. The nose is made from a large sausage, with two balls attached on each side of the base for nostrils.
9. Assess what you have done critically before proceeding further – this means looking at the head upside down as well. The detail should be bold and deep *(see fig. e)*, otherwise the features will be lost under the layers of paper added at the next stage.

Modeling with self-hardening clay

There are many self-hardening clays suitable for modeling on the market, all of which set hard after a few days at room temperature. The clay is easy to work with and gives a very smooth surface, especially if it is brushed with water at the end of modeling. Use it as a modeling medium like modeling clay, but bear in mind that the heads may be too heavy for the puppets. *(See also p.122.)*

Laminating with papier mâché

To create the laminated effect described earlier, you will need to cover the head you have modeled in layers of newspaper, torn into postage stamp-sized squares. You will also need a release agent, such as petroleum jelly or liquid soap; paste such as that used for wallpapering; gauze bandage or cheesecloth; white wood glue; a mixing bowl; water; a paste brush; and a modeling knife.

1. Mix paste with water according to the manufacturer's instructions. Use a heavy duty paste containing anti-

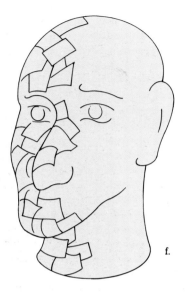

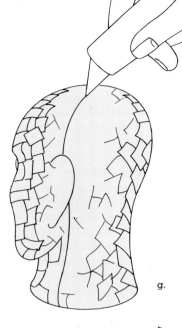

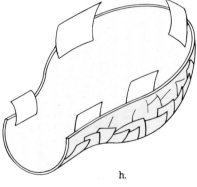

Laminated papier mâché *The modeled clay head is pasted with several layers of paper squares. When dry, cut the shell in half and glue strips of bandage in place, ready to join the two halves together.*

fungicide as this will prevent mold growing on the paper. Rub the surface of the head with petroleum jelly.

2. Cover the head with a layer of paper squares, pressing these firmly down into place *(see fig. f)*. Paste over the paper and cover with a further layer of squares. Use plenty of paste, rubbing it over the surface with your fingers so that it really soaks into the paper. Build up at least six layers, ideally stopping halfway through to let the paper dry, although this is not essential.

3. Leave the head to dry in a warm place, though you should avoid direct heat. Some shrinkage will inevitably occur and characteristic ridges will result.

4. Use a modeling knife to cut through the paper shell *(see fig. g)*. This is generally done from side to side, passing behind the ears, although in some cases the design

may involve working from front to back. If you have any difficulty prizing the papier mâché apart, a further cut from side to side, quartering the head, will help.

5. Leave the head pieces to dry on the inside for a few hours and then hold them up to the light to check for any weaknesses. If necessary, glue on strips of cheesecloth to the inside, or use more paste and paper.

6. Glue strips of cheesecloth around a cut edge with half the cheesecloth width projecting beyond the edge *(see fig. h)*. Leave to dry. Glue the matching cut edge, then bring the two halves together, and press the cheesecloth into the glue, using the handle of a long paint brush to reach right inside the head if necessary. Cover the joint on the outside with more paste and paper and leave to dry. Neatly trim the neck edge.

Painting papier mâché

Before you start painting the head, prepare the surface by rubbing it down with very fine sandpaper. Then seal it – the sealant prevents the paint from soaking into the paper. Ideally a white acrylic gesso primer should be used, but, if this is unavailable, use white acrylic primer or latex paint instead.

Paint the features with acrylic paints; these are waterproof, fast-drying and very easy to use. Thin them with water if you need to and clean your brushes with water when you have finished painting. To obtain a good flesh tone, mix red and white to get a basic pink, to which you add a little yellow and brown. Coat the entire head with the mixture, using two coats, if necessary, to get a good covering. Paint the eyeballs white with a very small amount of yellow added to take away the starkness. The features can now be painted according to the chosen character. Avoid excessive detail, as this simply will not be visible. Go for bold make up, eliminating the iris if necessary. You are aiming to create a sense of theater.

The final finish may need some attention as acrylics dry flat. You may decide to varnish the eyes and mouth to make them sparkle. The finished head can also be polished with clear furniture polish.

MAKING
HAND PUPPETS

Hand puppets have a universal appeal, especially when it comes to the fast-moving action of a British Punch and Judy show. Here, Punch and Judy are the puppets – the baby cannot be operated, even though its head is made of papier mâché. All it consists of is a stump bundled up in a wrap, a head and a bonnet, so start with this.

Judy is just a little more complicated, with a modeled head and a glove-like dress. By the time that you have made her you will be able to tackle the challenge of Punch and his strongly modeled features confidently.

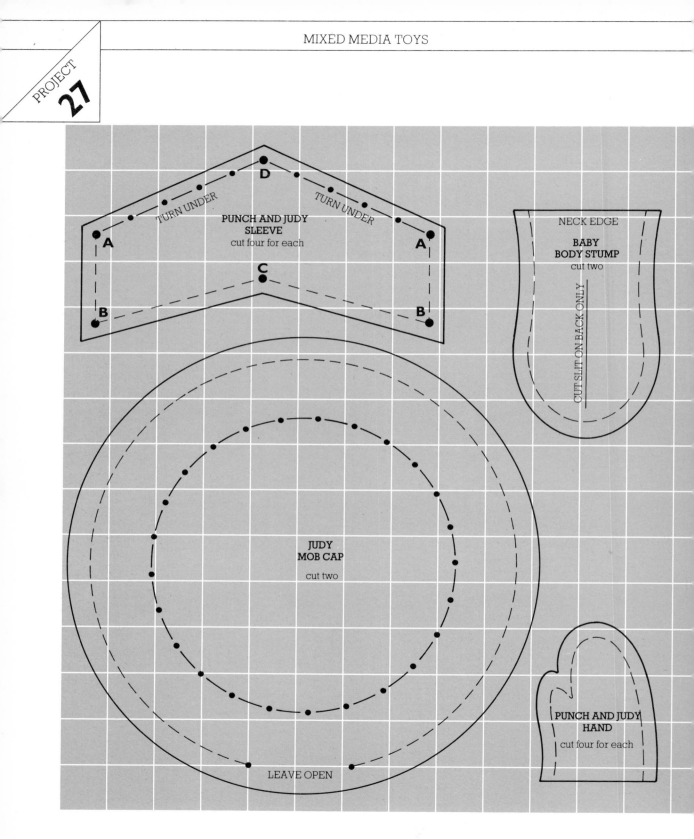

PUNCH AND JUDY
SLEEVE
cut four for each

TURN UNDER

TURN UNDER

D

A

A

C

B

B

NECK EDGE

BABY
BODY STUMP
cut two

CUT SLIT ON BACK ONLY

JUDY
MOB CAP

cut two

LEAVE OPEN

PUNCH AND JUDY
HAND

cut four for each

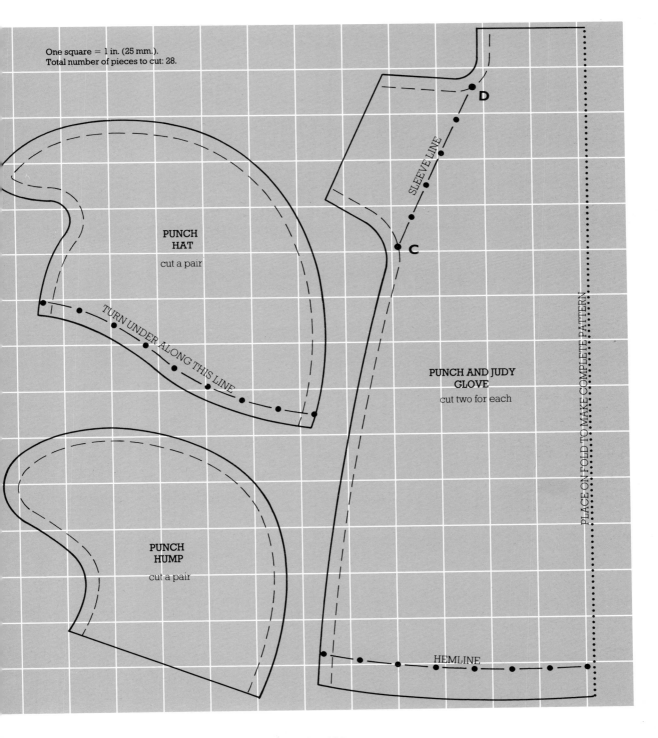

One square = 1 in. (25 mm.).
Total number of pieces to cut: 28.

PUNCH
HAT

cut a pair

TURN UNDER ALONG THIS LINE

SLEEVE LINE

D

C

PUNCH AND JUDY
GLOVE

cut two for each

PLACE ON FOLD TO MAKE COMPLETE PATTERN

PUNCH
HUMP

cut a pair

HEMLINE

Vinyl face mask

Clay head and neck

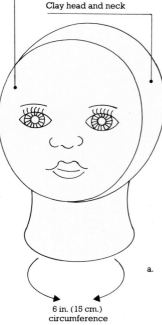

a.

6 in. (15 cm.)
circumference

Making the baby
Form a clay ball for the head
and then embed a vinyl face
mask (available from
toymakers' suppliers) onto its
front.
1. Follow the instructions given
on the previous pages to make
the papier mâché head. The
neck needs a circumference of
6 in. (15 cm.) to take the body
stump *(see fig. a).*
2. Paint on the features, starting
with brown pupils and
continuing with lighter brown
eyebrows and a soft, pink,
rosebud-shaped mouth. Put a
dot of red in the inside corner
of each eye and a spot of white
on each pupil as a highlight.
Fill the head with stuffing.
3. Make a full-size pattern *(see
p.12)* of the body stump from
the pattern grid and cut the
two pieces you will need from
the white cotton. Sew them
together around the curved
edge, then turn right side out.
Make a narrow hem on the
neck edge by folding toward
the inside and tacking.
4. Fit the stump onto the neck
and check for size, resewing if
necessary. Glue in place. Stuff
the stump through the slit in the
back, then close the opening
with ladder stitch.
5. Wind yarn over two fingers
to make a cluster of loops for
the hair *(see fig. b).* Backstitch

the loops together at one end,
then glue on forehead.
6. Cut a piece of cotton 8 in. (20
cm.) wide by 6 in. (15 cm.) long
for the bonnet and a circle 3 in.
(7.6 cm.) in diameter for the
crown. Fold bonnet in half
across the width and sew both
short sides together in turn.
Turn right side out.
7. Cut lace into three equal
lengths. Gather two to fit the
width of the bonnet. Sew one in
place along the folded edge

and the other just behind it
(see fig. c).
8. Run a gathering thread along
the open edge and pull up until
the bonnet fits the head.
Overlap the ends slightly and
fasten off *(see fig. d).* Run a
gathering thread around the
edge of the crown circle and
pull up tightly. Fasten off.
Flatten to form a small disk.
9. Gather edge of the third
length of lace and sew it
around three-quarters of the
crown *(see fig. e).* Place crown
over gathers of bonnet, thus
concealing them, and sew in
place. Sew ties onto each side
of bonnet, then place bonnet
on head and fasten.
10. Fold the wool square
diagonally in half and wrap
around the baby as a shawl.
Stitch in place.

Making Judy
Make a full-size pattern *(see
p.12)* of the body of the puppet,
or glove, as well as the sleeves,
hands and the fancy hat, known
as a mob cap, from the pattern
grid. Cut glove and sleeves
from striped cotton, hands from
felt and cap from white cotton.
1. When you model the head,
give it a strong nose and
prominent chin. There is no
need to model ears as they will
not be seen. Leave the mouth
area flat if this is your first
attempt at modeling.
2. Paint the eyes blue with
black pupils and outline the
upper edge of each eye with a
line of red, putting a dot of red
in the inside corners and
finishing with white highlights

*c. Gather up two
lengths of lace and sew
onto the bonnet.* **d.**
*Gather up the open
edge of the bonnet to
fit the head and fasten
off.* **e.** *Sew the gathered
edge of the third length
of lace onto the crown
circle.*

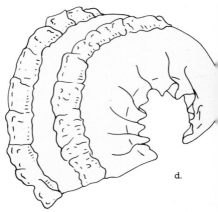

d.

b.

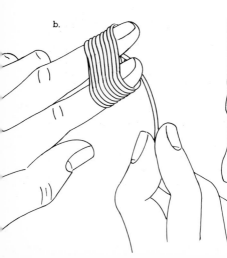

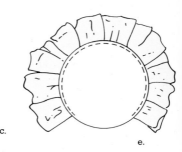

c.

e.

on the pupils. Paint the mouth. Give the cheeks some color by rubbing some lipstick on them.

3. Cut a strip of cardboard 8 in. (20 cm.) by 2 in. (5 cm.) and roll to fit the neck opening, which is approximately two fingers wide *(see fig. f).* Glue edges of roll with latex-based glue to hold it in place. Cover one end of the roll with scrap fabric and glue. Now glue the roll inside the neck opening, with the covered end right inside the head. Hold with clothes pins until the glue sets.

4. Glue a strip of felt around the outside of the neck and a second strip inside the roll. Sew the lower edges of both strips together for further security.

5. Sew glove pieces right sides together across shoulders and down each underarm and side seam. Make a double hem along the lower edge. Turn right side out, then fold under neck edge, making a single hem. Gather to fit over the neck. Backstitch in place, carefully working into the felt collar. Work a second row of stitching to secure. Cover stitching with gathered lace, which you glue in place with clear-drying glue.

6. Sew around the two felt hand pieces with a ⅛ in. (3 mm.) seam. Snip corner between thumb and fingers, turn right side out and stuff finger area lightly. Stab stitch finger divisions *(see p.14).*

7. Cut two pieces of cardboard 6 in. (15 cm.) by 1¼ in. (3 cm.). Roll these up, coat one end of each piece with glue and cover with scrap fabric. Glue the outside of the roll and gently ease the covered end inside wrist edge of hand *(see fig. g).* Complete the second hand in same way.

8. Feed hands into arm openings of glove with thumbs

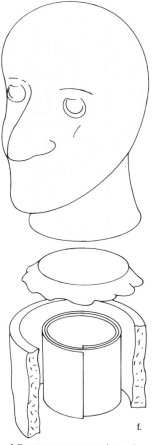

f. *For strong support at the neck, glue together a roll of cardboard and cover with a glued circle of fabric at one end. Glue the roll and insert into the head. Reinforce with strips of felt inside and around the neck.*

uppermost. Backstitch in position. Cover seams with gathered lace, again gluing into place.

9. Take two sleeve pieces and sew each underarm seam by folding A to A and B to B, then sewing from A to B. Turn one sleeve right side out and feed it inside the other sleeve, so that

PAINTING FACES

Prepare the surface by sanding with fine sandpaper and seal with a water-based primer. Use acrylic paint to mix a basic flesh tone, then add the features, keeping them simple and bold. Varnish the eyes and mouth and polish the flesh with clear furniture polish (see p.100).

right sides are together, seams pressed flat and all edges level *(see fig. h).* Sew wrist edges together from B through C to B. Open sleeve out so that all right sides are facing, then turn one sleeve inside the other, so that wrong sides are together.
10. Fold under a narrow hem on the shoulder edge of the sleeve and baste. Feed sleeve over hand and onto the glove, with D on neck seam and A on side seam of glove *(see fig. i).* Hem in place. Make and attach second sleeve in the same way.
11. Wind wool yarn into a 12 in. (30 cm.) long hank, using a book of the same height as the

g. Position of cardboard roll glued to the inside of the hand.

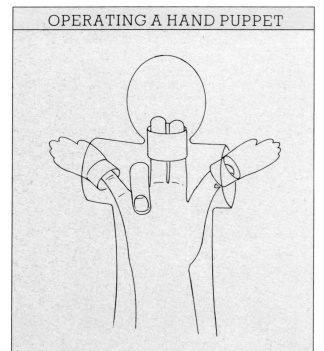

OPERATING A HAND PUPPET

Punch and Judy are planned to fit a large hand. The index and second finger support the head, while the thumb and little finger each operate an arm. The third finger remains bent down toward the palm. The cardboard rolls – called finger stalls by puppeteers – should ideally reach no further than the second joint of each finger and the first joint of thumb. This arrangement ensures maximum freedom of movement.

Practice clapping without hitting the chin, picking up and passing baby, hitting with the stick or even waving hands convincingly and bowing. Try operating two hand puppets together. Punch traditionally stays on the right hand, while all other members of the cast take turns on the left.

h. *Place one sleeve piece inside another with right sides together, seams pressed and aligned between B and A. Sew the wrist edges together from B through C to B.*

pattern. Wrap yarn over book 57 times, then slip hank off book and tie each end securely with strong thread. Backstitch a parting through the center of the hank *(see fig. j).* Now glue parting to the top of the head and then glue down each side of the face and around to back where the tie ends should come together. If there is a gap, conceal it with a bun.
12. Make the mob cap by sewing two circles together around the edge with right sides facing. Leave a small opening. Turn right side out, close opening and press cap.

i. *The sleeve is positioned over the glove, ready for hemming between D and A.*

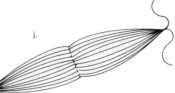

j. *The hair is wound into a hank, tied off at each end and sewn through the center to make a middle parting. The ties can be used to fasten the hank at the back of the head.*

Sew gathered lace around edge. Now run a strong gathering thread all around cap, 1¼ in. (3 cm.) in from the edge. Pull up to fit head. If necessary, put more stuffing in mob cap to give it shape, then sew cap in place through the gathering to the hair beneath. As a finishing touch sew ribbon to each side of the mob cap and bring it down to tie in a bow under the chin.

Making Punch

Make a full-size pattern (see p.12) of the glove, sleeves, hands, hump and hat from the pattern grid. Cut hands from felt and all parts of the costume from needle cord.

1. Because the head is so complex you may have to cut it off in four sections from the clay. Stress the characteristic curves of the nose and chin in your modeling and do not forget to model ears.

2. Paint the eyes brown with black pupils and outline the upper edge of each eye with a flamboyant red eyebrow. Finish eyes with white highlights. Paint the mouth with the same red as the eyes and paint the mouth opening white. You may like to add a black grid indicating teeth. Blush the cheeks and chin with more red paint or rub a little lipstick into them to heighten the color.

3. Make the neck roll, glove, hands and sleeves as you did for Judy, but this time using rick-rack for decoration, not lace.

4. Sew the two hump pieces together, turn right side out and stuff firmly. Run a strong gathering thread around the edge and pull up to roll raw edges inward. Cover seams with rick-rack. Ladder stitch the hump in place on the back of the glove.

5. To make the hair, you will need to cut a 9 in. (23 cm.) by ½ in. (1 cm.) central slot in the strong piece of cardboard as shown. Wrap wool yarn over cardboard approximately 130 times, then backstitch or machine the curls together through the slot. Break one end of the card and pull string of curls free. Glue hair around head, leaving a gap over the forehead.

6. Sew both hat pieces together, clip the curve and then turn right side out. Turn under lower edge and hem in place, then cover seam with rick-rack. Stuff hat, place on head and glue and stitch in place. Sew bell or yellow pompom to front of hat.

7. Attach head to glove. Cover the seam by gluing a simple collar over it, decorating the collar with rick-rack or a gathered ruff. If you like, you could even make a collar with tiny bells attached to it.

8. Finally, sand both ends of a length of doweling. Then tuck it under Punch's arm.

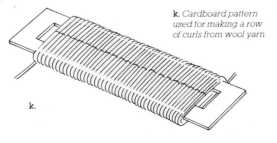

k. *Cardboard pattern used for making a row of curls from wool yarn.*

MATERIALS

For the baby:
modeling clay and acrylic paints
vinyl face mask, 2½ in. long, 2½ in. wide
1 yd. (1 m.) wool yarn for curls
2 oz. (56 g.) stuffing
12 in. (30 cm.) square of white cotton
24 in. (61 cm.) cotton lace
18 in. (46 cm.) square of coarsely woven wool
12 in. (30 cm.) white baby ribbon

For Judy:
a papier mâché head measuring 4 in. (10 cm.) from chin to top of head
ball of mohair wool yarn
9 in. (23 cm.) square of flesh-colored felt
½ yd. (0.5 m.) of 36 in. (92 cm.) wide striped cotton
1½ yd. (1.5 m.) gathered lace
12 in. (30 cm.) of 36 in. (92 cm.) wide white cotton
2 oz. (56 g.) stuffing
8 in. (20 cm.) square of thin card

For Punch:
a papier mâché head measuring 4½ in. (11 cm.) from chin to top of head
mohair yarn for hair
9 in. (23 cm.) square of flesh-colored felt
27 in. (69 cm.) of 36 in. (92 cm.) wide red pinwhale corduroy
6 oz. (168 g.) stuffing
8 in. (20 cm.) square of thin cardboard
approximately 2 yd. (2 m.) yellow rick-rack
strong piece of card 12 in. (30 cm.) by 2½ in. (6.3 cm)
small bell or yellow pompom for hat
length of doweling for stick

EQUIPMENT

Dressmaking shears, pins, needles, thread, tape measure or ruler, pattern-making equipment, paint brushes, knife, fabric and paper glue.

MAKING A
PUPPET THEATER

This toy theater is based on the traditional "Punch and Judy" hand puppet theater. However, it can also be used for small string puppets if it is turned upside down. It is designed to be easily adaptable – the removable playboard will provide both the external playboard needed for hand puppets, and the internal playboard that is used for string puppets.

The size of your theater
There are two things to consider before building your puppet theater: first, the size of the puppeteer (the measurements for this theater are suitable for a small child), and second, the size of the puppets, which will determine the size of the stage opening. If you want to make a theater to be used by adults for children's entertainment, simply enlarge the measurements. The string puppet described on p.112 is a large puppet that will require a much larger theater, so adapt the measurements of either the puppet or the theater. There is a wide range of commercially available string puppets that can be used with this theater.

Cutting the wood
Mark out the largest sheet of plywood and cut out the front, the two sides and the backboard. Use a panel saw, a portable circular saw or a power saber saw.

Make templates for the shelf supports. From the second piece of plywood cut out the parts for the string puppet rack; cut the parts for the playboard from the third piece. Cut battens to size, if this has not already been done.

Mark the slots in the shelf

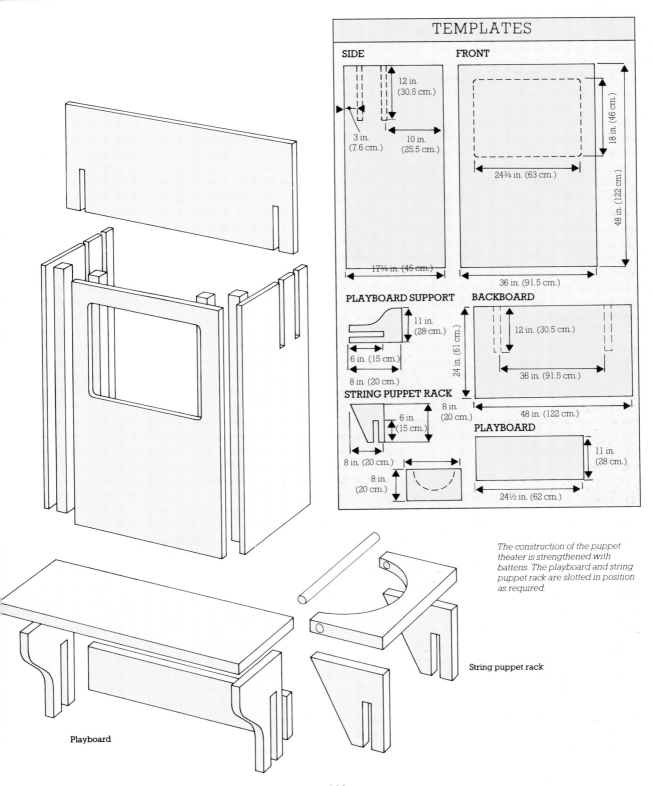

TEMPLATES

SIDE

12 in.
(30.5 cm.)

3 in.
(7.6 cm.)

10 in.
(25.5 cm.)

17¾ in. (45 cm.)

FRONT

18 in. (46 cm.)

24¾ in. (63 cm.)

48 in. (122 cm.)

36 in. (91.5 cm.)

PLAYBOARD SUPPORT

11 in.
(28 cm.)

6 in. (15 cm.)

8 in. (20 cm.)

BACKBOARD

12 in. (30.5 cm.)

36 in. (91.5 cm.)

24 in. (61 cm.)

48 in. (122 cm.)

STRING PUPPET RACK

8 in.
(20 cm.)

6 in.
(15 cm.)

8 in. (20 cm.)

8 in.
(20 cm.)

PLAYBOARD

11 in.
(28 cm.)

24½ in. (62 cm.)

The construction of the puppet theater is strengthened with battens. The playboard and string puppet rack are slotted in position as required.

Playboard

String puppet rack

PROJECT **28**

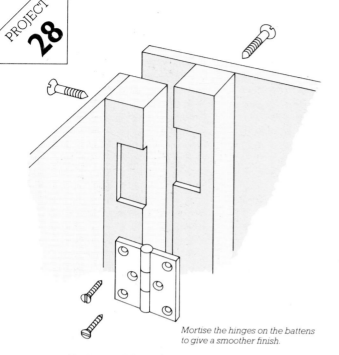

Mortise the hinges on the battens to give a smoother finish.

supports, the sides and the backboard and make ⅜ in. (10 mm.) wide cuts.

Now mark out the outline of the proscenium opening. Drill small holes in each corner and cut out the shape with a keyhole or saber saw. Smooth all of the edges with sandpaper before assembling the pieces.

Assembling the theater
The front and sides are put together first.
1. Tack the battens in position. Before screwing the pieces together, mark the position of the hinges. Use a pencil to outline each hinge, and score around each outline with a chisel to the depth of the hinge leaf. Chisel out the wood and tidy up the edges.
2. Attach the front to the side pieces by turning the screws in from the front, countersinking them, and making sure that the mortises for the hinges are accurately aligned. Install the hinges.
3. To assemble the playboard screw the crossbar to the two side supports, just in front of the slot. Glue the supports on

the playboard and secure with small nails or screws.
4. When the glue has dried, turn the cuphooks into the playboard. The hand puppets should be hung from these hooks when not in use.
5. Now assemble the string puppet rack, if required. Glue and screw the components together in the same way as for the playboard shelf (step 3). Drill a recess for the doweling and glue it in position.

Turn cuphooks into the underside of the playboard shelf.

Finishing and painting
6. All the sawn edges should be well-rubbed with sandpaper for a smooth finish. Check that none of the nails are protruding. Fill any holes with wood filler.
7. Seal the surface of the wood with a water-based primer. When dry apply a coat of white matte latex paint to all the pieces except the backboard. Give the playboard and the string puppet shelf a second coat of white paint, and paint the backboard a color of your choice, or paint a decorative background to add to the scenic effect. To paint neat and well-spaced stripes on the sides of the theater you will need to mask with tape. Tear off strips of masking tape 48 in. (1220 mm.) long and apply them at regular intervals down the length of the three sides of the theater. Give one coat of matte latex paint and when dry carefully peel off the tape. This will give a crisp edge to the lines.
8. Seal the paint with a coat of full-strength polyurethane varnish.

Making the curtain
9. Hem the edges of the material and sew curtain rings along one long edge. Thread

the rings onto a piece of doweling. (If felt is used for the curtains there is no need to make a hem.)
10. Screw cuphooks into the back of the front board of the theater at all four corners. You will need to be able to hang the curtain from either end of the opening, depending on how the theater is being used.

Using the theater for hand puppets
The theater should be assembled with the opening at the top. The backboard should be slotted into the back slot to allow room for the puppeteer to sit inside the theater. Fit the playboard onto the lower edge of the proscenium opening with the shelf projecting out of the theater. The puppets are hung on the cuphooks, where they are easily accessible.

Using the theater for string puppets
The theater should be set up so that the proscenium is in the lower half, the backboard is fitted into the slots positioned in the middle of the side pieces, and the playboard faces the interior of the theater to form a stage. Put the puppet rack in position on one of the sides.

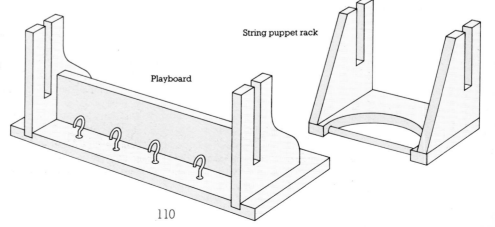

Playboard

String puppet rack

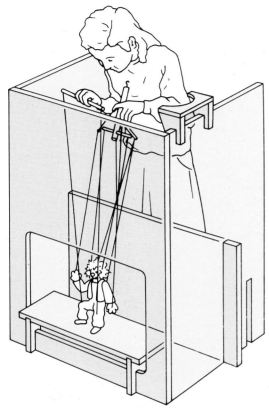

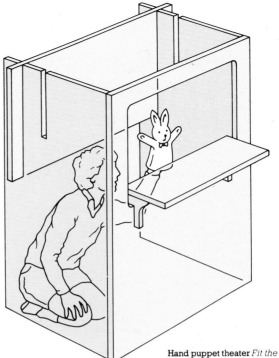

Hand puppet theater *Fit the backboard in the back slot to allow room for the puppeteer to operate the puppets from below.*

String puppet theater *Stand the theater on a raised surface to add height, making viewing more comfortable for the audience.*

Cuphooks installed at all four corners of the stage opening will allow the curtain to be hung from either direction, depending on how the theater is being used.

MATERIALS

Plywood:
1 sheet ⅜ x 48 x 96 in. (10 x 1220 x 2400 mm.)
1 piece ⅜ x 8 x 24 in. (10 x 200 x 610 mm.)
1 piece ⅜ x 11 x 40 in. (10 x 280 x 1020 mm.)
Softwood:
1 piece 1 x 1 x 48 in. (25 x 25 x 1220 mm.)
1 piece 1 x 2 x 23¾ in. (25 x 50 x 600 mm.)
1 piece 1 x 2 x 8 in. (25 x 50 x 200 mm.)
Hardware:
cuphooks
4 hinges and small screws
1¼ in. (32 mm.) woodscrews
matte latex paint (white and colors of your choice)
For the curtain:
4 large cuphooks
curtain rings
piece doweling 27½ in. (70 cm.)
1 39 x 21 in. (99 x 53.3 cm.) piece of fabric

TOOLS

Panel saw, power saber saw, hand drill, or power drill and drill bits, tenon or back saw, chisels, awl, screwdriver, ruler, masking tape.

MAKING A
STRING PUPPET

Here is a character that is sure to delight any audience, for clowns not only seem to have a natural charm all their own but they also are well able to hold the stage on their own. The stretch-knit fabric used for the body has been deliberately chosen to enable you to employ the typical puppet movement more often associated with carved wooden puppets.

Preparing the pattern for the body

Prepare a full-size pattern *(see p.12)* from the pattern grid. Cut head, face panel, body, arms and legs from jersey. Draw around the hand piece on a rectangle of doubled fabric, twice, for hands. Leave uncut until they have been sewn together. Cut shoes from squares of felt, keeping toes and soles in one color and remainder in a second color. The finished clown stands 22 in. (56 cm.) tall from feet to top of head.

Making the body

1. Start by sewing the front to the back body piece, from A to B on each side. Turn right side out and top stitch the double row that forms the waist hinge, either by machine or hand-sewn stab stitch. This hinge allows the clown to bow and bend naturally.
2. Stuff upper portion of body through the neck opening and the lower portion through the bottom one. Close each opening with slip stitch. Stitch three weights, such as heavy buttons, across the lower portion of the back.
3. Sew two leg pieces together on each side in turn from top edge to lower ankle edge.

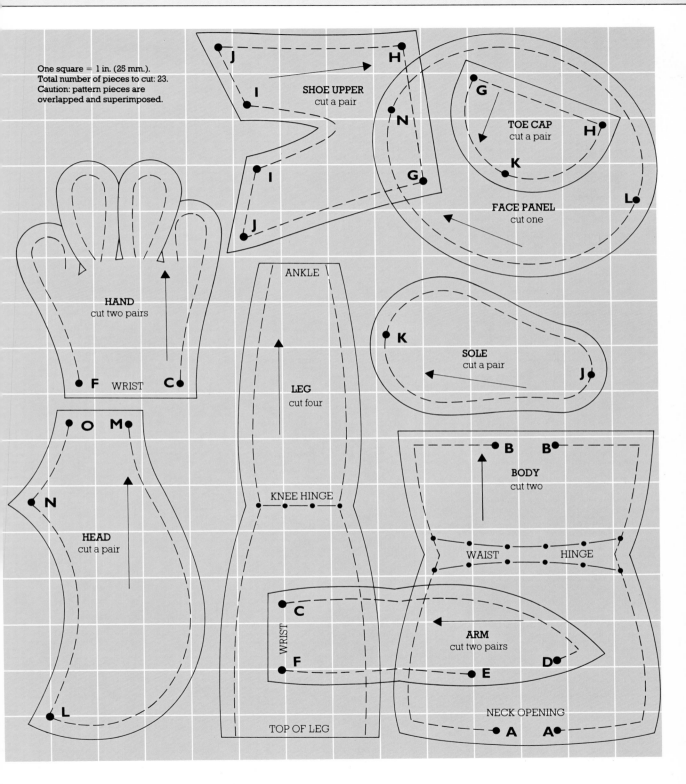

One square = 1 in. (25 mm).
Total number of pieces to cut: 23.
Caution: pattern pieces are
overlapped and superimposed.

SHOE UPPER
cut a pair

TOE CAP
cut a pair

FACE PANEL
cut one

HAND
cut two pairs

WRIST

ANKLE

LEG
cut four

KNEE HINGE

SOLE
cut a pair

BODY
cut two

WAIST   HINGE

HEAD
cut a pair

WRIST

ARM
cut two pairs

NECK OPENING

TOP OF LEG

Turn right side out and top stitch knee hinge. Stuff upper and lower sections of leg, then turn in top raw edges and slip stitch closed. Hold stuffing in lower leg temporarily with a pin. Cut an oval-shaped kneecap from foam and sew in place across the front of the knee hinge by catching on each side only. This kneecap will ensure that the knee only bends in the correct direction. Extra strength can be provided by gluing a small square of cardboard to the back of the foam, after first scoring it in half.

4. Make the second leg in the same way, then attach each leg to the lower edge of the body with buttonhole bars. These are simply strong thread straight stitches worked between body and leg, which are strengthened by having buttonhole stitch worked along the length.

5. Complete legs by sewing shoes. Sew toe cap to shoe upper from G to H, then make back seam by bringing I to I and J to J and sewing. Run a gathering thread around front edge of the toe cap, pull up until the shoe fits the sole between J and K and then sew in place. Turn completed shoe right side out and stuff toe area firmly. Wrap weights in stuffing and place in foot, directly below leg. Finish stuffing the foot.

6. Turn under ankle edge of leg, and then hand sew in place to the top of the shoe, covering the slit. Test to see that both leg and foot move freely by pinching the knee between your fingers and "walking" the leg along a table. If the toe drags when the leg "walks forward", the toe is overweight. When satisfied with the weighting, complete second shoe and attach in the

Foam kneecap backed with cardboard.

Assemble the body, then the legs, the arms, and finally the head.

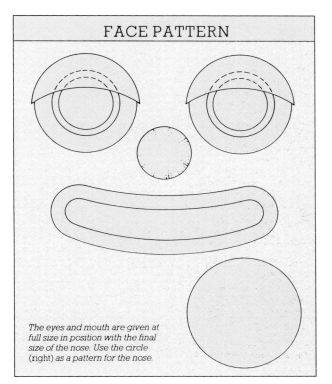

Use two pieces of fur fabric for the hair. Attach with glue, or by sewing.

FACE PATTERN

The eyes and mouth are given at full size in position with the final size of the nose. Use the circle (right) as a pattern for the nose.

same way.

7. Sew a pair of arm pieces from C to D and E to F. Turn right side out and lightly stuff, taking care not to distort the shape. Close opening between D and E with slip stitch and draw up waist opening with raw edges turned in. Now wind strong thread tightly around elbow and fasten off. This makes a flexible joint. Make the second arm in the same way.

8. Sew around hand pieces on rectangle of fabric, then cut out carefully, snipping corners between the fingers at the bottom of the slash. Turn hands right side out and stuff, again taking care not to distort the shape. Insert a weight into the palm of each hand. Turn in wrist edge, close and then attach to end of arm with buttonhole bars. ·

9. Place the arms at the side of the body and attach with buttonhole bars at the shoulders. If you feel that the arm is too long, you can compensate by shortening the shoulder. If it looks too short, make longer buttonhole bars.

10. Sew head pieces together from L to M and N to O. Run a gathering thread around the edge of the face panel and pull up to fit opening on head. Keep most of the gathers on the lower part around the chin area. Fit face to head matching

M to M and N to N, then sew.

11. Turn head right side out and stuff face first, carefully rounding out its shape before tackling the rest of the head. Leave neck area empty – this is essential as otherwise it will be impossible for you to nod the head and turn it from side to side. Turn under raw edges at bottom of neck and ladder stitch to top of body.

12. Cut out felt shapes for mouth and eyes, glue together and then glue in place on face, using clear-drying latex glue. Glue a sequin to the center of each eye. These will catch the light when the puppet moves. Cut a circle of red felt of around 1½ in. (3.6 cm.) diameter for the nose, gather up and stuff to make a ball. Slip stitch in place. Blush cheeks with face rouge.

13. Cut fur into a strip and wrap this around the head. Then cut a circle of fur to cover the top of the head. Glue or stitch fur hair pieces in place and brush into shape.

Preparing the pattern for the costume

Draw up a full-size pattern *(see p.12)* from the grid provided for the jacket and the rest of

the costume. Before cutting out the latter, check the size by laying the body of the clown against the pattern, as stretch fabrics alter so much in size when stuffed. Pay particular attention to length of sleeves and legs. Cut jacket pieces from felt.

Making the costume

1. Make a slit for the neck and then cut the center front open from neck to heel. The center back is only slit from heel to crotch. Hem the wrist edges of each sleeve. Sew underarm and side seams down to ankle, then seam each inside leg seam. Hem ankle edges.

2. Slip clown into costume and check again for fit. Gather each ankle edge and sew securely to leg beneath. Now sew a 2 yd. (2 m.) length of strong thread to each leg, just above

the knee. Do this beneath the costume by working through the front opening. These threads are for stringing the puppet and so must be attached securely. Pass threads through costume to outside and leave hanging for the time being.

3. Close front opening of costume and sew neck edge to body beneath. Cover neck seam by making a mandarin collar – this is simply a strip of material long enough to pass around the neck. It should be cut to twice the required height. Sew collar into a tube, then fold in half, turn under raw edges and sew in place.

4. Make the jacket by sewing front pieces to back on shoulders and sides. Edge jacket and sleeves with braid, then sew on sequins which will glint in the light.

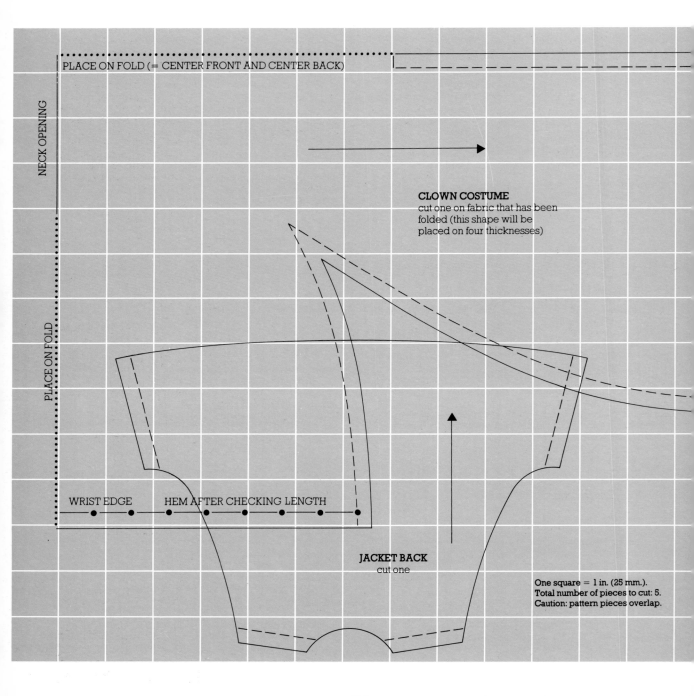

NECK OPENING

PLACE ON FOLD (= CENTER FRONT AND CENTER BACK)

CLOWN COSTUME
cut one on fabric that has been
folded (this shape will be
placed on four thicknesses)

PLACE ON FOLD

WRIST EDGE   HEM AFTER CHECKING LENGTH

JACKET BACK
cut one

One square = 1 in. (25 mm.).
Total number of pieces to cut: 5.
Caution: pattern pieces overlap.

angles to it. Then extend the diagonal of the original grid to intersect this vertical line. This will mark the height of the enlargement from which you can then draw the rectangle. Draw the grid on the enlargement rectangle by placing one end of a ruler at the bottom left-hand corner of the rectangle and aligning it with the furthest point of each vertical and horizontal line of the grid, then marking with a pencil where the ruler meets the edge of the larger rectangle. You can draw the enlarged grid using these markers.

3. The lines and shapes within each original square can now be plotted by eye in the corresponding square on the larger grid.

Working in miniature
Before you begin to construct the dollhouse it is essential that you understand the basic principles

related to working to scale and working in miniature. These principles are simply extensions of the squaring up method, but because of the size of the original measurements involved it means transferring those measurements from actual size to another medium. These principles can also be adapted to making furniture and furnishings for the dollhouse.

Scaling in proportion
The traditional dollhouse is often based on a real home and it is relatively simple to recreate your own, or a friend's home, in miniature. All traditional dollhouses are built to a scale of 1:12, so that 1 in. = 12 in.

(25 mm. = 30 cm.), and all fixtures, fittings and furniture that can be bought are made to this scale. This makes producing a realistic replica relatively easy.

Ideally, you should measure the house and draw up the plans accordingly. However, since this is generally not practical, the best way to overcome the problem is to take a series of photographs of the side and front elevations of the house, as square-on as possible, and scale up your plans from these using the method described earlier. To maintain the 1:12 scale, the squares of the grid that you draw over the photograph should correspond to a known dimension – the front door

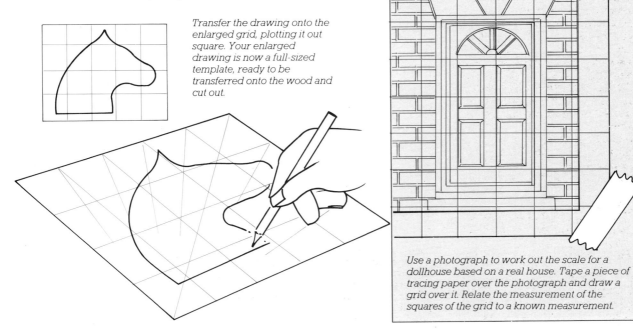

Transfer the drawing onto the enlarged grid, plotting it out square. Your enlarged drawing is now a full-sized template, ready to be transferred onto the wood and cut out.

SCALING A DOLLHOUSE

Use a photograph to work out the scale for a dollhouse based on a real house. Tape a piece of tracing paper over the photograph and draw a grid over it. Relate the measurement of the squares of the grid to a known measurement.

provides a convenient unit of measurement as it is probably the easiest to measure.

If, for example, the front door is 6 ft. (180 cm.) high, then it should measure 6 in. (15 cm.) high on your plans. So, ideally you should draw up your grid with the total height of the door corresponding to six squares. Whatever the size of the squares on the photo, you can easily work out how much they need to be enlarged to make 1 in. (25 mm.) squares on the plans. Depending on the size of the photograph, this may mean drawing a grid that has so many squares on it that it becomes impractical. If this is the case, halve the number of squares so that the 6 ft. (180 cm.) door corresponds to three squares on the grid, making each one worth 2 in. (5 cm.) on the plan.

Another method, which is not so accurate, is to take individual measurements from the photograph and increase each one by the percentage that you have worked out with the door – if the door in the photograph is 1 in. (25 mm.) high, multiply all measurements by six.

Whatever method you use, you will achieve a perfect scale replica of your chosen house. However, allowances have to be made when transferring real life to miniature. The average height of a modern room is about 8 ft. (240 cm.), but this will make the rooms in a dollhouse too shallow to easily place and maneuver objects, as well as making the room appear to be out of scale. There is no hard and fast rule, but it is safe to increase the height of the rooms by about 20% to give you plenty of space and a natural-looking room. Remember to take into account the fact that this will increase the overall height of the house. However, this will not affect the external proportions.

Miniature finishes
Wood is used for the basic construction of most dollhouses, but they get their individual character from the exterior and interior decoration that you give them. On pp.136-9 you will find details of external finishes and architectural details that will enable you to create anything from a stone cottage or a Tudor-style manor house to a modern brick building. Several materials are used, but the most versatile of all is self-hardening clay.

Self-hardening clay
This material is frequently used in the construction of both the exterior and interior of the dollhouse. There are a number of claylike modeling materials that are very convenient to use because they include binding and hardening additives which do away with the need to bake the clays at high temperatures in special kilns. Drying occurs over a period of days, the exact time dependent on a number of factors, such as the thickness of the clay, the size of the object made, atmospheric humidity, room temperature and the exact composition of the clay used.

Surface cracking
The clays dry without losing their shape, although there is sometimes a slight reduction of volume and some surface cracking. This is not quite the problem it might seem, for gaps and cracks are easily filled with glue and fresh clay.

The hardened surface is rather like plaster of Paris to work with; consequently, you may find yourself sawing, grinding, drilling and filling.

Preparing the clay
Self-hardening clays are sold in sealed packets which usually contain instructions for use. Read these carefully before starting, noting any special requirements. Prepare the work surface by laying down a plastic sheet, and have ready a bowl of water so that fingers and modeling tools can be kept moist.

Start by gently kneading the clay to make it pliable and, if necessary, add a little water. Work on small pieces at a time, combining them with each other until you have a sufficient quantity for your project. Any leftover clay can be wrapped in a plastic bag and stored in an airtight can for future use.

Forming
Clay can be shaped in many traditional ways. Perhaps the most popular method is pinching it to shape. More detailed shaping can be achieved by using the same tools as are used with modeling clay (see p.99). A modeling knife is particularly useful. Clay can also be flattened by hand or with a rolling pin, to make sheets for forming or cutting out flat shapes.

Yet another method of forming is to make long 'worms' of clay which are then built into shapes by coiling. This is the method used to make the flower borders in the dollhouse garden (see p.142).

Self-hardening clay can be modeled on a base or around a framework of a different material. Support can be provided by a wire framework (see tree-making on p.144), cocktail sticks and even pencils. This saves on the amount of clay used and also strengthens the object being made. Experiment, and if you do not like the form you arrive at the first time, simply roll it up and start again.

Surface textures
A smooth surface can be achieved by gently rubbing the clay with a moist sponge or damp finger before it dries. For a project that has dried you can use very fine-grade sandpaper and rub gently, wipe with

a damp sponge, then polish with a finger and dry with a soft cloth. Repeat this process several times, if necessary, to get a really smooth surface.

Interesting textures can be obtained by brushing the surface with different kinds of brushes, by stippling and even by drawing a comb or fork over the clay.

Patterns can be imprinted by pressing on lace or buttons, or simply by drawing with a fine knitting needle.

Drying
Allow air to circulate on all surfaces by placing the object on a foam rubber base or similar permeable substance.

If you want to change the shape or add a small piece, simply moisten the surface with a brush, smear with a little washed clay, then press the pieces together firmly and support them while they dry. Multipurpose glue can be added to the washed clay if necessary.

Sealing and painting
Self-hardening clays should be sealed with a coat of lacquer or paint to protect them from water. For painting, use acrylics (as used for the papier mâché projects, *see p.100*), tempera colors and matte latex or undercoat, followed by gloss.

Miniature style
The external finish of the dollhouse you build will have to be matched by its windows and doors. Close attention must be paid to these details if you want your dollhouse to be an exact replica. On pp.136-9, alternative doors of different periods which may fit in with your plans are shown. Otherwise it is a matter of reproducing in balsa wood the door of your chosen house. There is not as much detail to consider in the treatment of windows. Generally

only their size and shape have to be altered.

The problem of scale manifests itself most in the interior of the house with the wallpaper and carpets. Real carpet is too thick, and the designs on most wallpaper only really work when they are on full-size walls. Felt is a good substitute for carpet. It can be obtained in many different colors, remnants may be all you need, and it has the right texture for carpet. For wallpaper, wrapping paper often works well as long as the pattern is small and not too bold.

Lighting in miniature
A miniature lighting system will give the perfect finishing touch to your dollhouse.

For the dollhouse described in this section you will need just one central bulb fixed in the ceiling above the stairwell to illuminate the landing, stairs, hall and bedrooms.

You will need 36 in. (91 cm.) of thin electric cord, one small flashlight bulb and holder, one small simple switch and a dry cell with screw-down terminals.

Drill a ⅛ in. (3 mm.) hole through the landing ceiling section before the roof is put in place. This will take the two wires from the bulb in the landing ceiling to the battery and switch, which are placed in the attic area.

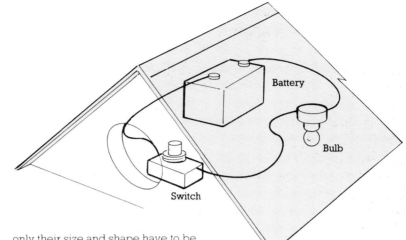

A simple miniature lighting system is arranged by fixing a screw-mounted bulb on the landing ceiling of the dollhouse. The light is controlled by a switch located in the attic.

SAFETY TIPS

For all their fun and suitability for the older child, these toys will almost certainly be used by younger brothers and sisters and by groups of children playing together. They are, after all, toys that encourage social contact. In this respect there is cause for some concern.

Check frequently to ensure that the playhouse is safe and sound and free from splinters, with all hooks firmly in place. Remember, too, that small objects in the dollhouse, especially pretend-food, might well prove dangerous to very young toddlers, who may be tempted to swallow them.

MAKING A
PLAYHOUSE

All children love having a home of their very own. This playhouse will give hours of enjoyment, not only keeping your children amused, but also providing them with something very important – an environment that is truly their own. The house can be used both indoors and outdoors. Made from oil-tempered hardboard, it is weatherproof yet lightweight, and, since it is hinged, it can be dismantled and stored easily.

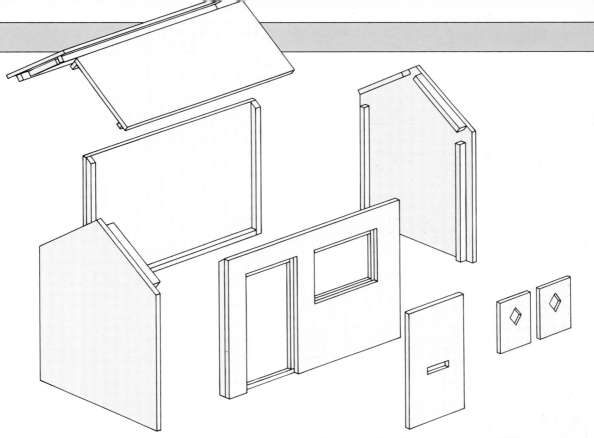

The battens strengthen the structure of the playhouse and provide the support for hinges and hooks.

Cutting the wood

Mark out the pieces for the sides, the front and back and the roof of the playhouse and cut out from tempered hardboard. Cut one roof, one side and a front or back from one sheet of hardboard (plywood can be used as an alternative for the sides and roof).

Mark out the door and window on one of the long sides. Drill holes at the corners and cut out with a saber saw. Take care when cutting out these pieces. Cut the softwood battens to size if you have not bought them precut to size.

Assembling the playhouse

1. Saw the tops of the four 39 in. (99 cm.) battens that will be the vertical supports for the back and front of the house at an angle of 45°, and sand them smooth (see fig. a). Make a

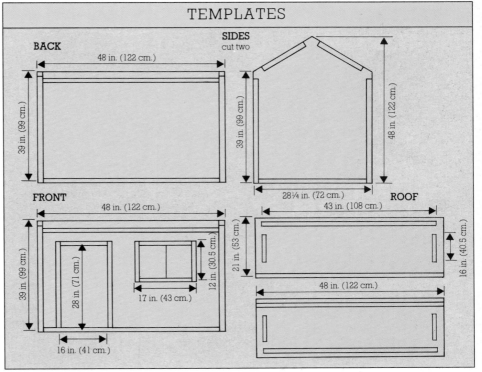

TEMPLATES

BACK
48 in. (122 cm.)
39 in. (99 cm.)

SIDES
cut two
39 in. (99 cm.)
48 in. (122 cm.)
28¼ in. (72 cm.)

FRONT
48 in. (122 cm.)
39 in. (99 cm.)
28 in. (71 cm.)
16 in. (41 cm.)
17 in. (43 cm.)
12 in. (30.5 cm.)

ROOF
43 in. (108 cm.)
21 in. (53 cm.)
16 in. (40.5 cm.)
48 in. (122 cm.)

PROJECT **30**

frame with two side pieces and a batten for the base using lap joints, nails and glue *(see fig. f)*, or a simple butt joint *(see p.58)* – if you use this alternative method you will need to cut the wood to size first. Screw the frame in position on the hardboard.

2. Make the frame for the front of the playhouse in the same way. Then make a frame for the door. Use the 32 in. (81 cm.) and 20 in. (51 cm.) pieces of 1 x 2 in. (25 x 50 mm.) wood. Fix the frame to give an overlap of ½ in. (12 mm.) so that it will keep the door from opening inwards.

3. Construct a frame for the window with the 21 in. (53.3 cm.) and 16 in. (41 cm.) battens, using lap joints. This frame should also be fixed to give an overlap of ½ in. (12 mm.). Screw the frame in position on the inside of the window *(see fig. g)*.

4. Now make the frames for the sides. The vertical pieces should be 1½ in. (3.8 cm.) shorter than the sides at the top edge and they should be positioned 1½ in. (3.8 cm.) in

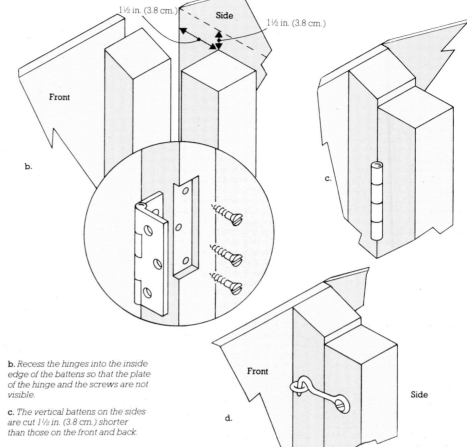

b. Recess the hinges into the inside edge of the battens so that the plate of the hinge and the screws are not visible.

c. The vertical battens on the sides are cut 1½ in. (3.8 cm.) shorter than those on the front and back.

d. Hooks are fitted onto battens at two of the corners and at the sloping sides of the roof.

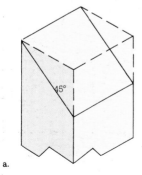

a. Saw the ends of the vertical battens for the front and back to an angle of 45° and sand them smooth.

from the sides *(see fig. b)*. The 16 in. (41 cm.) battens can be screwed in position on the short sides.

5. Sand all the edges.

6. Now assemble the front, back and sides. To make a playhouse that can be dismantled, two diagonally opposite corners are hinged and the other two corners fitted with hooks. Match up the pieces and mark the position for the hinges and hooks.

7. Fit the hinges. There should be three at each corner. Chisel a recess for each hinge on the inside edge of the batten and screw the hinges in position.

8. Fit the hooks and eyes at the opposite corners (two at each corner).

9. Now assemble the roof, using the 43 in. (108 cm.) battens. Screw one pair to the edges that will form the apex of the roof – one at the very edge of the roof piece, the other 1½ in. (3.8 cm.) from the edge. Screw on the second pair of battens 1 in. (25 mm.) from the opposite long edges of the roof pieces. Screw on the 16 in. (41 cm.) battens to the short edges of the roof, 1½ in. (3.8 cm.) from the edge.

10. Hinge the apex of the roof, using three hinges as for step 7).

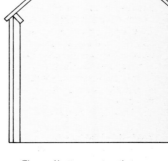

e. The roof battens rest on the angled ends of the vertical battens at the corners of the playhouse.

126

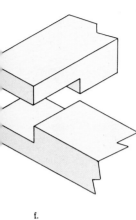

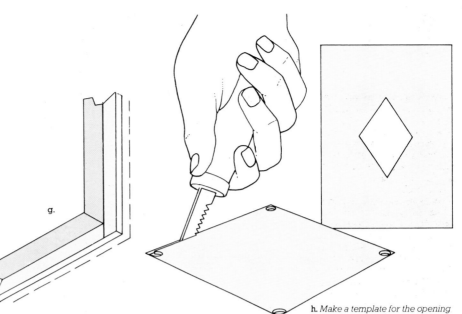

f. Assemble the frames with lap joints and then glue. They can be assembled independently and then screwed in position, or fixed directly on the main pieces.

g. The frame for the interior of the window should be 1 in. (25 mm.) smaller than the actual opening so that the shutters will close against it.

h. Make a template for the opening in the shutters and cut out with a keyhole saw.

11. Place the roof in position on the walls of the playhouse. The long battens rest on the angled vertical supports. Mark the position for the four hooks (two on either side, at the midpoint of the short sides) that will hold the roof firmly in position. Screw them in place.

12. Now fit the shutters. If you cut out the front piece carefully, you will be able to use the scrap for the window; otherwise cut a new piece from hardboard. Cut the wood in half and make a pattern for the diamond shape. Cut the shape from the two pieces, using a keyhole saw *(see fig. h)* or saber saw. Mark the position for the hinges and screw them in place (they do not have to be recessed).

13. Hinge the door in place.

Painting the playhouse
Prepare the playhouse for painting by filling any holes with a commercially-made filler and then sanding all

edges smooth. Apply a coat of oil-based primer, paying particular attention to the sawn edges. When dry, apply an undercoat, and then a final topcoat of paint.

Decide on a color scheme for your playhouse. Paint the walls inside and outside, and add brightly colored borders around the window and door frames. You might like to add details such as a brick or wood finish for the walls, or to create the illusion of a tiled roof.

Storing the playhouse
Simply unhook the roof and the two corners and fold up the three sections.

Making a permanent structure
If you intend to keep your playhouse outside in all weathers, give it extra weather protection by painting it thoroughly with exterior paint. Use water resistant resorcinol glue instead of water-soluble white glue.

MATERIALS

2 sheets 48 x 96 in. (1220 x 2400 mm.) oil-tempered hardboard
Softwood:
8 pieces 1½ x 1½ x 39 in. (38 x 38 x 1000 mm.)
2 pieces 1½ x 1½ x 48in (38 x 38 x 1220 mm.)
2 pieces 1½ x 1½ x 28¼ (38 x 38 x 720 mm.)
8 pieces 1½ x 1½ x 16 in. (38 x 38 x 410 mm.)
4 pieces 1½ x 1½ x 43 in. (38 x 38 x 1080 mm.)
2 pieces 1½ x 1½ x 48 in. (38 x 38 x 1200 mm.)
1 piece 1½ x 1½ x 24 in. (38 x 38 x 600 mm.)
2 pieces 1 x 2 x 21 in. (25 x 50 x 533 mm.)
2 pieces 1 x 2 x 16 in. (25 x 50 x 410 mm.)
1 piece 1 x 2 x 32 in. (25 x 50 x 810 mm.)
2 pieces 1 x 2 x 20 in. (25 x 50 x 510 mm.)
Hardware:
8 hooks
9 hinges with butt screws
6 face hinges with screws for the windows and door
white glue
resorcinal glue (optional)
wood screws and nails
oil-based primer, undercoat and topcoat

TOOLS

Panel saw, keyhole saw or saber saw, drill and suitable drill bits, hammer, screwdriver.

— MAKING A —
GO-CART

Though you can make a go-cart from any sturdy pieces of wood you happen to have, it is essential to use good quality, knotfree wood and to test the strength of the seat and the sturdiness of the construction before you allow your children to play with it. You can use any type of wheel, as long as it has a strong axle. Ballbearing wheels, such as those used for baby carriages, will go faster than ordinary wheels. If you are making the go-cart for very young children, it is a good idea to fix a baby carriage handle onto the back so that the go-cart can be pushed by an adult.

Making the go-cart

1. Saw the pieces of wood to the dimensions given on the templates.

2. It is important to round off all sharp corners and edges of the go-cart, as children will be jumping on and off it. Using a fretsaw, or a saber saw, round off the top front corners of the side pieces and the front corners of the center board. This is not only for reasons of safety, but because it will give the go-cart a racier appearance. Shape the ends of the brake levers to give a good hand grip. Sand them smooth.

3. Make the steering disk out of the square of plywood *(for method see pp. 80-1)*. Drill a ⅜ in. (10 mm.) hole through the center. The steering disk is not essential, but it will make the steering smoother.

4. To assemble the cockpit floor, position the side seats on either side of the center board.

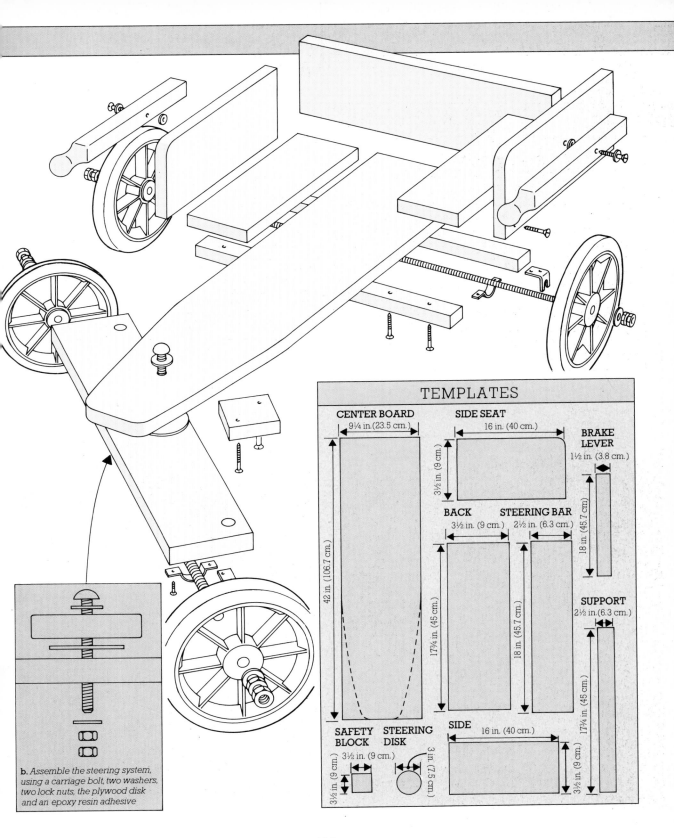

TEMPLATES

CENTER BOARD
9¼ in. (23.5 cm.)

SIDE SEAT
16 in. (40 cm.)
3½ in. (9 cm.)

BRAKE LEVER
1½ in. (3.8 cm.)
18 in. (45.7 cm.)

BACK
3½ in. (9 cm.)

STEERING BAR
2½ in. (6.3 cm.)

42 in. (106.7 cm.)

17¾ in. (45 cm.)

18 in. (45.7 cm.)

SUPPORT
2½ in. (6.3 cm.)

17¾ in. (45 cm.)

SAFETY BLOCK
3½ in. (9 cm.)
3½ in. (9 cm.)

STEERING DISK
3 in. (7.5 cm.)

SIDE
16 in. (40 cm.)
3½ in. (9 cm.)

b. *Assemble the steering system, using a carriage bolt, two washers, two lock nuts, the plywood disk and an epoxy resin adhesive*

129

Drill holes in the supports. Mark the center of each support and of the center board. Lay the supports across the cockpit floor, ensuring that they are square to the center board, as it is important for the back axle to be straight. They should also project beyond the edges of the side seat pieces, so that the wheels will clear the cockpit sides. Insert wood screws and screw the supports to the center board and side seats (see fig. c). Make sure that none of the screws project through the seat. If they do, file the ends flush with the surface of the wood.

5. To attach the back axle to the rear support, drill pilot holes for the brackets and saddle clips. The brackets prevent the wheels from hitting the sides of the go-cart and they should project slightly over the edge of the support. Place the axle, brackets and saddle clips in position and firmly screw in place (see fig.

d). If you use a commercially-made wheels and axles set, it will come complete with the necessary fittings. It is important to make sure that the axle is rigid and cannot move laterally.

6. Drill holes in the sides and back of the cockpit and attach them to the cockpit floor with glue and wood screws as shown (see fig. e).

7. Drill ³⁄₁₆ in. (4 mm.) holes through the brake levers. It is important to position the brake levers correctly or they will not work effectively. The screw holes should be approximately 1 in. (25 mm.) from the outer rim of the wheel (see fig. g). You will need washers on each side of the brake levers to ensure free movement. Insert screws as shown (see fig. f). To prevent the brake levers from dropping forward, insert two support screws into the sides just below the levers.

8. Attach the front axle to the steering bar with axle brackets

and saddle clips, as you did with the rear axle (see fig. h).

9. You will need a carriage bolt, two washers, the plywood disk and two self-locking nuts for the steering system. Drill a ³⁄₈ in. (10 mm.) hole through the front of the center board and the steering bar. Assemble as shown (see fig. b). Use an epoxy resin adhesive to keep the nuts securely in place.

10. The safety block will prevent the steering bar from

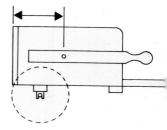

e. Attach the back and sides to the cockpit floor with glue and wood screws.

f. Fasten the brake levers to the sides with washers and screws.

g. The position of the screw should be approximately 1 in. (25 mm.) from the edge of the wheel.

d. Attach the rear axle to the back support with brackets and saddle clips.

c. To form the cockpit floor, position the seats on each side of the center board and screw the supports across the three pieces.

swiveling too far back and the wheels from hitting the center board. Find the correct position for the block by moving the steering bar. Drill holes in the safety block and attach with wood screws as shown *(see fig. h).*

11. There are several methods of attaching the wheels to the axles. If the axle is threaded, you can use a single lock nut – a nut with a nylon collar that holds it securely – or two ordinary nuts that are tightened against each other when in position. Use an epoxy resin adhesive as before. If the axle is unthreaded, drill a small hole through the ends of the axle, insert a cotter pin and bend up its ends. Whichever method you use, position a washer on each side of the wheel as shown *(see fig. i).*

12. Drill ⁵⁄₁₆ in. (7 mm.) holes in each end of the steering bar. Insert the ends of the length of nylon rope through the holes. To prevent the rope ends from unraveling, play a lighted match, or cigarette lighter, over each end until the strands melt together. Tie secure knots underneath the steering bar *(see fig. j).*

13. If the go-cart is intended for

very young children, drill holes in the sides and attach a baby carriage handle with wood screws.
Alternatively, build a push handle from two lengths of 1 x 2 in. (25 x 50 mm.) wood and a section of ¾ in. (19 mm.) dowel.

14. Paint or varnish the completed go-cart. It is worth applying several coats of polyurethane varnish to obtain a hardwearing surface.
Caution: Check regularly the nuts holding the axles and the steering system. Also check the rope for signs of fraying.

j. Add the steering rope to the steering bar and attach a baby carriage handle at the back of the go-cart if required.

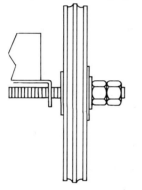

i. Attach the wheel to the axle with washers, lock nuts and epoxy resin adhesive.

MATERIALS

Softwood:
1 piece 1½ x 9¼ x 42 in. (38 x 235 x 1067 mm.)
1 piece ¾ x 3½ x 17¾ in. (19 x 90 x 450 mm.)
2 pieces 1½ x 3½ x 16 in. (38 x 90 x 400 mm.)
2 pieces ¾ x 3½ x 16 in. (19 x 90 x 400 mm.)
2 pieces ¾ x 2½ x 17¾ in. (19 x 63 x 450 mm.)
2 pieces ¾ x 1½ x 18 in. (19 x 38 x 457 mm.)
1 piece ¾ x 2½ x 18 in. (19 x 63 x 457 mm.)
1 piece ¾ x 3½ x 3½ in. (19 x 90 x 90 mm.)
Plywood:
1 piece ¼ x 3 x 3 in. (6 x 75 x 75 mm.)
Hardware:
1 ⅜ in. (10 mm.) carriage bolt, 2½ in. (6.3 cm.) long
2 ⅜ in. (10 mm.) nuts
2 washers
 1½ in. (3.8 cm.) wood screws
1 yard (1 m.) ¼ in. (6 mm.) nylon rope
1 baby carriage handle
4 wheels at least 6 in. (15 cm.) in diameter
2 axles approx. 24 in. (61 cm.) long
4 brackets
4 saddle clips
8 axle nuts and washers
 epoxy resin adhesive
 varnish or paint
 white glue

TOOLS

Tape measure, pencil, panel saw, fretsaw or saber saw, try square, drill and bits, screwdriver, wrench, paintbrush, sandpaper.

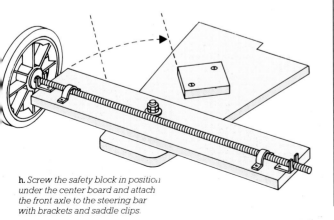

h. Screw the safety block in position under the center board and attach the front axle to the steering bar with brackets and saddle clips.

MAKING A
DOLLHOUSE

Dollhouses hold a special appeal for children of all ages, since they are the key to a whole miniature world of make-believe. Here is a particularly appealing example of an 18th-century English mansion with interior decoration and furnishings based on those of a modern family home. Its design, of course, can be modified to suit other periods and styles of house – including your own. The construction has been kept as simple as possible and the finished house is sturdy and durable.

Preparing the basic structure
1. With pencil and ruler, measure and mark out on tracing paper the 16 units that make up the house. The scale used is 1:12 (1 in. to 1 ft. or 25 mm. to 30 cm.).
2. Cut out the patterns for the units and position them on the sheet of plywood, using thumbtacks to secure them. Draw around the patterns.
3. Before you start sawing the

wood, secure it to your work bench with a C-clamp. This is both helpful and a safety precaution. Now cut out the units, using a medium crosscut saw. Sand down the rough edges and label each unit for future reference.
4. When all the units have been sawn out and sanded, you can cut out the doors and windows. Drill two ¼ in. (6 mm.) holes in diagonal corners of each door

and window. Insert the tip of a keyhole saw into one of the holes and cut to a corner. Then, from the same hole, cut to the other corner. Repeat this process from the second hole. Continue, until you have cut out all the doors and windows, with the exception of the gable windows. These are made with a brace and 1 in. (25 mm.) bit. Lightly smooth all rough edges as before. Be sure you save the scraps as some of them will be needed at a later stage of construction.

The chimney stacks and fireplaces should be constructed and fastened to the inner walls before the house is put together, as it will be difficult to work on them later.

Preparing the inner walls
1. You will need two 8½ in. (21.7 cm.) pieces of 1 x 3 in. (25 x 76 mm.) wood. Using wood glue, attach one of them to the center of a second floor inner wall. Cut the second block in half, sandwich the bathroom wall unit between the halves and then glue and nail together. Now glue them to the other second floor inner wall.
2. Next, cut out two 9 in. (23 cm.) pieces of the 1 x 3 in. (25 x 76 mm.) wood. These will be used for the fireplaces in the living room and kitchen. Using a coping saw, cut out a section for the fireplace measuring 3 in. (7.6 cm.) high and 2 in. (5 cm.) wide. Glue each chimney stack to the center of the first floor inner walls.
3. The kitchen fireplace has a brick finish. Use the same method as for the outside wall of the house (see p.136) and then paint it lightly with white matte latex. Give the inside of the living room fireplace a brick finish and paint it white as before. Paint the chimney

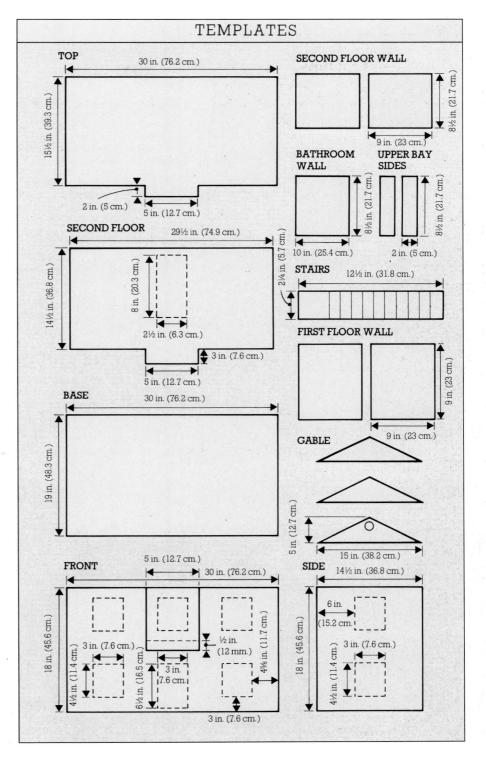

PROJECT
32

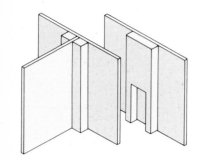

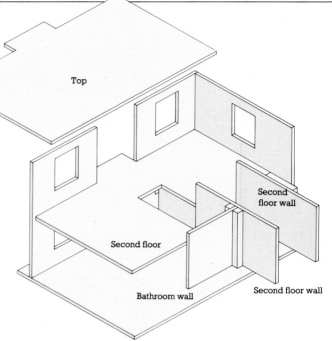

Attach the chimney stacks, fireplaces and the bathroom wall to the inner wall units

Top

Second floor wall

Second floor

Second floor wall

Bathroom wall

Second floor wall

stack the same color as the living room walls, leaving the front strip on either side of the fireplace unpainted. The mantel is made from a scrap of wooden architrave. Cut off a piece 3 in. (7.6 cm.) long. With a coping saw cut a section measuring 1 x 2 in. (25 x 50 mm.) out of the center. Glue the mantel above the fireplace, leaving it unpainted to create a stripped-pine look. Use two flat popsicle sticks for the pillars. Glue them in place with the rounded ends at the top.

Putting the house together
1. Before you start gluing and nailing the parts together, it is essential to check whether they all fit. When you are sure they do, give both sides of

each unit a coat of white matte latex paint. When dry, paint the inside walls according to your color scheme. It is much easier to paint the separate units. You could do it later, but you may find it difficult to reach the underparts and ceilings.
2. When all the units are completely dry, glue and nail them together. Use plenty of wood glue. Wipe off any drips with a damp cloth before the glue sets. Start the nail or brad holes with an awl. You only need a few – one near the corner of each unit and one in the middle should be enough.
First, attach the front to the side. Fix them to the base, leaving a 4 in. (10.2 cm.) overlap in front. Next, position the two inner first floor walls so

The second stage
The second floor should rest firmly on the first floor walls. Position the second floor walls and add the top.

that they are aligned on either side of the gap left for the upper bay. Leave a 3 in. (7.6 cm.) corridor between the inner walls and the front unit. Fix the second floor so it rests firmly on the inner first floor walls and projects through the upper bay gap. Now position

the inner second floor walls so that they are directly above the first floor walls. The second floor wall, with its previously attached bathroom wall, should be above the living room. Add the top unit and glue and nail two of the triangular roof supports to it. Leave the open end support loose to allow access to the flashlight battery in the attic. (This powers the lights and is inserted at a later stage, *see p.123*). Use small blocks of wood to strengthen the roof supports. Position and fix the blocks to the inside of the end roof support and on both sides of the middle roof support. Leave the house to dry overnight.
If you plan to leave the floors bare, the stairs can be made and inserted at this late stage of construction. But if you are planning a complicated décor you may wish to make them when decorating *(see p.139)*.
3. The roof is made from hardboard. Cut two rectangles, each measuring 9 x 30½ in. (23 x 77.5 cm.) Tape them together. Glue a strip of canvas to the underside of the join so that the unit is hinged like a

The first stage
Attach the front to the side. Fix them to the base, leaving a 4 in. (10.2 cm.) overlap in front. Next, position the first floor inner walls. Glue and nail after each step.

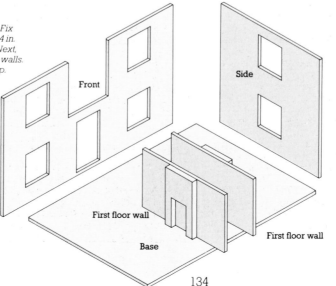

Front

Side

First floor wall

Base

First floor wall

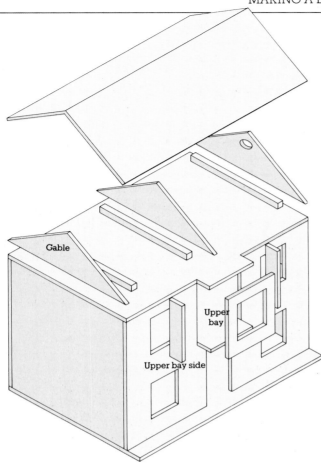

Gable

Upper bay

Upper bay side

The final stage
Fix two gables to the top and leave one loose. Construct the roof and attach it firmly to the gables. Add the three upper bay units.

book. When the glue has dried, place the roof on the triangular supports. Glue and nail. Remember to leave the open side roof support loose.

Insert the upper bay unit between the second floor and top unit projections. Fix it ½ in. (12 mm.) in from the edge. Put the two side strips in place. Glue and nail.

Front steps and pillars
1. Cut out and sand two strips of plywood, ½ in. (12 mm.) thick. One strip should measure 4 x 9 in. (10.2 x 23 cm.), the other 3 x 7½ in. (7.6 x 19 cm.) Center

the larger strip in front of the door opening and glue it to the projecting section of the base. Center the smaller strip and glue to the first one.
2. The pillars are decorative rather than functional, so they could be made from a variety of materials, such as a roll of stiff cardboard tube, rolled clay or papier-mâché. The best material however is wooden doweling with a diameter of 1 in. (25 mm.) – a broom handle would do. Cut two 6 in. (15.2 cm.) lengths. Using a drawknife, taper each pillar slightly and then sand them. Glue a square of ¼ in. (6 mm.) plywood to the ends of each pillar. Roll a thin band of self-hardening clay and coil it around each pillar end. Glue it to the doweling where it meets the ¼ in. (6 mm.) squares of

wood. Place a pillar on either side of the door opening. Glue to the top step. Fill the spaces between the tops of the pillars and the upper bay with two 1½ in. (3.8 cm.) cubes of wood.
3. Create an arch between the pillars to give the portico that final finishing touch. Measure the distance between the

cubes of wood and draw an arch on thick cardboard. Cut out, using a modeling knife. Paint with white matte latex. Next, cut a thick section of cardboard to form the underside of the portico. Shape the piece of cardboard into a curve and trim to fit the space. Glue into place and then glue the arch in front.

MATERIALS

1   ½ in. x 4 x 8 ft. (12 mm. x 1.2 x 2.4 m.) sheet plywood
1   ½ in. x 4 x 4 ft. (12 mm. x 1.2 x 1.2 m.) sheet plywood
2   x 2 ft. (61 x 61 cm.) sheet ¼ in. (6 mm.) plywood
1   small piece ⅛ in. (3 mm.) plywood
1   20 x 32 in. (51 x 81 cm.) sheet hardboard
1   12 in. (30 cm.) length doweling
    mixed balsa wood sheets – ¹⁄₁₆ in., ⅛ in., ¼ in., ⅜ in. sq (2 mm., 3 mm., 6 mm., 10 mm. sq)
    strips ½ in. (12 mm.) lath
1   length wooden architrave
1   ⅛ in. (3 mm.) acrylic plastic sheet
    cardboard (thick and thin)
    non-toxic multipurpose glue
    balsa wood glue
1   small packet self-hardening clay
    pre-mixed filler
1   tin white matte latex paint
    powder watercolor paints
1   brass cotter pin
2   short strips leather (or thin rubber)
33 ¼ in. (6 mm.) round wooden beads
33 tubular wooden beads, ¼ in. (6 mm.) long, ⅛ in. (3 mm.) diameter
2   flat popsicle sticks
1   roll masking tape
    tracing paper
    small strip of canvas
1   packet thumb tacks
1   box 1 in. (25 mm.) brads or slim finishing nails
    sandpaper

TOOLS

Pencil, medium crosscut saw, keyhole saw, saber saw, coping saw, hammer, C-clamp, brace and 1 in. (25 mm.) bit, awl, hand or power drill, ¼ in. (6 mm.) and ¹⁄₁₆ in. (2 mm.) bits, drawknife, modeling knife or scalpel, 1 in. (25 mm.) household paint brush, no. 1 pure sable paint brush, 1 yardstick (metre rule), tape measure.

PROJECT **33**

DOLLHOUSE
DECORATION

Finishing touches make all the difference to the final appearance of the dollhouse and whether or not it has a professional look. You will have great pleasure making the slate roof, brick exterior or window and door frames, knowing that ultimately these simple procedures will result in a truly period look. The color scheme for the interior has been left to your own personal choice, but, if you decide to follow the period style, keep to pink and blue for walls and white for ceilings.

The finishing touches
Allow all the glue used during construction to set before you start painting the exterior of the dollhouse.

Roof – slate finish
1. Cut thin cardboard into long strips ¾ in. (19 mm.) wide then cut off 1½ in. (3.8 cm.) lengths. This will give you tiles with the correct proportions.
2. Draw a line 1½ in. (3.8 cm.) from the bottom edge of the roof. Brush this strip with glue and apply a row of tiles across the roof. When this row is dry, pencil another line across the roof, ¾ in. (19 mm.) above the row of tiles.
3. Apply white or yellow glue and apply a second row of tiles. These tiles will overlap the row below. They should be

staggered so that each new tile is centered on the gap between two tiles in the row below. Continue until you reach the ridge of the roof. Repeat the process on the other side.
4. The roof ridge is made by folding a ¾ in. (19 mm.) wide strip of cardboard lengthwise. Glue along the top of the roof so that there is an equal amount of cardboard on each side of the ridge. Mix up some blue-gray paint using a white latex as a base and adding powder watercolor or liquid modeling paint. When coated over the paper tiles it will give the effect of slates. Paint the roof ridge gray so it looks like lead. Or, with a ruler and gray felt-tip pen rule parallel lines the length of the ridge before you

glue it to the roof. If the pen is worn, the effect will be more realistic.

Walls – brick finish
1. First, brush a thin coat of multipurpose glue over the front and side of the house. When the glue is dry, cover it with a thin skin of ordinary wood filler. If you mix the filler yourself, add the powder to the water and mix to a creamy paste.
2. While the filler is still slightly damp, you can score the brick

lines with a nail. The bricks are 3 x 9 in. (7.6 cm. x 23 cm.). You are working to a scale of 1:12, so you require ¼ x ¾ in. (6 x 19 mm.) lines. Pencil ¼ in. (6 mm.) marks on either side of the areas requiring a brick finish. Using a rule, score horizontal lines across the walls. Continue until both walls have been completely scored with lines ¼ in. (6 mm.) apart.
3. Now score short vertical lines ¾ in. (19 mm.) apart, between the horizontal lines. When you have done one row,

Roof ridge

Slate roof

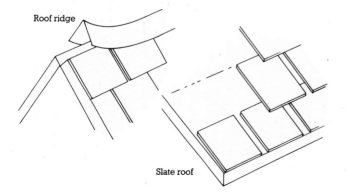

ALTERNATIVE ROOF FINISHES

Flat tile
1. *Cut long strips of cardboard about ⅜ in. (10 mm.) wide, then cut off 1 in. (25 mm.) lengths.* 2. *Lay the tiles in the same way as the slate tiles, applying glue along a pencil line drawn every 1 in. (25 mm.).* 3. *Paint a terracotta color with water paint.*

Ridge tile
1. *Cut long strips of corrugated cardboard 1 in. (25 mm.) wide.*
2. *Draw lines every 1 in. (25 mm.) from the edge of the roof and overlap the tiles.*
3. *Paint with terracotta colored paint.*

Thatched roof
1. *Cover the roof with multipurpose glue.*
2. *Apply self-hardening clay and, while still wet, texture with a comb or stiff brush to give a thatched look.*
3. *Paint with yellow latex paint.*

stagger the next, so that each vertical line is centered on the brick below. This will make the bricks look truly realistic. If the surface becomes too dry and difficult to score, dampen it with a brush dipped in water.

4. Color the wall surfaces with a terracotta latex paint or water paint. Make sure you paint lightly over the surface; your aim is to cover the bricks, but to leave the deep scoring clear to create the effect of pointing.

Plaster edges and window surrounds

1. Using a sharp blade, cut ½ in. (12 mm.) strips of thick white cardboard for the corners, edges and central divisions of the house. (Detergent boxes are ideal.) Glue the edges and surrounds in place and cover with multipurpose glue to seal them.
2. Make paper patterns for the gable, top and bottom floor windows from the diagram measurements. Position them on cardboard and cut out using a sharp blade. Glue the frames in place and seal with multipurpose glue. When the cardboard is dry, it can be painted with white latex paint.

Windows

Acrylic plastic makes an ideal substitute for glass. It is safe for children to play with and can be scored easily with a blade and then snapped off.
1. Make paper patterns of the window spaces. Place the patterns on the acrylic plastic, score around them and snap off along the lines.
2. The window frame can be made from white cardboard, balsa wood or semi-rigid foam plastic. Cut with a sharp blade and glue to the acrylic plastic. Use a clear balsa glue. Position each window centrally in its space and glue into place.

ALTERNATIVE WALL FINISHES

Stone wall
Make stone shapes and strips from clay and attach with glue, then paint gray and white.

Weather-board
Cut lengths of cardboard ½ in. wide, overlap in the usual way, then paint.

Tudor-fronted
Cut balsa wood strips as shown. Paint with black water paint and glue onto a pre-painted surface.

Stone wall with brick edge
*1. Make lumps of clay, attach with glue, paint white with dabs of black.
2. For the bricks, cut strips of cardboard ½ in. (12 mm.) long and alternately ⅜ in. (10 mm.) and 1 in. (25 mm.) wide. Paint terracotta and glue to the wall, alternating long and short.*

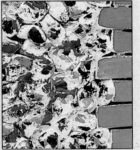

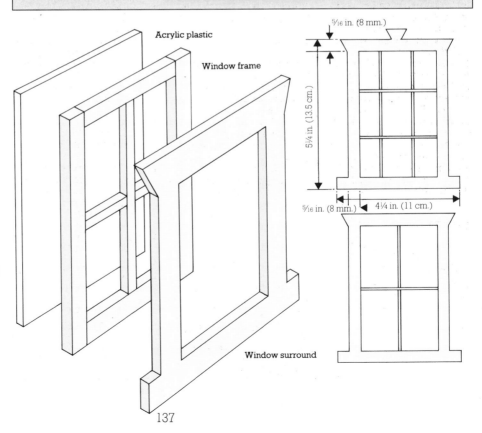

Acrylic plastic

Window frame

Window surround

⁵⁄₁₆ in. (8 mm.)

5¼ in. (13.5 cm.)

⁵⁄₁₆ in. (8 mm.)   4¼ in. (11 cm.)

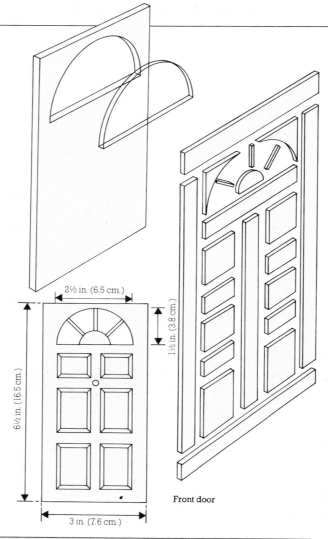

Front door

1. Cut out a 3 x 6½ in. (7.6 x 16.5 cm.) rectangle from a piece of ⅛ in. (3 mm.) plywood. Test it for size in the door space and trim if necessary.

2. Draw the shape of the fanlight using the measurements in the diagram. Drill a small hole. Insert the tip of your coping or fretsaw into the hole and cut out a semicircle.

3. Next, cut a semicircle of acrylic plastic increasing its size by ¼ in. (6 mm.) all around.

4. The trim and small details of the door are made from thin balsa wood, cut with a sharp blade, then sanded and glued into place as shown. Cut ¼ in. (6 mm.) strips for the edges and divisions. Cut six rectangles for the panels and carefully cut the trim for the fanlight.

5. Glue the edges of the acrylic plastic, place over the fanlight space and sandwich it between the plywood backing and the balsa trim.

6. Give the door an undercoat

and a topcoat of oil paint, just as you would a full-size door.

7. A brass cotter pin makes a good doorknob. Two small strips of leather or thin rubber will serve as hinges. Attach them to the inside of the door frame and to the back of the door. You can use a staple gun or glue. Leave overnight to dry.

Balustrade

There are various ways of constructing the short pillars that make up the balustrade. They can be made in wood turned on a lathe or molded and cast in plaster. However, the easiest and most effective method of producing uniform pillars is to assemble them from wooden beads, balsa wood, brads and clay. For each ¾ in. (19 mm.) pillar you will need: one round bead with a ¼ in. (6 mm.) diameter, one ¼ in. (6 mm.) long tubular bead with a ⅛ in. (3 mm.) diameter, two ⅜ in. (10 mm.) squares of ¼ in. (6 mm.) thick balsa wood, a brad and a tiny piece of clay.

1. Assemble abacus-fashion,

2½ in. (6.5 cm.)

1½ in. (3.8 cm.)

6½ in. (16.5 cm.)

3 in. (7.6 cm.)

Front door

ALTERNATIVE DOORS

Cottage door

1. *Make plank lines ½ in. apart with a shallow saw cut.*
2. *Cut plywood for the cross members, glue on and paint.*

Art Deco door

1. *Cut two pieces of plastic foam and one piece acrylic plastic to size. Glue together. Cut a shaped section at the top to show the acrylic plastic.*
2. *Glue three flat popsicle sticks to the door. Paint the door and the acrylic plastic for a stained glass effect.*

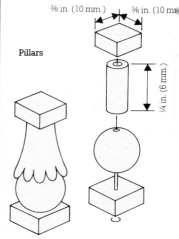

⅜ in. (10 mm.)   ⅜ in. (10 mm.)

Pillars

¼ in. (6 mm.)

Balustrade

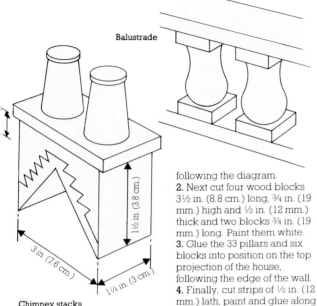

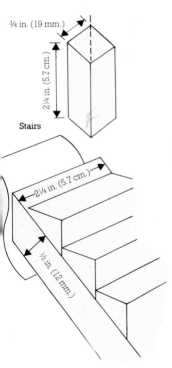

Chimney stacks

Stairs

following the diagram.
2. Next cut four wood blocks
3½ in. (8.8 cm.) long, ¾ in. (19
mm.) high and ½ in. (12 mm.)
thick and two blocks ¾ in. (19
mm.) long. Paint them white.
3. Glue the 33 pillars and six
blocks into position on the top
projection of the house,
following the edge of the wall.
4. Finally, cut strips of ½ in. (12
mm.) lath, paint and glue along
the top of the balustrade.

Chimney stacks

This is the final stage in the
construction of the exterior of
the house.
1. Cut two blocks of wood 1¼
in. (3 cm.) thick by 3 in. (7.6
cm.) wide by 1½ in. (3.8 cm.)
deep. Draw a line from the
bottom corner of each block to
form a triangle. The apex of the
triangle should be in the center
of the block, ½ in. (12 mm.)
from the top. Cut away the
triangle.
2. Give the stacks a brick finish,
using the same method as for
the walls. Then glue them in
place over the roof ridge.
3. The chimney pots are made
from a roll of clay about 1 in. (25
mm.) high and stuck onto the
roof.
4. Finally, cut strips of thin
cardboard for the flashing and
paint gray *(see diagram)*.

Stairs

These use the last of the 16
units cut from the exterior ½
in. (12 mm.) plywood sheet

1. Cut a 2¼ x 12¼ in. (5.7 x 31
cm.) strip and place diagonally
against the downstairs wall.
The angle will be 45°.
2. Cut nine steps from ¾ in.
(19 mm.) square lengths of
wood cut every 2¼ in. (5.7
cm.) then cut diagonally and
glued. Laid flat they resemble
a row of tents.
3. With wood glue attach the
steps to the strip and finish with
dark wood stain.
4. Sandwich a piece of cloth
between the stairs and landing
before gluing in place.

Walls, ceilings and floors

Walls and ceilings require
three coats of latex paint
except when wallpaper is
used. Then only one sealing
coat is required.

Wallpaper

Patterned wrapping paper is
used for this and is ideal
because the designs are suit
the scale of the house.
1. Make a paper pattern
of the wall area first, then cut
the wrapping paper to the
correct size.
2. Brush on a light coat of
wallpaper paste and apply.

Carpets

You will probably want to
carpet the living room, small
bedroom, large bedroom and
bathroom. Colored felt, sold in
24 in. (61 cm.) squares is best
for this. Iron the felt before
cutting, because ironing it,
especially with a steam iron,
can make it shrink.
1. Make a paper pattern of the
area to be covered, then cut
felt to the pattern.
2. Test for fit, then brush the
floor lightly with multipurpose
glue and attach felt.

Tile and wood floors

You can create the effect of
floorboards and tiles by
drawing lines on a piece of
semi-rigid foam plastic with
ball point pen and ruler.
1. Cut a paper pattern to fit the
floor area.
2. Cut foam to shape and fasten
with multipurpose glue.
3. Paint the desired color. The
foam plastic will take both oil
and water paints. For a
Mediterranean tile effect, paint
with terracotta poster paint.
For wooden areas like the hall
and landing, stain or varnish
the playwood.

MATERIALS

In addition to those for the exterior:
1 ½ x 2¼ x 12¼ in. (12 x 57 x 304 mm.) strip
  plywood for the stairs support
5 pieces wood 2¼ in. (5.7 cm.) long and ¾ in. (19
  mm.) square for the steps
2 sheets wrapping paper for wallpaper
2 24 in. (61 cm.) square pieces colored felt for carpets
1 sheet semi-rigid foam plastic for tiled floors
  dark wood stain, wood glue, latex paint for floors
  and ceilings
  wallpaper paste
  small piece of cloth for stairs

TOOLS

Same as for doll's house exterior

139

PROJECT **34**

DOLLHOUSE
GARDEN

No dollhouse, least of all this one, is complete without an appropriate setting. To complement the classical lines of its 18th-century facade you can create a walled garden with a central driveway and lawns with flowerbeds at each side. The whole garden is contained in a detachable base which fits onto the front of the house.

Preparing the base and walls

1. With tracing paper, pencil and ruler, measure and cut out the patterns for the base unit and six wall units, all of which are cut from ½ in. (12 mm.) plywood.

2. Now cut the units with a hand crosscut saw. Then, cut out the curves in the wall units with a saber saw. Smooth with sandpaper.

3. Glue the wall units to the base using wood glue. Set the front walls 2 in. (5 cm.) back from the front edge of the base. When dry, the wall units should be given a brick finish with wood filler in the same way as the house (see p.136).

4. Now that the wall units are in place make the two gate posts. Cut ¼ in. (6 mm.) balsa into two strips 8 in. (20.1 cm.) long and 1½ in. (3.8cm.) wide and glue to the front wall ends. When dry, smooth clay over them.

Cap and orb

1. With self-hardening clay, mold two caps 1½ in. (3.8 cm.)

square. Now mold two balls of clay 1¼ in. (3.2 cm.) in diameter. Pin and glue each cap and orb together when soft and leave to dry.

2. To finish, paint with stone gray latex paint mixed with a touch of sharp sand. When dry, pin to the top of the gate posts.

Cap and orb

1¼ in. (3.2 cm.)

¼ in. (6 mm.)

1½ in. (3.8 c

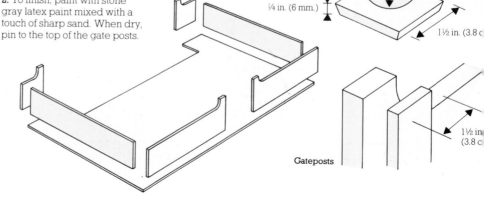

Assemble the basic garden area (right) following the proportions given before going on to add the decorative caps and orbs (far right) to the gateposts (bottom right) for a touch of authentic 18th century elegance.

Gateposts

1½ in (3.8 c

TEMPLATES

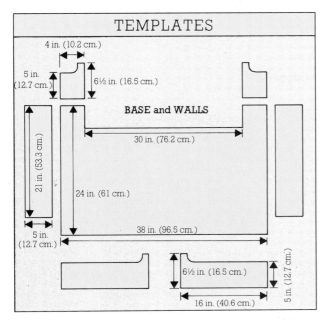

4 in. (10.2 cm.)
5 in. (12.7 cm.)
6½ in. (16.5 cm.)

BASE and WALLS

30 in. (76.2 cm.)
21 in. (53.3 cm.)
24 in. (61 cm.)
5 in. (12.7 cm.)
38 in. (96.5 cm.)
6½ in. (16.5 cm.)
5 in. (12.7 cm.)
16 in. (40.6 cm.)

The gate

This is made from ⅜ in. (10 mm.) thick balsa wood.
1. Carefully measure and cut out three strips ⅜ x 5 in. (1 x 12.7 cm.) for the horizontal slats; one strip ⅜ x 3 in. (1 x 8 cm.) for the right-side support one piece ⅜ x 6¼ in. (1 x 16 cm.) for the diagonal supportn and one curved piece ⅜ x 4 in. (1 x 10 cm.) for the left-side support. Cut two small vertical slats ¼ x ¾ in. (5 x 19 mm.).
2. Glue the pieces together with wood glue and when dry paint with undercoat, followed by a white gloss finish.
3. To make the gate hinge, bend two ¾ in. (19 mm.) bradsat right angles and insert into the side of the gate. These will fit into two staples secured on the left-side gatepost at the same level.

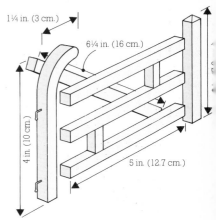

1¼ in. (3 cm.)
6¼ in. (16 cm.)
4 in. (10 cm.)
5 in. (12.7 cm.)

Garden plan

Before you begin to construct the components inside the garden, it is essential to draw a plan on the garden base. With a pencil and ruler, mark the correct dimensions and positions of everything within the garden as shown on the garden plan diagram.

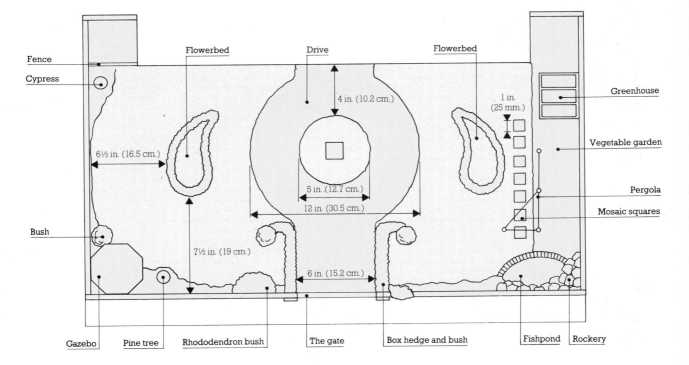

Fence
Cypress
Flowerbed
Drive
Flowerbed
Greenhouse
4 in. (10.2 cm.)
1 in. (25 mm.)
Vegetable garden
6½ in. (16.5 cm.)
5 in. (12.7 cm.)
12 in. (30.5 cm.)
Pergola
Mosaic squares
Bush
7½ in. (19 cm.)
6 in. (15.2 cm.)
Gazebo
Pine tree
Rhododendron bush
The gate
Box hedge and bush
Fishpond
Rockery

The lawns

These are made with self-hardening modeling clay.

1. Brush multipurpose glue onto the area which is to be grass.

2. Cut irregular outlines to mark out borders, then texture by brushing over with an old toothbrush. When the clay dries it will shrink and crack, so fill the gaps with glue, plug in more clay, and then texture in the same way.

3. When dry, paint with green latex paint mixed with a little sharp sand for more texture.

Hedges, borders, bushes and shrubs

1. Model clay to make the shapes shown in the diagram and texture the surface by scraping with a comb, or kitchen fork.

2. Glue in place with wood glue and when the clay is still soft, hand paint with green oil or latex paint.

3. To make rhododendron flowers, stick pieces of colored sponge here and there on the bush.

4. To make the border for the teardrop shaped flowerbed, make a roll of clay ⅝ in. (15 mm.) wide, 1 in. (25 mm.) deep and 14 in. (35.5 cm.) long. Fix in place on the garden base with multipurpose glue. Texture with a toothbrush.

Flowerbeds, vegetable garden, rock garden

1. You have already marked their positions on the base. Now dig up a piece of dry, earth from your own garden and remove the stones.

2. Mix the earth with a good amount of wood glue to make a glutinous mixture and press in place. At first it will look gray, but, when the glue dries, the earth will return to its natural color and be held and sealed in place.

3. For the border plants and flowerbeds cut sponge shapes and soak in water paint. Then fix. For the vegetable garden, simply glue pieces of green sponge in straight rows. Tomato plants can be shaped from modeling clay.

4. A convincing rock garden can be made by collecting small chips of stone, then fixing into clay with lots of multipurpose glue.

For plants, finish off with blobs of different colored sponge and dabs of paint. The best setting is in a corner with the wall for support.

Gravel drive

First brush wood glue over the surface and while still wet, sprinkle with sharp sand.

Fishpond

1. Cut a small semi-circular shape, 5 in. (12.7 cm.) across, from a sheet of acrylic plastic. Fasten in place with multipurpose glue.

2. Paint blue and green, then varnish.

3. To make a brick border for the pond, cut a 6 in. (15.2 cm.) strip of clay ½ in. (12 mm.) wide and ¼ in. (6 mm.) deep. Paint it brown to match the garden wall and mark off the bricks with a knife.

The gazebo

This is an octagonal structure built mainly from balsa wood strips and set on a raised plywood base. All parts are secured with multipurpose glue.

1. Draw the eight-sided base onto a circle of ½ in. (12 mm.) plywood, 4 in. (10.2 cm.) in diameter, with each side measuring 1½ in. (3.8 cm.)

2. Cut eight ¼ in. (6 mm.) balsa strips ¼ in. (6 mm.) wide and 4

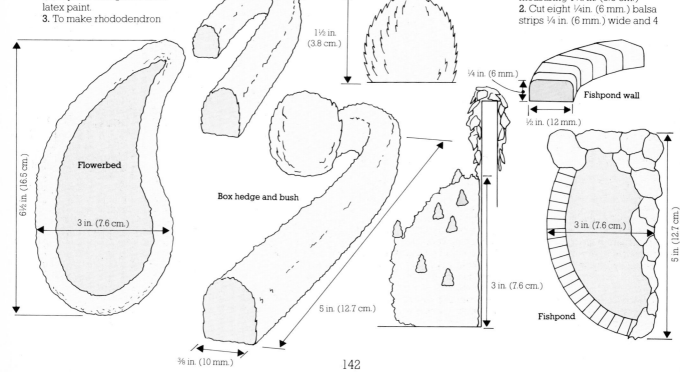

Flowerbed

6½ in. (16.5 cm.)

3 in. (7.6 cm.)

Box hedge and bush

1½ in. (3.8 cm.)

⅜ in. (10 mm.)

5 in. (12.7 cm.)

3 in. (7.6 cm.)

¼ in. (6 mm.)

Fishpond wall

½ in. (12 mm.)

Fishpond

3 in. (7.6 cm.)

5 in. (12.7 cm.)

142

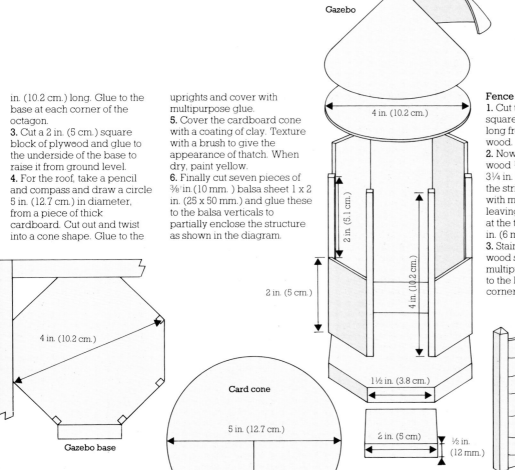

Gazebo

4 in. (10.2 cm.)

2 in. (5.1 cm.)

4 in. (10.2 cm.)

2 in. (5 cm.)

1½ in. (3.8 cm.)

2 in. (5 cm)

½ in. (12 mm.)

Card cone

5 in. (12.7 cm.)

Gazebo base

4 in. (10.2 cm.)

in. (10.2 cm.) long. Glue to the base at each corner of the octagon.

3. Cut a 2 in. (5 cm.) square block of plywood and glue to the underside of the base to raise it from ground level.

4. For the roof, take a pencil and compass and draw a circle 5 in. (12.7 cm.) in diameter, from a piece of thick cardboard. Cut out and twist into a cone shape. Glue to the

uprights and cover with multipurpose glue.

5. Cover the cardboard cone with a coating of clay. Texture with a brush to give the appearance of thatch. When dry, paint yellow.

6. Finally cut seven pieces of ⅜ in. (10 mm.) balsa sheet 1 x 2 in. (25 x 50 mm.) and glue these to the balsa verticals to partially enclose the structure as shown in the diagram.

Fence

1. Cut two posts ⅜ in. (1 cm.) square and 4¾ in. (12 cm.) long from a piece of balsa wood.

2. Now, cut eight strips of balsa wood ½ in. (12mm.) wide and 3¼ in. (8.25 cm.) long. Overlap the strips, fixing them together with multipurpose glue and leaving a gap of ½ in. (12 mm.) at the top of the posts and ¼ in. (6 mm.) at the bottom.

3. Stain the fence with dark oak wood stain and with multipurpose glue attach fence to the base and left-hand far corner of the garden wall.

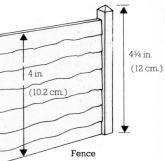

4¾ in. (12 cm.)

4 in. (10.2 cm.)

Fence

Pergola or shaded walk

The pergola is made from seven twigs, all cut to various lengths.

1. Cut the correct lengths then plan out their positions from the diagram.

2. Set each of the four upright sticks into a ball of clay mixed with multipurpose glue and fix the three cross members, taking care to glue them securely with multipurpose glue.

3. Once the glue has dried, the climber can be fixed in place, in this case a honeysuckle.

Honeysuckle

1. Cut a piece of brown electric cord of sufficient length to wrap around the frame of the pergola.

2. To make the foliage, mix a small quantity of sawdust with green paint and wood glue and stick on in blobs.

3. For the flower clusters, cut small pieces of sponge and immerse them in yellow water paint, then dry. All border plants and flowers are made with different colored sponges in this way.

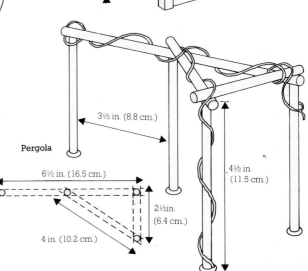

3½ in. (8.8 cm.)

Pergola

6½ in. (16.5 cm.)

4 in. (10.2 cm.)

2½ in. (6.4 cm.)

4½ in. (11.5 cm.)

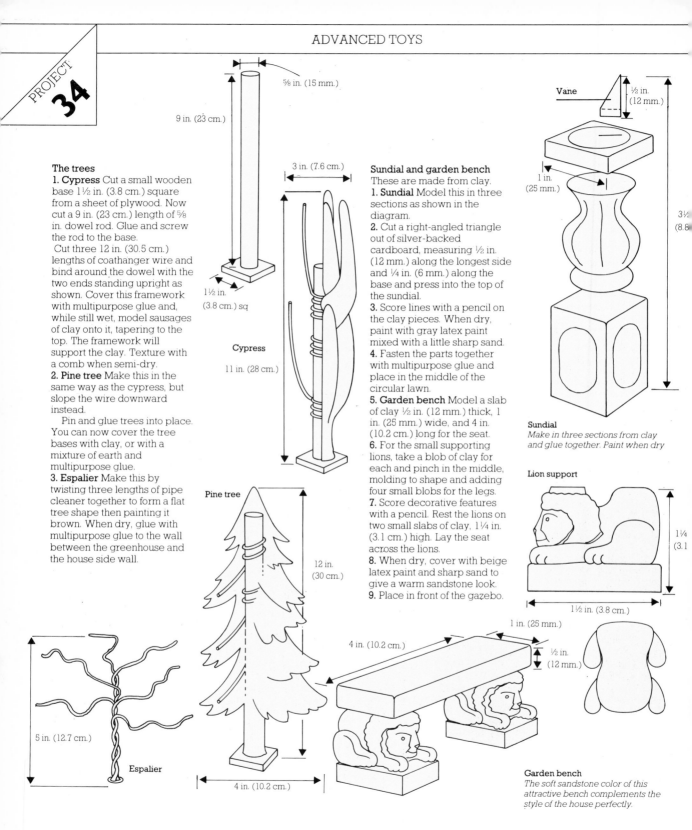

PROJECT **34**

The trees
1. Cypress Cut a small wooden base 1½ in. (3.8 cm.) square from a sheet of plywood. Now cut a 9 in. (23 cm.) length of ⅝ in. dowel rod. Glue and screw the rod to the base.

Cut three 12 in. (30.5 cm.) lengths of coathanger wire and bind around the dowel with the two ends standing upright as shown. Cover this framework with multipurpose glue and, while still wet, model sausages of clay onto it, tapering to the top. The framework will support the clay. Texture with a comb when semi-dry.
2. Pine tree Make this in the same way as the cypress, but slope the wire downward instead.

Pin and glue trees into place. You can now cover the tree bases with clay, or with a mixture of earth and multipurpose glue.
3. Espalier Make this by twisting three lengths of pipe cleaner together to form a flat tree shape then painting it brown. When dry, glue with multipurpose glue to the wall between the greenhouse and the house side wall.

9 in. (23 cm.)

⅝ in. (15 mm.)

3 in. (7.6 cm.)

1½ in. (3.8 cm.) sq

Cypress

11 in. (28 cm.)

Pine tree

12 in. (30 cm.)

4 in. (10.2 cm.)

5 in. (12.7 cm.)

Espalier

Sundial and garden bench
These are made from clay.
1. Sundial Model this in three sections as shown in the diagram.
2. Cut a right-angled triangle out of silver-backed cardboard, measuring ½ in. (12 mm.) along the longest side and ¼ in. (6 mm.) along the base and press into the top of the sundial.
3. Score lines with a pencil on the clay pieces. When dry, paint with gray latex paint mixed with a little sharp sand.
4. Fasten the parts together with multipurpose glue and place in the middle of the circular lawn.
5. Garden bench Model a slab of clay ½ in. (12 mm.) thick, 1 in. (25 mm.) wide, and 4 in. (10.2 cm.) long for the seat.
6. For the small supporting lions, take a blob of clay for each and pinch in the middle, molding to shape and adding four small blobs for the legs.
7. Score decorative features with a pencil. Rest the lions on two small slabs of clay, 1¼ in. (3.1 cm.) high. Lay the seat across the lions.
8. When dry, cover with beige latex paint and sharp sand to give a warm sandstone look.
9. Place in front of the gazebo.

Vane

½ in. (12 mm.)

1 in. (25 mm.)

3½ (8.8

Sundial
Make in three sections from clay and glue together. Paint when dry

Lion support

1¼ (3.1

1½ in. (3.8 cm.)

1 in. (25 mm.)

4 in. (10.2 cm.)

½ in. (12 mm.)

Garden bench
The soft sandstone color of this attractive bench complements the style of the house perfectly.

Greenhouse

This is made from 3/16 in. (3 mm.) thick acrylic plastic, as used in the house windows.

1. Cut out the four sections with a modeling knife – two side sections 3 x 5 in. (7.6 x 12.7 cm.); top section 3¾ x 4 in. (9.5 x 10.2 cm.); and front section 3 x 3½ in. (7.6 x 8.9 cm.).

2. To create the white wooden frame effect, cover the units with masking tape and draw on the white parallel lines.

3. Split the tape with a scalpel and peel off the strips, then spray the acrylic plastic underneath them with white enamel paint. When dry, scratch the crisscross lines for panes.

4. Glue the two side sections to the garden wall 3½ in. (8.8 cm.) apart. When dry, glue on the front section.

5. Hinge the roof in place with with masking tape and multipurpose glue.

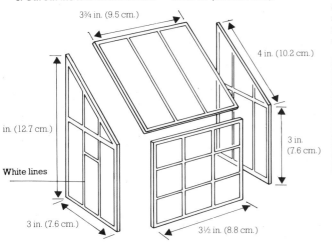

3¾ in. (9.5 cm.)
4 in. (10.2 cm.)
in. (12.7 cm.)
White lines
3 in. (7.6 cm.)
3 in. (7.6 cm.)
3½ in. (8.8 cm.)

MATERIALS

1 ⅜ x 24 x 38 in. (1 x 61 x 97 cm.) sheet of plywood ½ x 5 x
2 21 in. (12 mm. x 12.7 x 53.3 cm.) strips of plywood for the side walls
2 ½ x 4 x 6½ in. (12 mm. x 10.2 x 16.5 cm.) strips of plywood for two small curved side walls
2 ½ x 6½ x 16 in. (12mm x 6 x 16.5cm) strips of plywood for the two front walls
1 wood filler
  self-hardening clay
  assortment of balsa wood sheets ¼, ⅜, ½ in. (6, 10, 12 mm.) thick for the gazebo
1 can undercoat: white gloss, green, gray and beige, latex paint, yellow water paint, copper paint
1 ½ x 4 x 4 in. (12 mm. x 10.2 x 10.2 cm.) plywood block for the gazebo base
1 ½ x 2 in. (1.2 x 5 cm.) gazebo block support
  sandpaper
  masking tape
7 piece of thick cardboard
  piece of silver-backed cardboard 2 in. (5 cm.) square
1 multipurpose glue
  twigs of pencil thickness and length for the pergola
1 box 18 ga. 1 in. (25 mm.) brads
  brown electric cord
1 scrap of sponge rubber
  dowel and wire framework for trees
1 packet pipe cleaners
  stone chips
  mosaic squares
  sheet acrylic plastic ⅛ in. (3 mm.) thick for the greenhouse
1 can white enamel spray paint
  modeling clay
2 lollipop sticks
  varnish
2 1 in. (2.5 cm.) screws to fasten trees to the block

TOOLS

Pencil, saber saw, keyhole saw, hand crosscut saw, modeling knife, screwdriver, small household paintbrush, glue brush, snips, comb, compass, toothbrush.

GARDEN TOOLS

No garden is complete without tools. You can easily make a small spade and garden rake.

1. For the spade handle, make a ¼ in. (6 mm.) hole in the center of a piece of ½ in. (12 mm.) dowel with an electric drill. Then cut in half as shown.

2. Fasten a 2 in. (5 cm.) lollipop stick in the handle with multipurpose glue.

3. Cut the spade shape from a piece of silver-backed cardboard to measure ¾ x 1 in. (19 x 25 mm.). Glue the flap round the stick to fasten.

4. To make the rake head, cut an appropriate pattern from a piece of 1 in. (25 mm.) wide cardboard and glue the flap round a 3½ in. (8.8 cm.) lollipop stick.

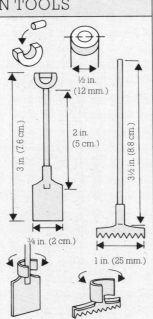

½ in. (12 mm.)
3 in. (7.6 cm.)
2 in. (5 cm.)
3½ in. (8.8 cm.)
¾ in. (2 cm.)
1 in. (25 mm.)

DOLLHOUSE
FURNITURE

Realism is all-important when you are creating a world in miniature for your children. If you have chosen to make a replica of your own home, you will enjoy the challenge of recreating its contents and décor. Simple methods are used to create pieces that range in style from a jardinière to a T.V. set and from antique to modern. They include soft furnishing, simple wooden furniture, clay work and ideas for adapting existing objects, such as matchboxes and buttons.

The kitchen units

The oven, stovetop and sink are made with 1¾ in. (4.5 cm.) square softwood.

1. Cut three pieces – one 7½ in. (19 cm.) long for the oven, and two shorter measuring 6¾ in. (17 cm.) for the stovetop and sink sections. Sand these blocks smooth and ensure that the ends are accurately squared.

2. Place the longer of the three blocks on end to make the oven, and arrange the other two longways around it as you think best, according to your overall kitchen design.

3. Mark off an area 1¾ in. (4.5 cm.) square for the stovetop. Paint it silver gray and stick on four flat red buttons without holes, or red spot transfers, to indicate burners. To make the outlines of the cupboards, sawcut vertical lines every 1¾ in. (4.5 cm.) on the stovetop and sink sections, making three along the stovetop side and two along the sink side.

4. To make the sink, chisel out a block 1½ x 3 in. (4 x 7.6 cm.) from the section to form a square cavity. Glue a lump of self-hardening clay firmly into the space. Pat into shape, scooping out a rounded rectangular shape with a

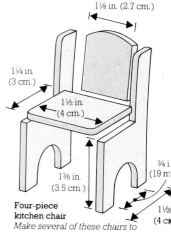

Four-piece kitchen chair
Make several of these chairs to furnish a busy family kitchen.

teaspoon to a depth of 1¼ in. (3 cm.). Make a drain hole in the clay with a nail head and then press the female part of a silver snap into the hole. Glue a cup hook into the wall side corner for a faucet. When the clay is dry, give it two coats of aluminum primer. Paint some thin cardboard with the primer and cut two strips for the worktops next to the sink and stovetop. Glue in place.

5. To make the 'see-through' oven door, saw two ³⁄₁₆ in. (5 mm.) cuts, one level with the work surface, the other parallel with it 2³⁄₁₆ in. (5.5 cm.) above. Cut away the unwanted center with a 1 in. (25 mm.) wood chisel and into the recess glue a picture of food cooking cut from a catalog or magazine.

To cover this, cut a piece of acrylic plastic (as used in the dollhouse windows), and glue it in place with multipurpose glue.

6. When all the sawing has been done and the sink made, paint the units with undercoat, followed by two top coats of ordinary gloss paint.

Wooden furniture

Most of the furniture has been made with ¼ in. (6 mm.)

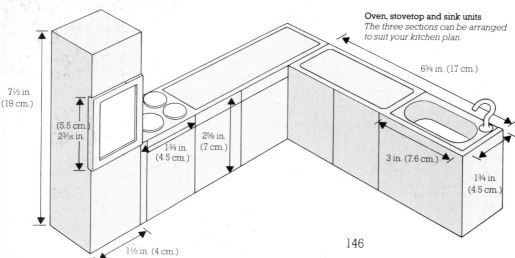

Oven, stovetop and sink units
The three sections can be arranged to suit your kitchen plan.

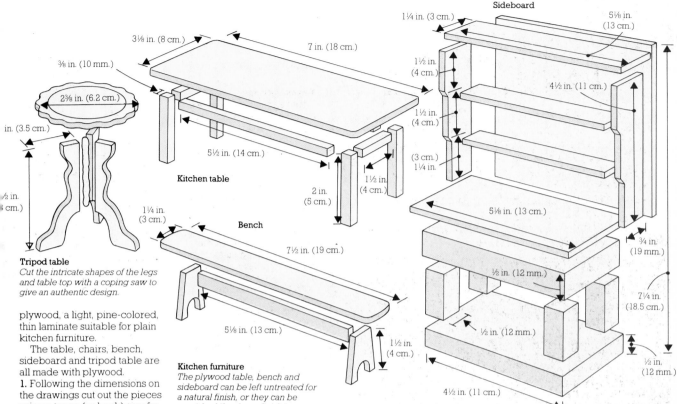

3/8 in. (10 mm.)

2 3/8 in. (6.2 cm.)

in. (3.5 cm.)

3 1/8 in. (8 cm.)

7 in. (18 cm.)

5 1/2 in. (14 cm.)

Kitchen table

2 in. (5 cm.)

1 1/2 in. (4 cm.)

1/2 in. cm.)

1 1/4 in. (3 cm.)

Sideboard

1 1/4 in. (3 cm.)

5 1/8 in. (13 cm.)

1 1/2 in. (4 cm.)

4 1/2 in. (11 cm.)

1 1/2 in. (4 cm.)

(3 cm.) 1 1/4 in.

5 1/8 in. (13 cm.)

3/4 in. (19 mm.)

1/2 in. (12 mm.)

1/2 in. (12 mm.)

7 1/4 in. (18.5 cm.)

1/2 in. (12 mm.)

4 1/2 in. (11 cm.)

7 1/2 in. (19 cm.)

Bench

5 1/8 in. (13 cm.)

1 1/2 in. (4 cm.)

Tripod table
Cut the intricate shapes of the legs and table top with a coping saw to give an authentic design.

plywood, a light, pine-colored, thin laminate suitable for plain kitchen furniture.

The table, chairs, bench, sideboard and tripod table are all made with plywood.
1. Following the dimensions on the drawings cut out the pieces using a tenon (or back) saw for the straight sections and a fretsaw for the few curved parts on the chairs and bench.
2. Sand all parts. They will all be glued with multipurpose glue, no brads are necessary. Leave all furniture overnight for the glue to set.

Chairs
Place the two side pieces onto a bed of modeling clay. This will hold them in position while the seat and back are glued in place.

Table and bench
Place table and bench tops upside-down, this time onto small blobs of modeling clay to hold everything in place. These can be removed easily when glue is hard.

Sideboard
The top is cut from 1/4 in. (6 mm.) plywood, the base from 1/2 in. (12 mm.) scraps.

Kitchen furniture
The plywood table, bench and sideboard can be left untreated for a natural finish, or they can be varnished if a glossy finish is required.

Assemble the top shelf section flat on its back so that the sides and shelves can be set in an upright position. Glue together the parts for the bottom section and allow it to dry overnight before assembling the top and the base. Stain or varnish the finished sideboard.

Tripod table
1. Cut all four parts to size with a coping saw since they are all curved.
2. Fasten the three legs together with a thin roll of self-hardening clay covered with multipurpose glue.
3. When the leg section is set, glue the table top in place.
4. Once the table is set, stain it with dark oakwood stain and finish it off with a circle of thin fabric 2 in. (5cm.) in diameter, cut to look like a fancy table cloth.

Matchbox dresser
1. Glue four matchboxes together with multipurpose glue as shown in the diagram.
2. Cut a strip of cardboard long enough to cover this unit, score fold lines and glue under the base, then cut a piece of cardboard to form the back and a mirror 2 1/4 in. (5.7 cm.) in diameter. Paint with matte latex.
3. Remove the drawers before you glue the back on. Punch a hole in each drawer for a brass cotter pin. Press these down inside.
4. Cut a small semicircle of silver paper and glue to the back for the mirror.

This simple method of making a small dresser can be surprisingly effective.

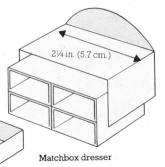

2 1/4 in. (5.7 cm.)

Matchbox dresser

PROJECT
35

Shelves
There are six shelves, three on either side of the fireplace.
1. Cut six shelves from a piece of ⅛ in. (3 mm.) balsa wood 3 in. (7.6 cm.) wide and 1 in. (25 mm.) deep. You will need some small triangular brackets to support them.
2. Paint white and with multipurpose glue fix in place. The two middle shelves are level with the mantle shelf, the bottom and top shelves are spaced 1⅜ in. (3.5 cm.) above and below.

Single bed
This is made from about eight flat popsicle sticks.
1. Cut a rectangle from ¼ in. (6 mm.) plywood to measure 3 x 5½ in. (7.6 x 14 cm.). Glue a ⅜ in. (10 mm.) square balsa wood frame underneath flush with the edges.
2. Place two 3 in. (7.6 cm.) popsicle sticks with rounded

Single bed
¼ in. (6 mm.) plywood and balsa wood is used for the base; popsicle sticks provide the supports and the headboard.

ends at the top of the bed so there is 1 in. (25 mm.) of leg below and the remainder above. Repeat at the foot of the bed with shorter sticks of 2 in. (5 cm.). Glue in place.
3. Place cross members on bedhead and foot and glue in place. Round both ends on these. Varnish finished bed.

Toilet seat
Cut this to the size on the diagram from ¼ in. (6 mm.) plywood with a coping saw. The projecting flange at the end of it is drilled for a brad to go through.

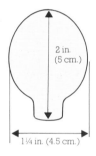

2 in. (5 cm.)

1¼ in. (4.5 cm.)

The living room and bedrooms can be enhanced with small ornaments made from self-hardening clay.

Clay furniture
The material used is self-hardening nylon reinforced clay, which has the advantage of hardening and keeping its form without being fired. It can be glued when wet and painted with matte latex, undercoat or gloss paints *(see p.123).*

Bathroom
1. Sink Following the measurements on the drawings use the basic modeling method, the pinch pot, where you roll a ball of clay in the palms and push the thumb into it to form a hole. This is then enlarged with the gentle pressure of thumb and forefinger. The basin is just a thumb pot with a flat side. The pedestal is a roll of clay, drawn out, waisted and one side made flat to fit the wall. Make a faucet from a bent piece of coathanger wire and the handles with brass cotter pin heads. When all units are dry, fasten them to the wall with multipurpose glue.

2. The toilet is made the same way as the sink using the pinch-pot method. Shape the base and lugs for the lid by adding lumps of clay. Pierce small holes through the lugs for the brad which holds the toilet seat. Smooth, leave to dry, then paint.
3. The bath is a mixture of wood and clay. Make a plywood box 2¼ x 2¾ x 6 in. (5.7 x 7 x 15.2 cm.) and brush the inside with multipurpose glue. Line with clay and smooth, making the drain and overflow holes with a nail. Press a silver snap over the drain hole. The faucet and handles are made as for the sink. Paint with white gloss inside and tile the sides and ends with sections cut to size from semi-rigid foam plastic.

Clay ornaments
1. The two jardinières are simply a roll of clay with a small thumb pot on top and scored with decorative lines. Dry and paint with latex. Make the plants from green plastic

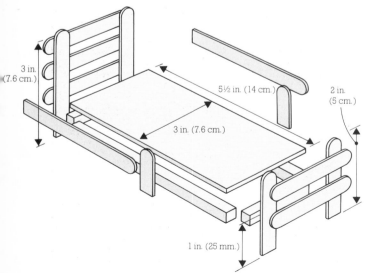

3 in. (7.6 cm.)

5½ in. (14 cm.)

3 in. (7.6 cm.)

2 in. (5 cm.)

1 in. (25 mm.)

148

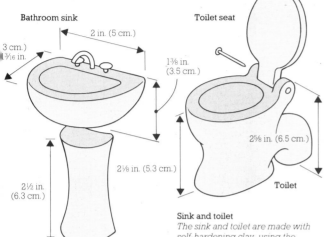

Bathroom sink

2 in. (5 cm.)

3 cm.)
³⁄₁₆ in.

2½ in. (6.3 cm.)

2⅛ in. (5.3 cm.)

Toilet seat

1⅜ in. (3.5 cm.)

2⅝ in. (6.5 cm.)

Toilet

Sink and toilet
The sink and toilet are made with self-hardening clay, using the pinch pot method.

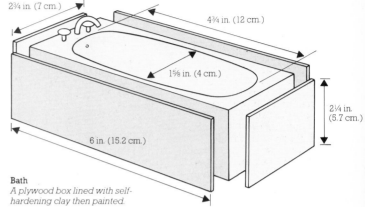

2¾ in. (7 cm.)

4¾ in. (12 cm.)

1⅝ in. (4 cm.)

2¼ in. (5.7 cm.)

6 in. (15.2 cm.)

Bath
A plywood box lined with self-hardening clay then painted.

cut into pointed strips and stick into multipurpose glue mixed with earth or sand.

2. The two dog ornaments are made from a ball of clay the size of a marble. Model two the same and paint the spots on with a small nail head.

3. Picture Glue a thin sausage of clay around the edge of a picture or photo, then with a match stick, press a pattern into it. When dry, paint with gold lacquer which will give a gilt frame effect.

4. The mini dollhouse. Start with a ball of clay and model a house 2 in. (5 cm.) high. Use a kitchen knife to sharpen it up. Make the windows by stamping the clay with an end section of wood into which is cut a 'cross' with a saw cut. This will leave the impression of a window frame pattern. Any ornamentation must be fastened on with multipurpose glue.

Wooden ornaments
The pine kitchen clock, living room clock, broom, T.V. and stereo, are all small objects which can be made

from the wood left over after the kitchen units have been made.

1. Pine clock and drawingroom clock The pine clock is a hexagonal piece of pine, each side measuring 1 in. (25 mm.) and glued onto a ⅞ in. (2.3 cm.) square block of pine. The curved-top clock is cut with a coping saw from a ⅜ in. (10mm.) thick block of pine and is 1½ in. (4 cm.) wide. Sand after sawing. Cut two clock faces out of a catalog or magazine, glue them on and then varnish. To make the pendulum for the kitchen clock stick a brass cotter pin on the front.

2. T.V. and stereo Simply cut two blocks of wood ⅜ in. (10 mm.) thick and 1½ in. (4 cm.) wide for the T.V., 2¾ in. (7 cm.) wide for the stereo. Sand and stain with wood stain. Now cut out a picture of a T.V. and stereo, stick in position and varnish.

3. Broom Cut the head off a toothbrush and round at the ends. Drill a hole in the center, glue in a 4½ in. (11.5 cm.) lollipop stick and paint.

MATERIALS

For the oven, stovetop and sink units:
1 piece square fir or pinewood 7½ in. (19 cm.) long and 1¾ in. (4.5 cm.) square
2 pieces square fir or pinewood 6¾ in. (17 cm.) long and 1¾ in. (4.5 cm.) square
4 buttons without holes for burners
3 silver snaps for sink, bathroom sink and bath drain
   self-hardening (nylon reinforced) clay
   aluminum primer
   a sheet of thin cardboard
   a picture of food cooking from a catalog
   small piece of acrylic plastic
   undercoat and household-gloss paints and gold lacquer
   paint, varnish, modeling clay, multipurpose glue
For the other furniture:
1 piece of ¼ in. (6 mm.) plywood 2 ft. (61 cm.) square for the wooden furniture
1 scrap of fabric for table cloth
   pictures of T.V. and stereo, one photo
   head of a toothbrush and a lollipop stick for the brush
1 piece ⅛ x 1 x 3 in. (3 x 25 mm. x 7.6 cm.) balsa wood for shelves
   flat popsicle sticks for the bed
1 piece ¼ in. (6 mm.) plywood 3 x 5½ in. (7.6 x 14 cm.) for the bath frame
4 matchboxes, silver paper and cardboard for the matchbox dresser
9 brass cotter pins for drawer knobs, pendulum and faucets
   brad for toilet
   small piece coathanger wire
   semi-rigid foam plastic

TOOLS

Wood chisel, tenon (or back) saw, coping saw, crosscut saw, scissors, paintbrush, sandpaper, modeling knife.

PROJECT 35

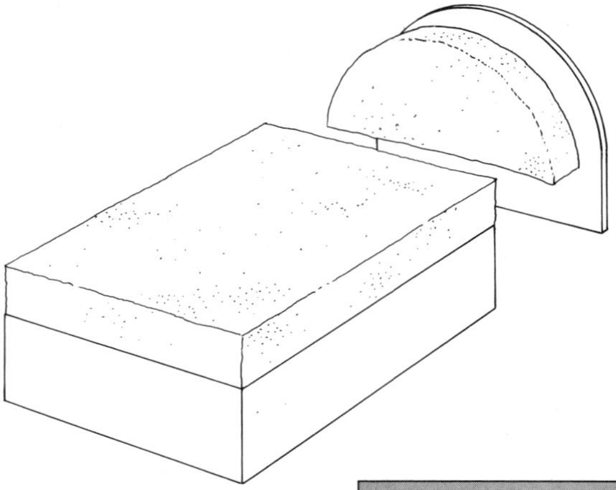

Making the soft furnishings

These are simple to make and include rugs, bed covers, chair covers and drapes. You will be able to ransack your sewing box for most of the materials.

Rugs

For the living room, bathroom and bedrooms.
1. Cut a piece of felt 3⅛ x 5⅞ in. (8 x 15 cm.) and a piece of iron-on interfacing the same size.
2. Now cut 100 strands of string 1⅜ in. (3.5 cm.) long.
3. Place 50 strands at each end of the felt and iron the interfacing on so the strands are sandwiched between felt and interfacing.

Knitted rug

1. Cast on 20 stitches in the yarn of your choice, knit 48 rows in plain stitch and bind off.
2. To make a fringe. Cut 24 pieces of yarn into 2 in. (5 cm.) lengths. Thread one strand through each stitch along the short sides of the rug and make a knot. Trim the fringe.

Crochet rugs

If you can crochet, a round or oval rug looks very good in the bedroom or in front of the fireplace.
1. **Round rug** For this, make six chains, gather them together, then half-crochet around in a circle until you arrive at the size you want. Change the yarn for the finishing row to give an edging.
2. **Oval rug** Start with 10 chains and work two rows of crochet, then half-crochet around in the same way until your width is adequate.

Double bed

1. Cut a block of plastic foam to measure 1¼ x 3½ x 5⅞ in. (3 x 9 x 15 cm.). A cardboard box

could also be used if you can find one of a suitable size.
2. Cut a piece of batting 3½ x 5⅞ in. (9 x 15 cm.) and glue on to the block, using a glue stick.
3. Now, cut a piece of fabric to fit over the base and glue on.
4. Make the bedhead in the same way as the armchair back but with a diameter of 3½ in. (9 cm.).

Comforter

1. Cut two pieces of fabric 5¼ in. (13½ cm.) long and 6 in. (15 cm.) wide, stitch around three sides with a simple running stitch, then turn to the right side and press.
2. Cut a piece of batting ⅜ in. (5 mm.) smaller all around than the fabric, put this inside for filling and oversew the open end.
3. With a running stitch, attach a piece of ribbon or lace around the edges of the comforter as a trim.

Pillow

Cut out two pieces of fabric 2⅜ x 4⅜ in. (6 x 11 cm.) and make in the same way as the comforter. Scatter cushions can be made this way too, but vary the sizes.

Single bed

Cut enough fabric and batting for a mattress, pillow and comforter. Make them up in the same way as the double bed but leave the lace trim off the comforter because the single bed has side supports *(see p. 148)*.

Armchairs

These are best made with a small print or plain fabric. Cut a block of plastic foam 1 x 2⅜ x 2¾ in. (2.5 x 6 x 7 cm.). Use a glue stick to glue all the pieces together.
1. Make a pattern from the diagram and cut out all the

fabric pieces.
2. Cut a piece of batting to fit the plastic foam and glue it on, then stick the piece of fabric for the seat of the chair to the base.
3. To make the back of the chair, cut a piece of cardboard ⅜ in. (10 mm.) smaller than the chair back fabric all around, and a piece of batting to fit the top half of the cardboard. Glue together. Now, put the chair back fabric right sides together and stitch, leaving the bottom half open. Turn to the right side and press. Insert the cardboard and the batting inside the fabric, turn up the fabric at the bottom end to form a neat edge, and glue to close. Glue the back of the chair to the seat, stitch down each side for strength and also along the bottom of the chair.
4. To make the armrests, put wrong sides together and stitch along the dotted line as shown in the diagram, leaving the bottom open. Turn to the right side of the fabric, fill with absorbent cotton and stitch to the chair.
5. To make the ruffle, hem the bottom of the length of fabric cut for this purpose. Fold over the fabric at the top and thread a gathering stitch through. Now gather the ruffle around the seat of the chair, and stitch on.

Make a further chair to match. If a sofa is required, make this twice as wide as the armchair.

Drapes

The easiest material to use is felt because it does not require stitching. If you decide on a different material, choose a small print or a plain fabric. Thin cotton crochet drapes make a good alternative too, as they have a miniature quality.

Master bedroom

Cut four pieces of fabric 3½ x 8⅝ in. (9 x 22 cm.) Stitch the sides either by hand or machine. Now, make a hem at the top and bottom, leaving the top edges open for the drape rod (a lollipop stick or dowel) to go through.

Small bedroom

Cut a piece of felt 1¾ x 5⅞ in. (4.5 x 15 cm.) and round off the

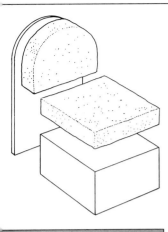

FABRIC TEMPLATES

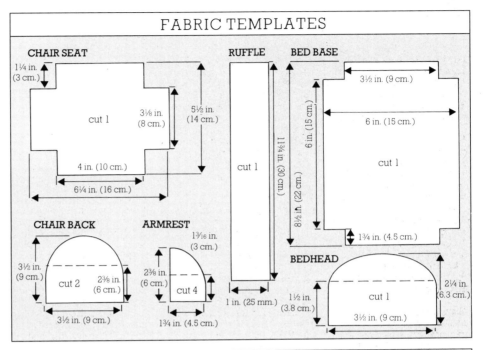

CHAIR SEAT

1¼ in. (3 cm.)

cut 1

3⅛ in. (8 cm.)

5½ in. (14 cm.)

4 in. (10 cm.)

6¼ in. (16 cm.)

RUFFLE

cut 1

11¾ in. (30 cm.)

BED BASE

3½ in. (9 cm.)

6 in. (15 cm.)

6 in. (15 cm.)

cut 1

8½ in. (22 cm.)

1¾ in. (4.5 cm.)

CHAIR BACK

3½ in. (9 cm.)

cut 2

2⅜ in. (6 cm.)

3½ in. (9 cm.)

ARMREST

1³⁄₁₆ in. (3 cm.)

2⅜ in. (6 cm.)

cut 4

1¾ in. (4.5 cm.)

1 in. (25 mm.)

BEDHEAD

1½ in. (3.8 cm.)

cut 1

3½ in. (9 cm.)

2¼ in. (6.3 cm.)

---

corners. Punch eight holes across the top with a hole puncher and thread a lollipop stick (or dowel) through.

Living room
Make these as for the master bedroom drapes, only a little shorter if you wish.

Kitchen
These are crocheted curtains.
1. Make 28 chains.
2. Crochet into the fourth chain from the hook.
3. Work one double, one chain, miss one chain, into next chain work one double, one chain. Repeat to end. Turn.
4. If you are good at crocheted work you can finish off the drape with a picot edging.
5. Make the second drape.

Landing
These are crocheted drapes.
1. Make 26 chains.
2. Use the same pattern as the kitchen drapes, but crochet 15 rows. Make two drapes.
3. Thread a lollipop stick (or dowel) through the holes at the top of the drape.

Fitting the drapes
You will need seven pieces of dowel or seven lollipop sticks cut to 4⅜ in. (11 cm.) in length, and 14 closed eyes (screw attachments with looped ends used to hang net drapes.)
1. Put one eye on either side of each window.
2. Thread the lollipop stick or dowel through the top of the drapes and through the eyes.
3. Cut pieces of lace or ribbon to match the color of the drapes and tie each drape to the side, then pin down with a matching colored thumbtack.

MATERIALS

For the floor coverings:
1 piece felt 3⅛ x 5⅞ in. (8 x 15 cm.)
1 piece iron-on interfacing the same size
  balls of string and yarn
For the double bed:
  plastic foam block 1¼ x 4⅛ x 6⅛ in. (3 x 10.5 x 15.5 cm.)
  glue stick
  batting
  fabric with a small print – remnants are good
  cotton to match bed fabric
  ribbon or lace
For the armchair:
  fabric with a small print
  plastic foam block 1 x 2⅜ x 2¾ in. (2.5 x 6 x 7 cm.)
  cardboard
  absorbent cotton
For the drapes:
  felt or fabric with a small print
7 pieces dowel or lollipop sticks 4⅜ in. (11 cm.) long
14 closed eyes

TOOLS

Knitting needles, scissors, crochet hook, hole puncher,

PROJECT
36

DOLLHOUSE
FAMILY

Every dollhouse needs figures to bring it alive and make it something that will appeal to the entire family. These figures have the great advantage of being both flexible and child-proof. Because they are made out of pipe cleaners, they can be bent whichever way you like, making them look relaxed and natural in their own home.

The family
The family figures should be made to the same scale as the dollhouse, 1:12 (1 in. to 1 ft. or 25 mm. to 30 cm.) so the adults will be about 5½ in. (14 cm.) high. The size of an adult's head goes seven times into its length.

You will need six 6 in. (15.2 cm.) pipe cleaners for each figure and some all-purpose clear adhesive. The heads and feet are made with wooden beads and wood. Self-hardening clay can be used as an alternative.
1. Look closely at the instruction layout and make the body framework as shown. Use one pipe cleaner for the head and shoulders, two for the legs, one for the hips and upper leg and two for the arms, crossed over to brace the chest.
2. Bind strips of stretch nylon cut from a pair of panty hose around the body frame for bulk.
3. To make the head, use a ¾ in. (20 mm.) bead for the adults, and a ⅝ in. (15 mm.) bead for the children. Glue the end of the head pipe cleaner into the bead hole. Paint the face with enamels in a simple Dutch doll style.
4. Cut two hand-shaped pieces of felt for each hand and glue on either side of the pipe cleaner, sewing to the binding at the wrist.
5. For shoes, drill small holes into a piece of doweling. Then

with a coping saw, cut small sections on the slant, about ¾ in. (20 mm.) long for the adults, ⅝ in. (15 mm.) long for the children. Now, shape with a blade and sand. Paint with enamels.
6. Glue the end of the leg pipe cleaner into the shoe hole.

Clothes for the family
These are all (with the exception of the boy's crocheted jacket) made by making paper patterns to the dimensions shown on the patterns and cutting from dress fabric with a small print, or from different colored felt.

Dress
1. Fold the fabric right sides together, stitch sides and sleeves, then make a hem.
2. Turn to right side and put the dress on the doll then edge each sleeve with a piece of lace.
3. Gather up the sleeves and stitch to the doll. Do the same with the neck then stitch a piece of lace around the neck.
4. To make the belt, fold the fabric in half lengthwise with wrong sides together. Turn in the raw ends and topstitch close to the edge.
5. The underskirt is made from a piece of 6 in. (15 cm.) x 2¾

in. (7 cm.) eyelet fabric. Fold in half and stitch the side, then hem the top and bottom. Thread a piece of elastic through the top hem and stitch a piece of lace to the bottom hem.

The dress for the daughter of the family is cut to half size and made the same way.

Trousers
1. Cut two pieces of felt, fold each piece with right sides together and stitch each leg.
2. Turn to the right side and sew the center back and front seams. Put the trousers on the doll and stitch them to the waist.

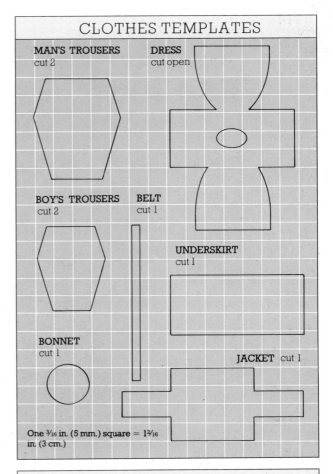

CLOTHES TEMPLATES

MAN'S TROUSERS cut 2

DRESS cut open

BOY'S TROUSERS cut 2

BELT cut 1

UNDERSKIRT cut 1

BONNET cut 1

JACKET cut 1

One ³/₁₆ in. (5 mm.) square = 1²/₁₆ in. (3 cm.)

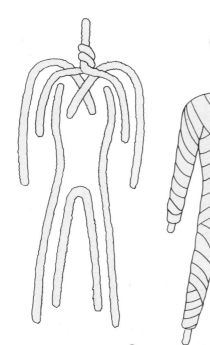

Drill small holes into doweling and cut on the slant.

Felt jacket
1. Fold in half, cut a small hole for the head then stitch sides and sleeves with a simple running stitch.
2. Cut two small pieces of fabric to fit around the bottom sleeves as cuffs. Glue onto the sleeves.
3. Put the jacket on the doll. Cut a small piece of fabric to encircle the neck as a collar and glue onto the jacket.
4. Glue the front opening.

Crocheted jacket
1. Make 12 chains, work six rows of half doubles. Now make nine chains either side for sleeves and work three rows of half doubles. Crochet to the middle. Now crochet

front left, working three rows of half doubles.
2. Decrease nine stitches, so you are left with six stitches. Work six rows of half doubles.
3. Do right side as left. Fold in half. Stitch sides and sleeves together. Turn to right side and put the jacket on the boy. Stitch the front to the doll. For the collar, cut a piece of felt and stitch around the neck.

Bonnet
1. Cut out a circle of fabric 2½ in. (6.3 cm.) in diameter. Fold in half, wrong sides together and stitch a piece of rick-rack along the folded edge.
2. Turn bonnet edges in and run a line of tiny basting stitch around the edge, then gather.

MATERIALS

1 package pipe cleaners
 all-purpose clear adhesive
1 pair old panty hose
2 ¾ in. (20 mm.) beads for adult heads
2 ⅝ in. (15 mm.) beads for children's heads
 doweling 12 in. (30 cm.) long for shoes
 enamel paints or felt-tip pens for painting faces
 dress fabric remnant and felt for clothes
1 6 in. (15 cm.) piece of elastic
1 6 in. (15 cm.) piece of lace
1 2¼ x 6 in. (5.7 x 15 cm.) piece of eyelet fabric
1 ball of yarn
1 2½ in. (6.3 cm.) piece of rick-rack
 spool of matching thread

TOOLS

Hand or power drill, coping saw, a very fine paintbrush, modeling knife, scissors, crochet hook, needle.

GLOSSARY

Acrylic paint A quick-drying water-based paint, available in a wide range of colors. It is ideal for papier mâché and wood.

Actual size Term referring to the size of wood that has been planed and prepared by the lumberyard. Most wood is sold already planed smooth from nominal size. Thus 1 x 2 in. (25 x 50 mm.) nominal size will measure about ¾ x 1½ in. (19 x 38 mm.) when planed to actual size. Ask for actual sizes to make the projects in the book.

Awl Used for making starting holes for screws before using a screwdriver. Large screws will need a drilled hole. See *pilot hole*.

Backsaw A saw used for all fine cutting and jointing. It is a rigid saw with a strongly braced back to the blade.

Backstitch Used for strong, handsewn seams.

Balsa The model maker's wood – it is extremely light and can be cut and shaped easily with a modeling knife. Joints are made by using balsa cement.

Base coat Layer of paint applied after the primer has dried. It provides a good base for the top coat. Use the correct primer for the type of paint used.

Basting A temporary stitch used to hold fabric edges together ready for seaming.

Batting Sheet padding used as stuffing in quilting.

Bias Any diagonal line in relation to the warp and weft threads of a fabric. A true bias is made by folding the selvage at right angles across the fabric.

Bias strip Used for binding raw edges of fabric. The strip will fold over a curved edge smoothly without twisting or pulling.

Bracing Technique used to hold splaying legs in close to a body on a soft toy. Ladder stitch is worked on the surface. Alternatively an optional dart can be made in the wrong side when seaming the skin.

Butt joint A simple wooden joint made by nailing or screwing the end of one piece of wood to another.

Buttonhole stitch Embroidered stitch with a rope edge appearance.

Calico A lightweight, plain weave cotton fabric sometimes printed with small floral patterns. A natural color is used for making doll's bodies.

Compass Instrument for drawing circles.

Control Apparatus to which strings of a marionette are attached. The string puppet is manipulated by operating the control.

Coping saw A versatile saw for cutting curves and irregular shapes. Blades are narrow and set with teeth facing the handle. They are adjustable, which makes cutting easier.

Countersink The action of shaping the top of a screw hole so that the head of a flathead screw lies flush with the surface of the wood.

Crown joint Style of jointing soft toys for use with hardboard disks and cotter pins.

Dado joint Strong joint where end of a cross piece is recessed into the side of an upright. A stopped housing joint is used where appearance is important because the overlap conceals the cut-out.

Darts Darts are used in sewing to provide fullness at strategic points. They can be curved, straight, single or double pointed.

Dowel or doweling A hardwood molding, machined to a round section.

Dowel joint Joint made between two pieces of wood by using short lengths of dowel as pins which are tapped and glued in place.

Dressmaker's graph paper Large sheets of paper covered with a 2 in. (5 cm.) grid.

Drill stand Will ensure accuracy for any drilling job and also allow you to drill to predetermined depths by means of fitted stops. Doweling holes will also be true and square.

Embroidery thread Six-stranded cotton thread used to embroider facial features on the soft toys.

Enamel paint A hard-wearing paint with a high gloss finish, available in small quantities.

Epoxy resin A very strong two-part adhesive consisting of a resin and hardener which are mixed in equal parts. The resulting chemical reaction creates a strong, waterproof, durable bond which is set after about 48 hours.

Felt A fabric produced by matting short fibers. Felt does not fray but will tear when damp, consequently it is not advisable to wash felt toys.

Fretsaw This saw has a greater range of cut and more maneuvrability than a coping saw. It is used for wood, particularly plywood up to about ¼ in. (6 mm.) thick and cuts on the downward stroke.

Gloss paint Oil-based paint used on wooden toys. Paints must be lead-free to meet safety regulations.

Grain The lay of the wood fibers, which is along the length.

Grain line Soft toy patterns are marked with an arrow. The line should run parallel to the selvage which shows the direction of the lengthways grain, or warp, of the fabric.

Hardboard Manufactured board constructed from softwood pulp which has been compressed under high pressure.

Hardwood Comes from deciduous trees such as ash, beech, maple, oak and cherry. Generally harder to work than softwood, but it is stronger and longer lasting.

Hemming Handsewn finish to a single edge of fabric.

Holesaw A drill attachment that is a combination of a center pilot bit and a ring-shaped saw for cutting large diameter holes through wood. Useful for making wheels.

Interfacing A thin layer of fabric which is sewn or fused to a soft toy skin to add strength.

Invisible thread Nylon thread for making whiskers on soft toys.

Keyhole saw The only saw able to cut a hole in the middle of a large panel. The saw bends easily and is difficult to control.

Ladder stitch Used for closing openings, attaching parts such as tails and for bracing limbs. It should be worked with a strong thread.

Lap joint Half the depth of each corresponding piece of wood is removed. Sawn edges are smoothed with a chisel then fastened together with glue and wood screws.

Latex adhesive A natural rubber glue used for bonding fabrics, paper and porous materials. It is white and dries to a translucent film. There is some yellowing with age.

Lumber-core plywood
Manufactured sheet material made from rectangular strips of softwood glued together side by side and sandwiched between single or double veneers of wood.

Machine stitches Straight stitch is used for sewing seams, a zig-zag stitch for attaching elastic direct to fabric removing the need for a casing.

Marionette A string puppet.

Measurements Standard and metric measurements are given. Do not mix them.

Modeling clay Modeling material that may be used over and over again.

Muslin Loose woven cotton fabric similar in appearance to gauze.

Nap The soft, down-like surface of a fabric that is produced by brushing the surface. It has come to describe all fabrics which must be cut with the pattern pieces facing in the same direction, whether or not they have a true nap.

Needle modeling A soft sculpture technique that provides shaping to a stuffed, fabric object by the placement of stitches which are then pulled tight and fastened off.

Nominal size The size of wood as it leaves the sawmill. Drying and surfacing reduce the actual dimensions, but the width and thickness are still given in terms of the nominal size.

Optional darts Preparation of the toy skin in place of external bracing stitches.

Overcasting A basting stitch used to hold two or more fur fabric pieces together prior to seaming.

Panel saw Saw for cross-cutting (across the grain) and ripping (sawing along the grain).

Papier mâché Made by soaking strips of paper in wallpaper paste and pressing into a shape. It dries to form a tough, durable material.

Particle board Manmade board constructed from small wood chips which have been coated with resin and compressed together under high pressure and heat.

Pile In soft toys, a fur-like fabric.

Pilot hole A small starting hole for screws made with an awl or a drill.

Pincers Long handled tweezers used to reach narrow extremities inside soft toy skins which would be otherwise difficult to stuff.

Playboard The shelf on which hand puppets perform in a puppet booth.

Plywood Manufactured board constructed from an uneven number of thin layers or veneers which are bonded face to face, with the grain running in alternate directions.

Polyester fiber Good quality, white stuffing material.

Polyurethane varnish Synthetic varnish used to give a clear gloss finish to toys painted with water-based paint. It also can be used directly on unpainted wood to enhance and protect the natural features of the wood.

Power saws 1. Circular saw, for all basic cutting. **2.** Saber saw, used primarily for cutting curves. The fine blade allows quite intricate work.

Prepared wood See *actual size.*

Primer Used to seal sawn wood preparatory to painting. White latex paint is the most popular.

Proscenium Part of puppet theatre where the puppets appear and perform.

Release agent Substance, such as petroleum jelly, that prevents molding materials from sticking together.

Rickrack A zig-zag braid used for decorating clothes.

Running stitch A long running stitch is used for tacking. A short running stitch can be used for a seam where strength is not important.

Safety eyes Two-part component consisting of a plastic eye and a metal washer. Once fixed in place they cannot be pulled out of a toy by a child.

Sandpaper Abrasive material that comes in a variety of grades from very coarse to superfine. Always sand the wood in the direction of the grain, and not against it.

Satin stitch Straight stitches worked close together to fill a shape.

Seam allowance A seam allowance of ¼ in. (6 mm.) is allowed for on all fabric pattern pieces except for felt pieces which have an allowance of ⅛ in. (3 mm.) (and dollhouse projects).

Seam ripper A small tool used for cutting out seams and threads.

Seams The joining of two or more pieces of fabric sewn by machine using a straight stitch or by hand, using backstitch.

Self-hardening clay Modeling material that sets hard on exposure to air. It does not need to be fired in a kiln.

Selvage Edge of a woven cloth.

Slip A mixture of clay and water that is used as an adhesive for joints in clay. It is applied by brush.

Softwood From cone-bearing trees with needle-like leaves such as pine, fir and spruce. It is generally lighter and easier to work than hardwood.

Stab stitch Similar in appearance to a small running stitch, traditionally used on felt.

Standard size See *nominal size.*

Stem stitch An embroidered outline stitch ideal for facial features.

Strong thread Used for closing stuffing openings and attaching any part of a soft toy to the body. Also used for stringing puppets. Examples are button thread, crochet cotton and upholstery thread.

Topcoat The final application of a paint or varnish.

Try square Used for working out straight lines and right-angles on wood.

Vinyl face mask A dollmaking accessory that may be purchased from craft shops and larger handicraft departments.

Wallpaper paste A cellulose paste used for bonding layers of newspaper together to make papier mâché.

Warp 1. A twist in wooden boards or sheets that is due to internal or surface tensions. **2.** Fabric threads that lie parallel to the selvage of the cloth.

White glue Water-based polyvinyl acetate glue that will bond paper, wood and hardboard. Setting time is about one hour and some projects may need to be clamped while the glue is setting. Remove excess glue with a damp cloth once it sets.

Zig-zag stitch A machine stitch used for neatening seams and attaching elastic.

INDEX

Page numbers in *italic* refer to illustrations and captions.

M

mallets, wooden toymaking, *54-5*
maple, 54
masking, painting, 59
matchbox dresser, 147, *147*
materials, soft toymaking, 11-12
measurments:
  enlarging, 120
  reducing, 120
measures:
  soft toymaking, *11*
  wooden toymaking, *54-5*
miniature:
  dollhouse, 132-53
  finishes, 122
  lighting, 123
  scaling in proportion, 121-2, *121*
  style, 123
  working in, 121-3
mixed media toys, 98-119
modeling:
  in modeling clay, 99, *99*
  stands, 98-9
modeling clay, modeling with, 99, *99*
modeling knives, wooden toymaking, 12
mouths, embroidered, 16
muslin, soft toymaking, 12

N

nailing, wooden toymaking, 58
nails, wooden toymaking, *54-5*, 58
needles, soft toymaking, *11*
noses, embroidered, 16
nursery ted, 22, *22-3*

O

oak, 54
outdoor toys:
  go-carts, 128-31, *128-31*
  playhouse, 124-7, *124-7*
  swings, 82-3, *82-3*
overcasting, 14, *15*

P

paddle steamers, 88-91, *88-91*
painting:
  acrylic paint, 59
  enamel paint, 59
  fine lines, 59
  gloss paint, 59
  masking, 59
  papier mâché, 100
  preparing the wood, 59
  self-hardening clay, 123
  stenciling, 59
  techniques, 59
  wooden toymaking, 59
panel saws, wooden toymaking, *54-5*, 56
paper punches, soft toymaking, *11*
papier mâché:
  painting, 100
  puppet heads, 99-100, *100*
particle board, 56
pastes, 58
patchwork balls, 19, *19*
pattern grids, enlarging, *12*
pattern layouts, soft toymaking, 13, *13*
pattern templates, soft toymaking, 12-13, *12*
patterns:
  keys, *14*
  transferring, *12*
pencils, soft toymaking, *11*
pens, ruling, 59, *59*

pergola, miniature garden, 143
photocopying, transferring patterns, *12*
pictures, miniature, 149
pillows, miniature, 150
pin hammer, wooden toymaking, *54-5*
pinafores, rag dolls, 47
pine trees, miniature garden, 144
pipe clamps, wooden toymaking, *5-5*
pipes, wooden toys, 64, 66, *66*
planes, wooden toymaking, *54-5*
planing wood, 57
playhouse, 124-7, *124-7*
pliers:
  soft toymaking, *10-11*
  wooden toymaking, *54-5*
plywood, 56
  wheels, 58
polyester fibers, stuffing soft toys, 12
polyurethane varnish, 59
power drill, wooden toymaking, *54-5*
power tools, wooden toymaking, *54-5*
Punch and Judy, making, 101-7, *101-7*
punches, soft toymaking, *11*
puppets, 98-119
  hand, 101-7, *101-7*
  heads, 98-100
  Punch and Judy, 101-7, *101-7*
  string, 112-19, *112-19*
  theaters, 108-11, *108-11*
puzzle balls, 20-2, *21*
puzzles, jigsaws, 62-3, *62-3*

R

rabbits, soft toys, 28-31, *28-31*

rag dolls:
  clothes, 44-7, *44-7*
  making, 40-3, *40-3*
rattles, wooden toys, 64, 66-7, *67*
reducing measurements, 120
redwood, 54
rip-sawing, 56
rock garden, miniature, 142
roofs, dollhouse, 134-5, 136, *136*
rubber latex glue, soft toymaking, *11*
rugs, miniature, 150
ruling pens, 59, *59*
running stitch, 14, *15*

S

safety, 123
  wooden toymaking, 59
safety eyes, 15, *15*
sandpaper, wooden toymaking, *54-5*
satin stitch, 15, *15*
saws:
  using, 56-7
  wooden toymaking, *54-5*
scaling in proportion, 121-2, *121*
scaling up, 120-1, *120-1*
scissors, soft toymaking, *10*
screwing, wooden toymaking, 57-8
screws, wooden toymaking, *54*, 57-8
seam ripper, soft toymaking, *10*
seams, easing curved, *14*
self-hardening clay, 122-3
sewing, soft toymaking, 14
sewing machines, soft toymaking, *11*
shelves, miniature, 148
shoes, rag dolls, 41
shrubs, miniature garden, 142

Acknowledgments

The authors and publisher would like to thank the following people and organizations for their kind help in the production of this book:

Jane, Sam, Katie and Amber Wood; Stanley Tools Ltd, Sheffield; and the students of the Thamesside Adult Education Institute and the Tonbridge Adult Education Center who tried out many of the soft toys.